BUS

ACPL ITEM
DISCARDED

D0796505

Heavy Traffic

Daniel Madar

Heavy Traffic:
Deregulation, Trade,
and Transformation in
North American Trucking

UBC Press / Vancouver and Toronto
Michigan State University Press / East Lansing

© UBC Press 2000

All rights reserved. No part of this publication may be reproduced, stored in a retrieval system, or transmitted, in any form or by any means, without prior written permission of the publisher.

Published in the United States by Michigan State University Press.

Printed in Canada on acid-free paper ∞

Canadian Cataloguing in Publication Data

Madar, Daniel R., 1941-
  Heavy Traffic
  (Canada and international relations, ISSN 0847-0510; 12)
  Includes bibliographic references and index.
  ISBN 0-7748-0769-5 (cloth); ISBN 0-7748-0770-9 (pbk.)
  1. Trucking – Government policy – Canada. 2. Trucking – Government policy –
United States. I. Title.
HF 5635.A6M32 2000   388.3'24'0971   C00-910102-0

Library of Congress Cataloging-in-Publication Data

Madar, Daniel, 1941-
  Heavy traffic : deregulation, trade, and transformation in North American
trucking / Daniel Madar.
  p. cm.
  Includes bibliographical references and index.
  ISBN 0-87013-556-2 (alk. paper)
  1. Trucking – Deregulation – United States. 2. Trucking – Deregulation – Canada.
3. Trucking – Deregulation – North America. 4. Free trade – North America. I. Title.
HE5623 .M253 2000
388.3'24'097 – dc21   00-036776

This book has been published with the help of a grant from the Humanities and Social Sciences Federation of Canada, using funds provided by the Social Sciences and Humanities Research Council of Canada. UBC Press acknowledges the financial support of the Government of Canada through the Book Publishing Industry Development Program (BPIDP) for our publishing activities.

UBC Press
University of British Columbia
2029 West Mall, Vancouver, BC V6T 1Z2
www.ubcpress.ubc.ca

Michigan State University Press
1405 South Harrison Road, Suite 25
East Lansing, Michigan 48823-5202
www.msu.edu/unit/msupress

Contents

Preface

This project originated in conflict. A dispute between Canada and the United States over trucking deregulation and the treatment of foreign carriers proved surprisingly contentious and difficult to settle. The industry was an important one, and there were no bilateral agreements covering it. The dispute, and its resolution, lay in domestic regulation, and politically experienced and articulate interests were involved on both sides. For the American government the issue was reciprocity; for the Canadian government it was sovereignty. For an international relations person with a life-long interest in transport the issues were irresistible.

Since the stakes were regulatory, understanding them meant understanding regulation, and this meant gaining knowledge of the regulated industry – particularly its organization, economics, technology, and clientele. Appreciating the political appeal of deregulation required a tour through the critical literature. Grasping the politics of change led into public policy, and trucking's provincial jurisdiction in Canada brought federalism into play.

These issues were fused by events. The United States deregulated in 1980. The imbalance with still-exclusionary Canada led directly to complaints and a bilateral dispute. As Canada was successfully defending its regulation, the federal government was becoming greatly worried about trade and competitiveness. Those concerns led eventually to free trade negotiations with the United States. Meanwhile, transport reform was making its way forward. Both came to fruition in 1987 as a draft free trade agreement and a revised Motor Vehicle Transport Act. Since trucks are the prime vehicles of Canada-US trade, international competition was very much on the minds of deregulation's supporters and opponents.

Both the United States and Canada deregulated just as a serious recession was beginning – 1980 for the United States and 1990 for Canada (it wasn't until 1989 that all provinces had implemented the Motor Vehicle Transport Act). Trucking, a derived-demand industry, is immediately affected by economic slowdowns. Combined with the disruption of deregulation, both Canadian and American industries went through severe adjustment. As free trade took effect and the 1990 recession ended, transborder traffic burgeoned. Traffic patterns reflected not only trade, but also the adoption by Canadian and American industries of integrated and high-speed logistics. Trucks were naturally suited to be the prime mode of transportation. Together, deregulation and trade have transformed the trucking industry.

Here we have a medley of ingredients. For people interested in public policy it shows the dimensions of reform and change in key industries. For people interested in international relations it shows the dimensions of economic interdependence – with an added leavening of complex dispute resolution. For both, the industrial element adds a realistic appreciation of the world at work. My hope is that the curiosity and discovery that supported my excursions will be conveyed to the reader, whom I hope approaches the book with the same sense of the open road.

Acronyms

AIB	Anti-Inflation Board
ATA	American Trucking Associations
CAMCA	Canadian-American Motor Carriers Association
CCMTA	Canadian Council of Motor Transport Administrators
CEA	Council of Economic Advisers
CITL	Canadian Industrial Transportation League
CLC	Canadian Labour Congress
CMA	Canadian Manufacturers Association
CTA	Canadian Trucking Association
DOT	Department of Transportation
FIRA	Foreign Investment Review Agency
FTA	Canada-United States Free Trade Agreement
GATT	General Agreement on Tariffs and Trade
ICC	Interstate Commerce Commission
LTL	less-than-truckload
MFN	Most Favoured Nation
MVTA	Motor Vehicle Transport Act
NEP	National Energy Program
NIRA	National Industrial Recovery Act
NITL	National Industrial Transportation League
NTA	National Transportation Act
OHTB	Ontario Highway Transport Board
OTA	Ontario Trucking Association
PCV	Public Commercial Vehicles
QTA	Quebec Trucking Association
TL	truckload
TMI	Trucking Management Inc.
UPS	United Parcel Service
USTR	United States Trade Representative
WTO	World Trade Organization

Heavy Traffic

1
Introduction

Canada and the United States exchange the world's highest level of bilateral trade, valued at $1.4 billion a day, and two-thirds of it travels in trucks.[1] Within a day's truck journey of Toronto is a market with US$2 trillion of disposable income and over US$1 trillion in retail sales. The American portion of that market is seventeen times the size of the Quebec and Manitoba portion, and Toronto's share of it exceeds Boston's, New York's, and Detroit's.[2] Two reforms facilitated this development. Free trade removed restrictions to commerce, and deregulation removed restrictions to transportation.

Speed, adaptability, and price favour trucks as the primary mode of transportation. The industry's structural diversity provides an assortment of transport services, and competition keeps rates low. That potential had always been present but had been hampered by regulation. Route and commodity controls restricted service competition, and rate controls restricted price competition. Discontent with regulation, backed by cogent economic arguments, became a political force in both countries in the 1970s. The United States deregulated with the Motor Carrier Act, 1980. In Canada the Motor Vehicle Transport Act, 1987, set out new regulatory standards, and by 1989 the provinces had implemented them. Deregulation allowed motor carriers to offer the services they wished and to negotiate prices individually with shippers. Since then carriers have learned to move in the fast and changeable currents of an open market.

Integrated service between the two countries would not be possible without transborder operations. Those, too, are a product of deregulation. Previously, parallel restrictions had made it difficult for carriers from one country to offer service in the other, and most motor freight was simply transferred at the border. Through service became possible when deregulation in the two countries granted entry to carriers of either nationality. Cabotage rules reserve purely domestic service to domestic carriers, but foreign carriers can circumvent them by using domestic equipment and drivers. Facilitating easy movement is a highway network that connects Canadian and American traffic centres. Traffic has burgeoned under free trade. Between 1989 and 1997 transborder truck revenues increased by 148 percent, and transborder tonnage more than doubled.[3]

Domestic long-haul shipments were also transferred from carrier to carrier because the same regulatory restrictions discouraged nationwide operations. Expansion meant appearing before regulatory boards, which presumed against new service, and facing carriers hostile to new competitors. In exchange carriers enjoyed secure and predictable business conditions in carefully apportioned markets. The regulatory rationale was to maintain a stable and prosperous industry – a rationale that most truckers firmly supported.

When deregulation exposed motor carriers to the full force of competition, their worst expectations came to pass. In the face of demands for cheap rates and adaptive service, the standardized and complacent efforts that had sufficed under regulation were no longer adequate, and the previous cost structures were now unbearable. Carriers unable to adjust closed their doors, often after years of struggle, producing the industry's highest rates of failure since the Depression.[4] Worse, in both countries deregulation coincided with a serious recession – 1980-2 for American deregulation and 1990-2 for Canadian deregulation. For Canadian carriers, the recession accompanied the initial phases of free trade, blending disruption with opportunity.

Free transborder movement did not begin amicably. American deregulation ended a symmetrically restrictive arrangement and created a unilateral advantage for Canadian carriers. The Interstate Commerce Commission (ICC) granted free entry to the interstate market on a non-discriminatory basis, and Canadian carriers were pleased to accept the hospitality. The Canadian government meanwhile retained its tight controls. American carrier complaints about Canadian restrictions touched off the Trucking War, which began in 1981 and became a significant bilateral dispute by mid-1982. Like other conflicts in which some ordinary commodity – beer, chickens, turbot – becomes a martial adjective, the Trucking War involved an important industry, politically articulate economic interests, opposed preferences, and ample portions of perceived unfairness and injury.

Resolution was hindered by trucking regulation's solely domestic jurisdiction. With no bilateral agreements or international trade standards covering trucking services, restoring a balance meant either the ICC restricting Canadian entry or Canada adopting parallel liberalizations. Any effort to apply a special standard to Canadian applicants, Ottawa pointed out, would be discriminatory. And any expectation that Canada should change its regulation, Ottawa insisted, infringed on its sovereign prerogative to manage transport. Although the dispute ended when both sides signed an agreement pledging full, fair, and equitable treatment of each other's carriers, Ottawa interpreted the agreement to mean continuation of its existing practices, which already met those standards.

Canada did subsequently deregulate, although the connection to the Trucking War and free trade is not as obvious as it might seem. Canadian initiatives in transport deregulation had preceded American ones by thirteen years. Canada partially deregulated rail rates with the National Transportation Act, 1967, and the railways' improved performance was one consideration supporting the Staggers Rail Act, 1980, which deregulated American rail carriers. Research on both sides of the border documented ample amounts of inefficiency and waste in trucking. In the stagflationary climate of the 1970s, these burdens became politically insupportable.

In deregulating first, the United States was guided by prospective benefits. Trucking had been under tight controls since its infancy, and aside from the small sector that handled exempt agricultural commodities, the only experience the industry had with open markets was during the worst years of the Depression. Returning to open markets, American carriers believed, was a policy experiment with them as subjects. Adding to the Canadian case for deregulation was the ongoing demonstration across the border. While Canadian shippers contemplated improved prices and service, however, Canadian carriers contemplated serious competition. More feared than new Canadian competitors were new American ones.

Regulation and the State
Trucking regulation in both countries stemmed from the Great Depression and from government efforts to remedy the same problems – distress in the railway industry and turbulence in the trucking industry. Both governments at the time believed that unregulated motor carrier competition caused the problems and that tight controls would cure them. Both applied the same basic regulatory standard of public convenience and necessity, a venerable test in common law. Backed by shared understandings, that standard supported nearly symmetrical regimes of motor carrier regulation for almost fifty years.

Regulation made the state the pivotal actor – indeed, regulated trucking was an exemplar of an industry moulded and organized by the state. From the industry's earliest years, regulation had partitioned it by national and subnational jurisdictions and allocated exactly specified segments of the public roads, dividing up territory in an industry whose natural mobility is universal. The same apportionments of cargoes and conditions of service organized the industry by sector. The influence was pervasive. In the words of an American carrier executive, "our decisions, plans, growth and even market definition depended largely on our ability to meet or guide ICC standards of what motor carriers ought to be and ought to do. In that system, customers became a third party to our business. Both they and we addressed their needs through our regulator."[5]

Institutional analysis treats the origins, effects, and persistence of rules, and Canadian and American trucking regulations were elaborate edifices of rules. The supporting regulatory model, however, had simply been transferred from the railways and never did match trucking's economic characteristics. Although the industry's support was one reason for the model's half-century of persistence, institutional support came from the belief that regulation was rational and effective and that the industry's normal condition was tightly controlled. The origins and effects of these rules and assumptions are the topic of Chapter 2.

One measure of the state's latitude to act is the ability to implement important changes. States enjoy that ability in policy sectors where authority is centred in a single agency that has clear jurisdiction. Ability to act diminishes when authority is scattered among a number of agencies and across levels of government. Deregulation presents contrasting portraits. In the United States, the American Trucking Associations (ATA) and the Teamsters had prospered under regulation and were its strongest defenders. Their success in resisting occasional reform initiatives in the 1950s and 1960s earned them the reputation of being powerful special interests. Their adversary, once it became set on reform, was the ICC. The ICC's behaviour was a striking demonstration of its ability to act. It began in-house regulatory reform in the late 1970s. Congress – partly to avoid being overtaken – became involved and passed the Motor Carrier Act, 1980. This measure stopped well short of complete deregulation, but the ICC, bent on completing the task, simply continued on its own with thoroughgoing reform. American deregulation is the topic of Chapter 3.

On the other hand, Washington's management of the Trucking War, in the words of an ATA official, was a "rugby game" of bureaucratic disorder. Initially divided sentiment in the executive branch crystallized in opposition to coercive measures, but Congress backed a moratorium on Canadian entry. The Department of Transportation – attentive to charges of unfair competition but opposed to blanket measures – worked to get flexible language in the moratorium so that it could be lifted. Unwilling to become involved in an international dispute, the ICC stayed as far on the sidelines as possible, even though the executive branch preferred a regulatory solution. The Office of the United States Trade Representative, mindful of the trucking industry's structural complexity, opposed any effort to negotiate a sectoral agreement and wound up with the unpromising task of arranging a dignified exit. The Trucking War is analyzed in Chapter 4.

The emphases are reversed on the Canadian side. Ability to act showed in Ottawa's diplomatic management of the Trucking War. Adamantly refusing to harmonize Canada's regulation, Ottawa firmly took charge, even though the regulatory rules at issue were established and well-defended provincial prerogatives. On the other hand, Ottawa had never exercised its legal jurisdiction over interprovincial trucking, and, when it did decide to deregulate, it could not legislate reform directly. The Motor Vehicle Transport Act, 1987, represented a set of liberalized regulatory standards, which the provincial governments were expected to adopt. Parliament, following extensive representations in legislative hearings by truckers and shippers, duly passed reform legislation. Most of the provinces were willing to streamline their trucking regulation, but not all were willing to abandon it. That made truckers allies of the provinces, two of which were resolved to continue protecting them from competition. The result was a protracted sequence of compliance. Ottawa's only resource was to threaten to take up its latent jurisdiction. Its lack of enthusiasm for actually doing so led to an inelegant and disjointed implementation. As procrastination continued in the holdout provinces, those that had already deregulated began complaining about non-reciprocity – the same grievance that had sparked the Trucking War seven years earlier. Canadian deregulation is the topic of Chapter 5.

The exit of the state has made carriers and shippers directly interactive. Product offerings and prices no longer emerge from regulatory decisions but from a "process of definition and recognition" among carriers and shippers of transport needs and service offerings.[6] For shippers the point of reference is the carriers' ability to meet specific requirements and the availability of substitutes. In deciding what to supply, carriers focus on both shipper needs and the offerings of other carriers. The process in such conditions is one of comparison, trial, and error.[7] Trucking's structural diversity complicates the process with an array of transport products and a variety of cost structures and prices.[8] These conditions produce a fluid and contingent business life for motor carriers. The ones that have survived in this deregulated environment epitomize nimbleness and opportunism – the corporate watchwords of the 1990s. Life after deregulation is examined in Chapter 6.

Deregulation and Trade

Trucking is an exemplar of a derived-demand industry. Carriers, regardless of what they do, cannot create demand for their services; that demand is created by shippers. The nature of that demand, in turn, is shaped by the actions of the state. Trade barriers between Canada and the United States, managed as part of their economic and foreign policy, directed much of that demand to national markets, which shared the same jurisdictional borders as did regulation. Trucking developed for over fifty years within the exact confines of regulatory controls, and it did so within national markets shaped by trade controls. When the two states deregulated trucking, they withdrew their controls on the movement of transport vehicles; and when they removed tariffs and other trade barriers, they withdrew their controls on the movement of goods. Deregulation and free trade were parallel and complementary liberalizations. Carriers, for their part, followed the goods.

Connecting deregulation and trade is the fact that cheap transportation lowers the costs of trade and increases a state's number of tradable goods. A good is tradable when its domestic price is lower than its price at the export point of delivery. If the costs of transportation to the point of delivery eliminate that margin, then the good is non-tradable. If transportation costs are low, however, then previously non-tradable goods become practical to export, and a state's trading opportunities multiply.[9] Globally, efficient and cheap transportation has supported a massive expansion of international trade. Trucking's role as the main conduit of Canadian-American trade makes rates pivotal, and deregulation drastically lowered them.

Regulatory reformers expected cheaper rates, but more comprehensive results actually ensued.[10] The first of these was a revolution in industrial logistics. Shippers discovered supply-chain management, in which production is organized in a closely coordinated network of suppliers, assemblers, and distributors. Transporters furnish the connective linkages. The most familiar feature, referred to as just-in-time, reduces costs by shifting inventory backward in the production sequence and replenishing it as needed. Production is timed to the arrival of parts and components during brief "delivery windows." Flow-through logistics achieve the same benefits on the distribution side, with producers supplying statistically predictable requirements at retail outlets on a continuous schedule, thus reducing the need to hold goods at intermediate points. The optimal version is a straight transit from producer to store shelf. Large retailers such as Wal-Mart have been adopting these arrangements with their suppliers, assigning them and their transporters the task of keeping items stocked at a specified level. On both the manufacturing and distribution sides, these arrangements generate rapidly moving inventories, requiring suppliers to keep pace with changeable requirements and requiring transporters to be exactly punctual. Carriers have had to adapt. Much of the standardized, one-size-fits-all service fashioned by regulation has given way to customized logistics in which carriers and shippers work together to manage transportation. Taking advantage of their experience in designing specialized services, many carriers now include logistics planning and management in their offerings.

Rationalizing production under liberalized trade extends supply-chain networks across national boundaries. Since adoption of the Canada-United States Auto Pact in 1965, General Motors, Ford, and Chrysler have shipped parts and components among widely dispersed production facilities in the two countries and were early adopters of just-in-time. The automakers' recent efforts to reduce vertical integration have brought more external suppliers into their networks and expanded logistics requirements. The results show in traffic. Automotive products are Canada's largest export commodity group and the largest commodity group crossing the border in trucks.[11] Highway 401 is the main logistical corridor, and most of the existing and all of the new automotive plants are located along it. The more general importance of manufactured exports makes Ontario the centre of transborder trucking. Distribution favours Ontario as well. Seeking economies of scale, firms have begun centralizing their distribution and delivering from huge regional centres on an overnight or two-day basis. That, too, has been rationalizing under free trade and requires fast, adaptive transportation. The size of the Ontario market, and its proximity to the heart of the vast American market, shows in overall traffic levels. Revenue on transborder shipments from Ontario accounts for almost half of the transborder total for Canada. At 22 percent of that total, shipments from Ontario to the north central American states remain the largest single block of traffic.[12] Reflecting free trade's diversifying effects, Ontario's relative share of southbound traffic has marginally decreased since 1989, while those of other provinces have grown. The region experiencing the largest increase – 281 percent – is the Prairie provinces. The largest destination remains the north-central states, but revenue on shipments to the American south has increased by 364 percent.

Deregulation and Integration

The second unexpected consequence of deregulation has been integration in the two countries' motor carrier industries. One American regulatory reformer, as will be noted in Chapter 4, did report foreseeing that Canadian entry could become a problem, and the Canadian Trucking Association (CTA) did warn of unbalancing the existing arrangement. At the time, however, deregulation was not on the Trudeau government's agenda, and without free movement in both directions integration could not occur. It was even less possible to foresee that a bilateral free trade agreement would be in place ten years later and would be highly compatible with a radically changed trucking industry.

That same compatibility was true of American and Canadian carriers themselves. Having developed under symmetrical regulatory regimes, they entered the opened transborder markets with comparably structured firms and similar experience. Their common operational forms and practices, together with shared pools of traffic, provided the basis of integration. The industry is too large and diverse to speak of pervasive integration, but trade patterns, regulatory openness, and the industry's own universal mobility allow carriers in all niches, from family firms to billion-dollar operations, and from single-commodity haulers to general freight carriers, to develop international business. An excellent highway system facilitates widespread movement, and electronic technology, including satellite-linked dis-patcher-to-driver communication and on-line data interchange among car-riers and shippers, facilitates widespread coordination. Truckers' websites post available loads by origin, commodity, and destination, allowing carri-ers and shippers across North America direct access to one another. By elim-inating high brokerage fees, the websites democratize the market by supplying even the smallest carriers with a common pool of information. Because of the effects of free trade, and because of the derived-demand nature of trucking, integration ultimately reflects the transition from state to market. Integration stems from no master program but from thousands of individual carriers exploiting opportunities and responding to market forces, producing an almost perfectly aggregate result.

2
The State in Action: Regulation's Origins and Effects

The State, Order, and Rationality

Motor carrier regulation was a quintessential instrument of the state. It controlled entry to the industry, the domains of each carrier, terms of business with shippers, and the conditions of growth and change. Entry controls governed the number of carriers, and route controls specified exactly which segments of the public roads they might use. Commodity controls governed what they might haul on which segment and in which direction, and rate controls specified what they could charge. Altogether, motor carrier regulation produced a highly structured industry, with each sector serving particular parts of an elaborately partitioned market. In these visible and practical ways, trucking regulation was the state in action.

Although these controls imposed considerable costs and restrictions, carriers fortunate to be in the industry preferred them. The desire to be regulated arises from the "very uncertainty of the exchange process itself" and increases with the "number of potential participants and the level of turnover."[1] The early years of trucking were indeed uncertain, as we will see momentarily. Regulation creates stability by standardizing relationships. It brings market conditions, inputs and outputs, and technology under a common jurisdiction and makes individual firms part of a collective system.[2] Regulation reduces uncertainty by providing "stable expectations ... and a way to predict the behavior of others."[3] By doing so, regulation "buffers organizations from turbulence" and enhances their prospects for survival over time.[4] Preferences for such protection are part of broader efforts by firms to create favourable environments.[5] The firms with the strongest interest in doing so are those with weak market power. Fledgling motor carriers in the early 1930s exemplified that position.

Trucking's structure is complex, and its array of services qualifies it as a multiproduct industry.[6] Regulation helps stabilize such industries, whose differing market conditions, technologies, or products create conflicting interests and division. Unclear boundaries among sectors and unstable market shares within sectors increase contention and instability. Significant division undermines common action and fragments trade associations into specialized and sometimes adversarial groupings.[7] The ATA formally recognized that diversity by using the plural form in its name. Problems of unity faced both the Canadian and American trucking associations as they sought to represent increasingly different sectors of a structurally complex industry. Following deregulation, in fact, two specialized carrier groups left the ATA. While regulation was in place, the ATA's task was made easier by enforced and clear sectoral divisions and careful apportionments of the market. One benefit of state involvement was a stable basis of collective action.[8]

Sovereign state power over regulation creates a "bounded system" of organizations and exchange.[9] Jurisdiction was centralized federally in the United States when the ICC was given authority over interstate trucking in 1935, and truckers wishing to do business across state lines made a single application to it. In Canada's decentralized system truckers have always had to secure permission from each province. The two systems were also bounded internationally. The same entry controls were applied to foreign carriers and produced separate Canadian and American markets. Because the two systems were based on such similar rules, however, they fostered twin motor carrier industries that shared the same basic sectoral organization, common operational practices, and a standardized technology.

Regulation becomes institutionalized when its rules assume a "taken-for-granted" character, becoming part of daily calculations and, more broadly, fixtures of an understood and expected order.[10] More fundamentally, regulation "confers the force of myths and cultural understandings upon the functioning of organizations," providing a common justification for their status and activity.[11] Supporting these understandings is the belief that they are rational and effective.[12] These understandings may be readily espoused by members of the industry and by regulators themselves. Sharing these understandings, industries and regulators can become both "architects and products of the rules and expectations they have helped devise."[13] The trucking industry's stability and prosperity was long credited to regulation, and it was only when economists began showing the true costs of regulation in the 1970s that this belief began to be questioned. Tampering with a successful formula was the basis of the carriers' opposition.

Much of the critique that brought trucking regulation into question challenged its economic rationality. Trucking regulation did represent a fusion of two different purposes: one stemmed from controlling natural monopolies to ensure fair prices and to prevent abuses, and the other stemmed from managing vital industries so as to maintain dependable operation. The two converged in the 1930s, with falling revenues for the railways and cut-throat competition among truckers. By extending railway regulation to trucks, the Canadian and American governments intended to protect the former and to stabilize the latter. The result was incongruous. Measures designed to prevent monopolistic abuse by railways were used to prevent excess competition among truckers. How those measures came to be applied is an interesting story.

An Uptsart Industry

The motor carrier industry began with the discovery that gasoline-powered vehicles were ideal for transporting light cargoes. Trucks became a part of military logistics during the First World War, and after the armistice a pool of surplus army vehicles enabled civilians to begin businesses as motor carriers. The roads of the time were a principal limitation, with rain and melting snow turning unpaved ones into mire and with narrow widths limiting vehicle size.[14] That made urbanized regions the centres of trucking industry development. The trucks themselves were a second limitation. Although early truckers were ingenious in adapting small vehicles, existing technology still limited cargo size and variety, thus restricting clientele and service.

As the automotive age brought public demands for better roads, the state and provincial – and later the federal – governments of the two countries began programs of highway construction and developed trucking's technological base. Vehicle design also improved. The biggest advance in truck capacity was the development of diesel power and semi-trailers in the 1930s.[15] As these improvements proceeded, motor carriers expanded into intercity and then into interstate and interprovincial freight markets – previously the unchallenged domains of the railways.

The growth of trucking was becoming a serious concern. Having spent decades assembling massive physical plants, the railways faced an industry where the costs of getting started were almost nominal. Truckers had no equivalent to the railways' outlays on private rights of way because highway construction was a public expenditure. Trucks, the major capital item, were inexpensive both in absolute dollars and in proportion to potential business. Operators who could not afford new trucks could buy used ones. There was no minimum organizational size, and business could be started with one vehicle. Growth was easy to manage. Trucks are small cargo containers, and volume is increased simply by adding more trucks. With these small and inexpensive increments of expansion, firms could grow vehicle by vehicle.

Also attractive was the industry's atomized structure, with no firms having the resources or market power to ruin competitors or dominate large blocks of traffic. There was a loose assortment of state and provincial regulatory controls, but most did not restrict entry. There was no federal regulation. Altogether, these advantages made trucking an industry wherein ordinary people could become entrepreneurs, and carriers proliferated.

Speed and convenience made trucking a new and appealing mode for small-shipment general freight and package express. On the railways these commodities travelled under the highest rates and were premium traffic. The road network did limit the truckers' challenge to short- and medium-haul markets, but that too was premium territory. American and Canadian railway regulation cross-subsidized less profitable service with high rates in short- and medium-distance markets. By entering them, truckers disrupted the railways' carefully balanced rate structures.[16]

This was not orderly progress. Many of the new motor carriers possessed little experience and only a loose knowledge of their costs, making them aggressive, if not reckless, rate cutters. When the Depression began reducing intercity traffic volumes, truckers cut rates even further. With thin margins and shallow finances they failed easily, but low entry barriers continued to attract newcomers. Advocates of regulation could point to a list of unhealthy conditions: high rates of entry and exit, an atomized structure of small firms and one-vehicle operators, unreliable service, shrinking markets, and destructive price warfare. Together with the railways' grievances, these conditions invited regulation.

Regulatory Advent in the United States

In the United States, trucking regulation had an irregular development during the 1920s, as individual state governments imposed a variety of measures. For the most part these were intended to prevent misuse of public roads and unsafe operations, although some states were also sympathetic to railways seeking to limit the growth of trucking. The jurisdictional reach of state regulation was defined in 1925 in two Supreme Court decisions, *Buck* v. *Kuykendall* and *Bush* v. *Moloy,* which held that state regulation could not be used to impede interstate trucking, even in the absence of any federal regulation.[17] The rationale of regulation was expanded in 1932 in *Stephenson* v. *Binford,* when the Supreme Court upheld the state of Texas's right to apply restrictive entry controls to truckers and to use different standards for different sectors. The decision opened the way for those practices at the federal level, which the Motor Carrier Act authorized in 1935.[18]

Besides the railways, state regulatory agencies and organized labour supported federal regulation. State regulators were concerned about national highways and interstate trucking operations, which were beginning to cross their jurisdictions, and the lack of common controls. Unions favoured regulation to achieve order and stability for collective bargaining and better working conditions. Regulation was opposed by a coalition of shippers, vehicle manufacturers, and most of the motor carriers.[19]" We will see the carriers' reasons momentarily.

By 1935 the ICC had acquired a broad mandate over the railways. Its mission under the Act to Regulate Interstate Commerce, 1887, was controlling monopolistic practices, but that was expanded by the Transportation Act, 1920, to managing the railways as vital industries. With concern shifted from excessive rates to adequate profits, the ICC took a sympathetic view of behaviour that would have invited antitrust prosecution in the absence of the Transportation Act's new understanding of the public interest. That interest was a stable and prosperous industry.[20] The same understanding would guide the ICC's later management of trucking.

Initially, the ICC saw no need for regulation. In an investigation of transport in 1928, the ICC found that the railways were, indeed, losing traffic to trucks but that they were also enjoying increasing volume from a growing automobile industry. The Depression changed that assessment. A similar ICC investigation in 1932 found transport in oversupply and a need for regulation of all of its modes.[21] Excess competition, the ICC was convinced, was the main issue. Responding in 1933 to a shippers' petition to investigate high railway rates, the ICC held that the real problem was unregulated trucking.[22]

Applying the Railway Formula

Congress intervened with the Emergency Railroad Transportation Act, 1933, which created the Office of the Federal Coordinator of Transportation to examine the situation and to recommend legislation. President Roosevelt appointed an ICC commissioner, Joseph Eastman, as coordinator of transportation. Mr. Eastman shared the ICC's view that the problem was excess competition and believed that the ICC, already responsible for the railways, was the natural agency to manage trucking.[23] Regulation would be based on "the same general theory as developed for the railroads: transportation is basically monopolistic in nature and that is true for all agencies of transport."[24] He explicitly rejected the alternative of withdrawing railway regulation and creating a free transportation market.

Extending a regulatory remedy from one industry to a very different one reflects the historical dimension of rules and experience.[25] As a young administrator in the Progressive era, Eastman believed in the regulatory state.[26] Later, as a senior official at the ICC, he worked within a comprehensive set of rules and assumptions for managing the railways. Shaping his views were "his philosophy of public control, his experience with commission regulation, and his understanding of railroad history."[27] Even the Depression's drastic effect on traffic levels did not change his views: it merely exacerbated underlying structural conditions.[28] That settled the question of what measures to apply. In preparing draft motor carrier legislation, Eastman's office simply copied the Interstate Commerce Act's principal provisions, which were written for railways.[29]

Not all agreed that the new regulation was rational. James C. Nelson, an economist who began studying motor carrier competition in the 1930s, believed that it was clear in 1935 that motor carriers "were organized as many-firm competitive industries, not as monopolies or oligopolies." For that reason, he believed, applying railway regulatory measures to trucking was wholly misguided. Congress knew of trucking's structural diversity and inherent competition from hearings on a series of regulatory proposals that began in 1926 and from the ICC's own report in 1928. Since these features – cited forty years later to support deregulation – were so apparent at the time, Nelson asserts, economics cannot explain why trucking was regulated.[30]

From the perspective of the ICC's governing assumptions and rules, however, trucking was a naturally analogous case.[31] In both industries, stable competition required state intervention. The measures and rationale were contained in existing law and practice for the railways. With regulation enjoying apparent success there, it was reasonable to expect the same success in trucking. In the view of institutional analysis, arrangements that have evolved without serious failures are easily regarded as rational and effective. It is just as easy to assume that new applications will carry their benefits forward. When that assumption is widely shared, it represents "cause-effect relationships embodied by political culture."[32] Governments believed that establishing agencies such as the ICC articulated "general principles of industrial order," which could be used in new policies for new problems.[33] Those principles frame individual choices such as Eastman's. When institutional rules and understandings are the guide, attention is on what is appropriate within their terms.[34] Railway regulation, in that perspective, was the model to use.

In Congress the motor carrier legislation was supported by the ICC, the railways, many state regulatory commissions, and, in a decision based on a close vote among its membership, by the National Industrial Traffic League (later to become the National Industrial Transportation League), an organization of shippers. Some of the large motor carriers also came on side. Having taken advantage of federal funds to establish the ATA under the National Industrial Recovery Act (NIRA), they decided to support the Motor Carrier Act only after the Supreme Court declared NIRA unconstitutional in 1935, making it illegal for truckers to regulate their industry themselves.[35] The Motor Carrier Act's opponents were farmers organizations – which insisted on and got exemptions for agricultural commodities, leaving the road transport of those products unregulated – the National Highway Users Conference and the Automobile Manufacturers Association. Without the strong backing of the ICC and the ATA, which would have preferred self-regulation under NIRA and saw the legislation as a second-best option, the railways' pressure alone would probably not have been enough for the Motor Carrier Act's passage.[36] For its part, the ATA had developed quickly under NIRA and, by 1934, had succeeded in achieving a measure of common purpose among many carriers. This was reflected in the unusual harmony that prevailed during its first convention in 1934 and that marked a change from previous division and disunity.[37] Even under the ATA's aegis, trucking retained its sectoral plurality, which regulation entrenched.

Together with state controls over intrastate trucking, the advent of federal regulation of interstate trucking formed a neatly hierarchical arrangement. Carriers seeking to do business within a particular state applied to that state's regulatory commission, and carriers seeking to do business between states applied to the ICC. The same entry standards were used at both levels, and jurisdictional domains were clearly marked. When federal deregulation came in 1980, as we will see in the next chapter, the ICC had a wide and recognized field of reformist action.

Regulation and Federalism in Canada

Trucking in Canada developed quickly in the 1920s, and in 1928 the two national railways began a concerted political effort to get truckers regulated. As in the United States, in Canada the railways held that truckers enjoyed unequal capital cost, labour, and service advantages. The same argument of injury to a vital public resource was used, and the same solution of comprehensive regulation of transport was demanded. The railways' view was not accommodating: "No trucking company should be authorized to operate in a market then served by rail."[38] As the Depression began to shrink traffic and revenues, the railways' calls for regulation became keen.

The provincial governments had begun regulating motor carriers in the 1920s, but in contrast to the United States, where Supreme Court decisions established a federal jurisdiction for interstate trucking in 1925, in Canada that question was not judicially determined until 1954. That left three decades for the provincial regulatory systems to take root. In the early years the federal government saw no particular need to intervene because only a small portion of trucking was interprovincial. Ottawa was not completely uninterested, and when railways demanded relief during the Depression, the Duff Royal Commission was convened to investigate the situation in transport and to propose remedies. The commission's report acknowledged that the railways' problem was "due in many cases to the fact that conveyance by road is intrinsically a more suitable form of transport." Still, traffic diversion to truckers "free from regulations analogous to those imposed on other forms of transport ... may very well be opposed to the best interests of the country's welfare."[39]

Emphasizing the role of the railways in maintaining economic unity, the commission held them to be a necessary "quasi-monopoly," requiring "a measure of protection from long distance road competition," along with "an equalization of the conditions under which short distance traffic is carried."[40] The report recommended a national system of licensing and, for common carriers, proof that their operation would serve the public interest. (Common carriers, along with trucking's other sectors, will be addressed shortly.) Truckers supported entry controls as a way of stabilizing competition, but they were suspicious of any federal regulation.[41] The Royal Commission accordingly recommended that trucking regulation remain in provincial hands.

This influential report identified the very same problem – truck competition – that the American federal coordinator of transportation identified a year later. The regulatory assumptions were also the same: the railways were vital national resources, and their prosperity was in the public interest. Also the same were assumptions about the trucking industry: its capital structure and the largely out-of-pocket nature of its costs disposed it to excessive rates of entry, cut-throat competition, high rates of failure, and unreliable service.[42] To bring transport under a common order, regulation should be extended to trucking. As in the United States, in Canada a model assumed to be successful in one industry was applied "largely through projection" to a new industry.[43]

No economic analysis was officially articulated. "It is impossible to explain why trucking, in comparison to certain other industries, is in need of economic regulation from a search of the origins of motor carrier regulation."[44] And there was scant justification in the statutes themselves. The first substantive written decision of the British Columbia Motor Carrier Commission in 1973 acknowledged: "It is a curious aspect of the regulatory system with which we are concerned that the principles on which it is to be operated are neither apparent from the two statutes concerned ... nor have been laid down in recorded decisions. We have found ourselves at this late date obliged to seek the purpose which may properly be ascribed to the legislation."[45] The underlying rationale, however, had simply carried on from the 1930s: "No concept, whether it is openly called 'destructive competition' or whether it is simply implicit in a board's reasoning or a statute's wording, is more pervasive in the continuing justification for the need for economic regulation."[46]

As the industry's growth began to spill across provincial boundaries, the provinces simply began regulating the traffic themselves and discouraged federal involvement. In 1937 a Senate bill that would place all transport modes under a federal regulatory commission was defeated in the face of strong opposition from the provinces and from the recently organized CTA. Supporting them was the fact that there existed no clear constitutional mandate for federal controls. Interpretations at the time presumed that the provinces' ownership of roads gave them jurisdiction for regulating road transport. A 1939 brief submitted to the Royal Commission concerning dominion-provincial relations, for example, stated: "To date it has been generally accepted that provincial control [over highway transportation] is complete."[47] The federal government decided to leave trucking regulation to the provinces, even though motor carriage was increasingly able to operate widely.[48]

The result was a decentralized arrangement, with the provinces regulating both intra- and interprovincial trucking. Instead of producing the American hierarchy of federal and state jurisdictions, province-based regulation produced a set of adjoining ones. Internationally, the provinces controlled their segment of the border with the United States. Carriers seeking to do business beyond their province had to apply to each board involved, and, along with restrictive entry controls, they faced boards sympathetic to local carriers. Assembling an operation across several provinces involved multiple proceedings and multiple occasions for denial. Later, the same decentralized arrangement complicated deregulation, as we will see in Chapter 5.

A Judicial Gift Surrendered

The outcome of *Winner* v. *S.M.T. Eastern Ltd.* in 1954 squarely placed authority over interprovincial carriage in the hands of the federal government; and, in response, the federal government legislated that authority back to the provinces. This episode is worth examining briefly because the structure it established was in place during deregulation and remains in effect now. It also sheds light on the problems of national regulation within a decentralized federal system.

These are the elements of the case: The New Brunswick Motor Transport Board, upheld by the New Brunswick Court of Appeal, ruled that a bus company providing a service between the United States and Nova Scotia by way of New Brunswick could not pick up or discharge passengers in New Brunswick.[49] The bus operator challenged the ruling on jurisdictional grounds in the Supreme Court of Canada. The case attracted participants far from New Brunswick, with the attorney general of Ontario as well as representatives of the two national railways taking part in the proceedings. The Court ruled that the province could restrict the intraprovincial operations of the company but that it could not interfere with its extra-provincial operations. The Court's decision established both provincial and federal jurisdictions and ended the constitutional ambiguity. The portion of highway transport under federal jurisdiction rose from 2 percent to 50 percent.[50]

The decision was appealed to the Judicial Committee of the British Privy Council, with the provinces of Ontario, Alberta, New Brunswick, and Prince Edward Island supporting the appeal because of their loss of extra-provincial and international jurisdiction. The judicial committee's decision, one of the last it made as Canada's court of final appeal, went even farther: extra-provincial highway transport is under federal jurisdiction, but so are the intraprovincial operations of companies engaged in extra-provincial transport. In the committee's laconically instructional words: "The province has indeed authority over its own roads, but the authority is a limited one and does not entitle it to interfere with connecting undertakings. It must be remembered that it is the undertaking (the actual movement of goods and passengers), not the roads, which comes within the jurisdiction of the Dominion."[51]

That decision established the same principle as did the American Supreme Court in 1925: regardless of the regulations a province may impose on road transport, it "must not prevent or restrict interprovincial traffic."[52] The federal government, however, did not use this new authority. On the day following the decision, the federal minister of transport announced that a system of divided jurisdiction was not in the public interest. Fearing a "chaotic condition in the field of highway transport," the federal government convened a federal-provincial conference several months later.[53] The provinces favoured keeping their regulatory powers as they were. Strongly supporting full provincial control were the national and provincial trucking associations, who were long convinced that the federal government was inveterately pro-railway and that the provincial governments were their natural guardians.[54]

The federal government's solution was the Motor Vehicle Transport Act, which delegated regulatory authority over intraprovincial, interprovincial, and international motor carriage to the provincial governments. Each province, therefore, could regulate trucking within and across its borders as it saw fit. With the federal government excluding itself, there was no Canadian equivalent of the Interstate Commerce Commission to regulate interprovincial trucking. Provincial boards treated applications for operations outside the province "as if the extra-provincial undertaking operated in the province were a local undertaking" – in effect acting as if they were a federal board.[55] Without federal statute on interprovincial trucking, it was not obvious what a province could actually grant. Extra-provincial authority is legally complex and has produced a large amount of litigation.[56] The Supreme Court of Canada, however, has consistently upheld the Motor Vehicle Transport Act.[57]

Ottawa has never taken up trucking regulation, even though it has always viewed transportation as an important national policy area and, since the National Transportation Act, 1967, has had the statutory power to do so. In order to have a workable system of interprovincial trucking in the absence of federal regulation, the provinces depend on voluntary interprovincial cooperation. When the federal government liberalized entry and rate controls in the Motor Vehicle Transport Act, 1987, it depended on the provinces to put those new standards into effect. With no single political arena for deciding the issue, as had been the case in the United States Congress, Canadian deregulation took place in a chain of secondary arenas, with the trucking associations continuing to look to the provinces for protection.

Regulation and Sectoral Organization

One of regulation's most potent effects was maintaining sectoral boundaries in a naturally fluid and adaptive industry. Trucks can travel anywhere. They can operate on fixed schedules or go, as needed, to particular destinations; and they can handle freight in truckload or small-lot quantities. Their services can be offered to the general public (on a for-hire basis) or to individual shippers (on a for-rent basis). Although there are advantages to specialization, particularly in handling bulk commodities, the industry's inherently flexible technology makes it possible for one firm to conduct a variety of operations with the same pool of equipment. Operations are not difficult to change. The service life of trucks is brief, and leasing makes equipment immediately available. Terminal networks do represent fixed capital, but only one of trucking's sectors uses them. Deregulation, as we will see in Chapter 6, has allowed carriers to deploy their resources as they choose, but, until then, the industry was tightly structured. Although regulation hobbled a naturally mobile industry, it did manage conflict and spared carriers from sorting out territories and market shares among themselves. Not all sectors, however, enjoyed regulation's benefits equally, and the prime advantages went to common carriers. Overall, the system of rules and sectoral divisions shows the regulatory state at work.

Common Law, Common Standards, Common Carriers

Common carriers were the most stringently regulated because they served the general public. Canadian and American regulation of common carriers was based on public convenience and necessity, a common law test that requires a proposed service to satisfy an actual need.

The ICC established entry standards for common carriers in its *Pan American Bus Lines* ruling in 1936, with Joseph Eastman sitting as a senior commissioner on the panel hearing the application. Invoking public convenience and necessity, the panel ruled that a new operating authority should "serve a useful public purpose, responsive to a public demand or need."[58] Then came the restrictions. If existing carriers could provide the proposed service themselves, then there were grounds for denying the application regardless of any competitive benefits. The burden of proof was on the applicants, who had to bring forward shippers willing to certify that existing service was so unsuitable that it could only be remedied by granting the application. There were also grounds for denial if an application was shown to be "endangering or impairing the operations of existing carriers."[59] One endangerment was price competition. In *Wellspeak Common Carrier Application* a year later,[60] the ICC ruled as inadmissible an applicant's attempt to show that it would offer lower rates.[61] The ICC allowed carriers already holding operating authority grants (hereafter referred to as authorities) to protest new applications even if they were not directly affected.

Applications to extend or modify existing authorities faced the same hurdles, making it difficult for carriers already in the market to get even modest expansions. Promises of improved service were no advantage. The ICC would deny route changes that would give an applicant shorter transit times than his competitors. In deciding any particular application, the ICC had wide discretion, since the wording of *Pan American* was general enough to "support about any holding."[62] These provisions were reflected in state-level regulation, with all but three requiring a public convenience and necessity test for common carriers. The result was a widely consistent set of rules at both levels of government.

The ICC regulated commodities by specifying what goods carriers could handle. The practice began in 1935, when the ICC, awarding operating authorities to existing carriers under the Motor Carrier Act's grandfather clause, simply wrote in the commodity lists submitted by carriers. In 1952 the ICC adopted a uniform system of fifteen cargo categories and a large number of subcategories, and this resulted in much more specific controls. Route regulation was based in the Motor Carrier Act itself, with the requirement that operating authorities specify the routes, terminals, and intermediate points served.[63] These provisions meant that operating authorities were written in very particular terms, listing exactly which sections of which highways and access roads a carrier could use and exactly which items out of dozens a carrier could transport on which section and in which direction.

Reflecting different operational patterns in trucking, ICC regulation distinguished between regular and irregular route common carriage. Regular-route carriers operated service on fixed schedules between sets of destinations. Their authorities accordingly specified particular segments of the roads used. Irregular-route carriers served particular regions, often from a central point, and did not travel in fixed point-to-point patterns. Their authorities gave them general permission to use regional roads. Combining these provisions with all the commodity subcategories produced extensive rules, intricate competitive prospects from new applicants, and alert scrutiny from all parties at proceedings. In the late 1970s an internal review at the ICC and negative decisions from federal courts brought the *Pan American* standard into question, and the Motor Carrier Act, 1980, formally abandoned it. For the previous four decades, however, *Pan American* served as the ICC's touchstone.

Ontario introduced entry control in 1933 by amending its Public Commercial Vehicles Act to require applicants to show that their service would be in the public interest. This was done partly as a response to the Duff

Royal Commission's recommendation to bring trucking under regulation and partly in response to pressure from trucking companies to limit entry. The regulatory assumption was stated in the 1934 Annual Report of the Ontario Municipal Board, which noted positively that it had corrected the problem of granting licences "in excess of public demand."[64] Similar measures appeared in the highway transport statutes of the other provinces later in the decade. There was wide variation in specific entry criteria. The four Atlantic provinces and British Columbia had legislation specifying the factors that the provincial boards might consider in assessing an entry application, including the effects of new entry on existing carriers. Alberta's and Quebec's legislation contained no entry criteria. Ontario's, Manitoba's, and Saskatchewan's legislation did not mention entry criteria but granted the boards of those provinces backstop powers to approve entries on the basis of public interest. In all provinces, the highway transport boards were given "wide ranging, subjective powers to approve entry case by case."[65]

Except for Alberta, which has never restricted entry into the intraprovincial market (beyond requiring proof of insurance and financial responsibility), all other provinces have, in practice, followed the test of public convenience and necessity. As in the United States, proof required submitting evidence that the new service was necessary, and all provincial boards allowed interested parties to protest new entries. When Ontario began using these procedures in 1933, representatives of the railways and already-certificated truckers became regular attenders of board meetings.

Their protests have often been decisive. A study of the Ontario Highway Transport Board's decisions in 1977-8, for example, found a pattern of protecting truckers already holding operating authorities in the province. The number of protesting carriers was a primary factor accounting for denial. Applicants who were willing to modify their proposal to accommodate objections, the study found, were much more likely to be granted operating authority. Shipper support had "virtually no influence on the probability of a license being granted."[66] Offering lower rates did not help an applicant's case. "If pressed, most regulatory boards would probably deny the admissibility of rate issues in the determination of the public interest."[67] Canadian boards had a more general latitude within which to consider prospective harm to existing carriers, and some required proof that "other transportation services will not be adversely affected."[68] The Ontario and Quebec boards were regarded as being the most restrictive.[69] Protecting certificated carriers was the Quebec Transport Commission's "overriding concern."[70] New operating authorities in Quebec were "almost totally reserved to existing firms," who were able to share the industry's growth among themselves.[71] In Ontario, there was actually a decrease over time in the number of operating authorities in seven of the ten licence classes.[72]

Another index of the boards' discretionary powers was latitude not to publish the reasons for their decisions. The Ontario board, which possessed perhaps the broadest discretion, would only publish the results of its decisions, leaving no public case law on the meaning of public convenience and necessity as established by precedent. Canadian courts, in common with their American counterparts, were extremely reluctant to challenge provincial highway transport board decisions.

In both countries, the common carriers' route networks were incremental creations. They took form through years of piecemeal extensions of routes and commodities, through mergers with other carriers, and through the cautious and reluctant accommodation of new entrants. Regulators did not grant absolute monopolies, although they did allow small numbers of carriers to become predominant in particular areas. That made no carrier's domain either exclusive or exactly coextensive with another's; rather, the pattern was overlapping. Making things even more complex was the diversity of firm sizes, which ranged from small carriers on a handful of routes to large operators covering whole regions. The domains of the large overlapped those of the small, producing variegated networks across the two countries. For service beyond a carrier's territory it was necessary to interline with other carriers either by transferring the cargo at a terminal or by giving the loaded trailer directly to the next carrier. Before deregulation, almost all international motor freight was interlined at the border. Overall, common carriage was closely controlled and protected. The degree of protection showed in operating authorities' considerable cash value. To critics of regulation, that value reflected the excess profits possible in restricted markets.

Although common carriers could be licensed to handle goods in truckload (TL) quantities, their business tended to be less-than-truckload (LTL). Consolidation into volumes large enough to fill trailers requires terminals where shipments can be collected, classified, assembled, loaded, and dispatched. Nationwide common carriers had large terminal networks. In the United States, Yellow Freight Lines, one of the three largest, had 350 terminals; and in Canada, CP Express and Transport had fifty-six. Common carriers operated much like airlines, with fixed routes, regular schedules, and departures for particular destinations. Under deregulation, both airlines and common carriers rationalized their networks into hub-and-spoke systems.

Terminals and cargo handling figure significantly in common carriers' costs: a survey of fifty-four common carriers found terminal and platform costs averaging 26 percent of revenues.[73] That is a significant burden in an industry in which line-haul costs – primarily fuel and labour – predominate, although rate regulation, while it was in place, provided ample compensation. Terminal-centred operations also made common carriers the most territorially fixed of trucking's sectors. That was not a disadvantage under regulation because permission to expand or change operations was difficult for any carrier to obtain. For both costs and service, terminal-centred operations became a serious impediment under deregulation, as we will see later.

Private Carriage: The In-House Option

Private carriers are fleets assembled by manufacturers, distributors, and retailers to transport some or all of their goods themselves. Since they do not offer services for sale, neither Canada nor the United States has regulated them. The only restriction is that they must own the goods they carry, and this prevents them from hauling for hire or leasing their vehicles to other carriers or shippers. Freedom from entry, route, and commodity restrictions allows the vehicles to be used as needed, and freedom from dealing with for-hire carriers provides complete control over the goods. Instead of adapting to for-hire carriers' offerings and requirements, firms can manage transportation according to their own production and traffic patterns. Charging customers for shipping can recover capital and operating costs, and in many applications the premium-quality transportation available with private carriage is a sales advantage.

The spatial organization of private carriage is determined not by regulation but by traffic patterns. Private carriage is used in production for moving components from one facility to another and, in distribution, for supplying retail outlets. There is no competition between private carriers because they do not operate for hire; rather, competition is among the products their parent firms sell. Private carriers do compete with other trucking sectors, and the contest is over the respective ways of organizing and using fleets of trucks. Because of the capital commitment of establishing private fleets, traffic lost to them from for-hire carriers may be difficult to recover, particularly if the for-hire alternatives are less attractive. That was the case under regulation, with common carriers steadily losing traffic to private carriage. By the 1970s private carriers were moving the largest portion of Canadian and American motor freight.

Only the fact that private carriage was not equally attractive to all shippers limited the erosion. Establishing a private fleet requires a capital investment, and operating costs must be kept proportional to service benefits. Those costs depend on the logistical patterns of the parent firm. Balanced traffic patterns may produce efficient operations, but unbalanced patterns – usually found in shipping to distributors and retail outlets – mean empty miles and high costs. Common carriers, in the absence of one-way restrictions, were free to solicit backhaul cargo in order to balance operations. Because balance is so important, they have been willing to discount rates on backhauls and, under deregulation, have been free to do so. In the absence of regulation, private carriers would also be able to balance traffic by leasing their trucks and drivers to other carriers or shippers, converting themselves temporarily to for-hire carriers. The period could vary from a trip lease for a single journey to longer leases for slack periods. The prospect of such latitude and efficiency made private carriers solid supporters of deregulation. To regulatory reformers, private carriage's prime share of intercity traffic was evidence that regulated trucking was overpriced. To common carriers, deregulation promised even more traffic diversion. As attractive services developed under deregulation, however, many firms returned to for-hire carriers – one of the transitions examined in Chapter 6.

Contract Carriers: Marginal but Mobile

Contract carriers serve individual shippers on the basis of negotiated agreements. They differ from common carriers in that they offer rented transportation to particular clients and do not hold out their services to the general public; and they differ from private carriers in that they haul for hire.

American regulation subjected contract carriers to a lower entry standard. Instead of showing a specific need, as common carriers were required to do, it was enough to demonstrate that the proposed service would be in the general public interest. In practice that required evidence of insurance, responsibility, and a useful purpose. The legal basis had been set in *Stephenson* v. *Binford,* in which the Supreme Court upheld the state of Texas's lower barrier for contract carriers. The public interest test was used at both levels of government, with all but eight states requiring it. Offsetting this generous treatment was the ICC's "rule of eight," which limited a contract carrier to that number of shippers. Being found to be serving more than eight, or not to be "standing aloof from the lure of public calling," risked an ICC order to discontinue the illegal operations or be reclassified as a common carrier.[74]

The rule of eight kept contract carriers small and marginal, and they were far fewer in number than were common carriers. In 1955, for example, there were 2,646 ICC-certificated contract carriers in the United States compared to 15,686 common carriers.[75] They accounted for only 7 percent of ICC-regulated motor freight.[76] Because contract carriers posed so little competitive threat, the ICC's liberal entry standard did not harm common carriers. Shippers, however, were affected. For adequate and steady volume, the contract carrier's incentive was to fill the quota with the largest shippers available. For shippers too small to afford their own private fleets, common carriers were the only choice. For contract carriers themselves, the need to deal only with large shippers closed off much of the potential market.

Access to backhaul traffic was also curtailed, since it had to be available from one of the eight clients. Shippers with predominantly one-way traffic flows were unattractive customers. For them, too, since one-way flows raise the cost of private carriage, using common carriers was the only option. These regulatory effects, critics argued, entrenched the advantages of common carriers.[77] To make contract carriage widely available, reformers advocated ending the rule of eight.

Released from their regulatory limitations, contract carriers could compete directly with common carriers. Their advantages are mobility and a low cost structure. Shippers integrate contract carriers directly into their logistics. If a shipper uses the vehicles in regional distribution, then that is the carrier's domain. If the use is inter-regional or continent-wide, then those are the carrier's domains. Operating according to shippers' timetables keeps overheads low, supporting small firms and uncomplicated management.[78] This is one sector of trucking in which it has always been possible for newcomers to begin operations with a modest investment. A used tractor is affordable by family-car standards, and a used trailer costs even less. Some shippers supply their own trailers. These features make contract carriage simple, cheap, and adaptive. Used in a well-run logistics system, contract carriage is potentially very efficient. American contract carriers understood these advantages and supported deregulation.

The regulation of contract carriage in Canada has been less well defined than it has been in the United States. Contract carriers were governed by the same controls as were common carriers, and all provincial regulatory boards have the discretionary power to attach conditions and restrictions to individual operating authorities, including the names of the particular shippers to be served.[79] In Ontario contract carriage was recognized as a separate form of business, but, in more recent years, the province tended simply to award individual carriers authority to serve both the general public and specified individual shippers, allowing firms to be both common and contract carriers and eliminating some of the elaborate partitioning of American practice.[80] Because of that blurred distinction, contract carriage was rarely mentioned in the studies that Transport Canada and the Canadian Transport Commission commissioned in the early 1980s to supply an analysis upon which to base reform. It also did not appear in the annual reviews of the National Transportation Agency (discontinued in 1994), and it is not listed as a category in Statistics Canada's annual survey, *Trucking in Canada*.[81]

That does not mean a lack of awareness. In 1969 the Ontario Highway Transport Board, departing from its practice of not issuing justifications for its decisions, cited contract carriage as a reason for denying entry to firms offering lower rates. If such rates became available, the board stated, then shippers would begin clamouring for more contract carriage and threaten the business of common carriers.[82] In the decade before deregulation, provincial boards began authorizing contract carriage much more generously, partly in recognition of the mode's efficiencies.[83]

Owner-Operators: Semi-Free Agents

Independent owner-operators, who buy and maintain their own trucks, were free in both countries to haul exempt commodities, primarily unprocessed agricultural products, without operating authorities. Hauling regulated commodities required owner-operators to lease their vehicles and services to a certificated carrier. Canadian owner-operators needed a lease in force in order to use the public roads, while American owner-operators with expired leases could travel in search of new ones. Motor carriers pay owner operators an agreed portion of the trip revenue, usually on a per-mile basis. Leasing allows owner-operators to be engaged or let go as traffic requires, providing carriers a flexible and low-cost source of equipment and labour. Whether leasing offers an owner-operator stable employment depends on the carrier. Lapses in traffic or bad faith in providing enough work represent serious risks. A particularly bad situation occurs when one is stranded far from home without a return load. Owner-operators stood to benefit from liberalized leasing rules that would give them access to other for-hire carriers, private carriers, and shippers, and so they supported deregulation.

Because a fleet of trucks can be used in so many different applications, these regulatory partitions were to some extent artificial. By removing the partitions, deregulation allowed the industry to reorganize according to actual capabilities and demand. The most striking change was the rapid emergence of TL carriers in both countries. These firms haul full-trailer consignments directly from shipper to receiver, eliminating the common carriers' costly and slow terminal networks and adapting readily to tailored service. TLs operate for general hire but share contract carriage's simpler operating structures and unlimited mobility. Contract carriers, with the exception of some firms such as Ryder, continue to be small, but their market share has grown. Both contract and TL carriers are appealing substitutes for private carriage. The private carriage operations that continue enjoy favourable traffic balances (which can be augmented through trip leasing) or serve highly particular requirements. Even so, the substitutability of for-hire carriage is a constant consideration.

In the face of these changes, common carriers – known, since deregulation, as LTL carriers – had to streamline their operations in order to survive. The task was formidable because TL and contract carriers can undercut LTL rates and provide faster service. The adjustments were so wrenching that most of the large LTLs closed, leaving only three fully nationwide operations in the United States and none in Canada. Enjoying simpler networks and lower overheads, regional LTLs have expanded rapidly in the two countries and are quite profitable. We will see these transitions in more detail in Chapter 6. For now it is enough to remember regulation's structuring effects and the industry's underlying characteristics.

Standard Rates and Collegial Consultation

Both Canadian and American regulation allowed carriers to form organizations for setting common rates. As with entry controls, the purpose was a stable and prosperous industry. Carriers would ensure adequate profits for themselves, and regulators would ensure fair and reasonable rates for the public. Collusive price setting is illegal in both countries, but American and Canadian courts held the truckers' activity not to be a crime as long as there was regulatory supervision. Under regulation common carriers did well financially. The American sector's return on equity averaged 17 percent to 18 percent.[84] The national average for manufacturing industries is 12 percent to 15 percent.[85] The Canadian trucking industry as a whole enjoyed a 15 percent return on equity in 1988, the year before full-scale deregulation took effect.[86] One reason for that performance was rate regulation predicated on adequate earnings.

After the Motor Carrier Act's passage in 1935, truckers began establishing regional rate bureaus, following the practice of the railways and the urging of the ICC.[87] Rate bureaus provided a common forum and produced rates to which all could agree. Rates were specified for every commodity according to an elaborate system that classified cargo by size, density, and distance. The bureaus published rate books for shippers and, as required by the Motor Carrier Act, filed their rates with the ICC. The commission's power of rate review enabled it to deny or modify those it deemed unreasonable.

In keeping with its practice with the railways, the ICC used a standard figure to assess motor carrier profitability when deciding to approve rate increases. That figure was the carrier's operating ratio, which is the percentage of revenue claimed by operating expenses. It continues to be used as a handy index of performance. An operating ratio of 100 shows no profit and a ratio over 100 shows net loss. The ICC's standard for motor common carriers was ninety-three, and rate increases filed to keep firms at that level were granted automatically.[88] To put that figure into perspective, LTL operating ratios since deregulation have run in the mid-to-high nineties. In that competitive environment, as Chapter 6 will show, an operating ratio of ninety-five shows efficiency and cost control. A ratio below ninety is extremely impressive. With much less need for efficiency under regulation, the ICC's figure of ninety-three was quite comfortable.

Collective rates raised antitrust questions. Congress removed that exposure in 1948 with the Reed-Bulwinkle Act, which it passed over President Truman's veto. The Reed-Bulwinkle Act exempted regulated motor carriers participating in collective rate agreements from antitrust prosecution, provided their rates had ICC approval. Although the act allowed carriers to file independent rates, the rate bureaus, backed by the ICC, allowed other members to file protests. The virtual certainty of that happening strongly discouraged departures from bureau rates.[89] By the 1950s there were more than 100 rate bureaus in the United States and an elaborate, complex, and closely coordinated set of rates. That arrangement deluged the ICC with several thousand rates a day. The result of being so overwhelmed was that the ICC tended to approve rates automatically and, in 1977, rejected only 1 percent.[90]

Tariff bureaus in Canada have reflected the diverse provincial practices of rate regulation. In provinces where the regulatory boards have prescriptive power over intraprovincial rates, the tariff bureaus have sought to represent their members before the boards. Until recently, the Manitoba, Saskatchewan, and Newfoundland boards specified rates.[91] The other provinces required only that rates be filed with the provincial boards, and Alberta had no rate-filing requirements. Only Newfoundland and Quebec showed concern about extra-provincial rates.[92] Price fixing was illegal under the federal Combines Investigation Act, although court interpretation allowed the activity if rates were filed according to law. Courts also presumed regulated rate filing to be in the public interest.[93]

Provinces spent far less on rate regulation than they did on entry control.[94] In Ontario fewer than half of the certificated carriers bothered to file tariffs at all.[95] In Quebec there was so little rate enforcement that the price behaviour of the industry actually approximated competition.[96] To some extent this represented a compromise between controls and an open market. Shippers fearing price discrimination by truckers and truckers fearing "rate chiselling" by large shippers had a common interest in standard prices.[97] At the same time, enforcement of the myriad rates produced by route and commodity regulation would be prohibitively expensive. As a solution the boards depended on the tariff bureaus to establish standard rates and on carrier self-interest to police discounting. Carriers would hear of rate cutting from shippers or receivers. Although there was the option of bringing legal charges, the more common remedy was to have carriers in the tariff bureau put pressure on the discounter to stay in line.[98] The view in the trucking industry was that this system was somewhat flexible in practice and made the transition to price competition after deregulation less drastic in Canada than it was in the United States.[99]

In both countries, rate, service, and entry regulation allocated territories and market shares within each sector and kept transportation products distinct. Because Canadian and American regulation was so similar, it structured the two industries in strikingly parallel ways. As we will see in Chapter 6, that correspondence formed the basis of integrated transborder service, which developed rapidly once the regulatory barriers were removed. Until then, their protective effects had made regulated truckers keen to preserve the system. The two trucking associations were strong advocates of regulatory barriers.

The Trucking and Shippers Associations

Regulation's effect on the industry's sectoral structure showed in the ATA's use of the plural in its title. The ATA is a group of affiliated carrier conferences. Under regulation they represented common, contract, and private carriers along with specialized sectors such as tank truck carriers. Owner-operators have their own associations. Common carriers were the ATA's principal constituency under regulation, and their position as the industry's largest firms gave their interests and economic support special weight. The ATA's firm opposition to deregulation was based on the common carriers' interests – not those of contract and private carriers. At the same time, the ATA sought collective action in a diverse industry, pooling its members' resources, setting common policies, representing carrier interests in Congress and, most important, acting as an interested party in ICC proceedings. The industry's structural diversity and its thousands of carriers made that a considerable achievement.

In Canada, federal divisions made the provincial trucking associations the predominant carrier organizations. Until recently the CTA, the national trucking organization, was small and had no responsibilities with the federal government in the area most crucial to truckers – economic regulation. Until deregulation and American entry became an issue, the CTA had defined its mission as continuing the fight, begun in the 1930s, against regulatory advantages for the railways.[100] The provincial associations reflected the size of their carrier industries. The Ontario Trucking Association has always been the largest and best-funded. Private carriers and independent owner-operators have their own associations. Canadian trucking associations had a similar stake in maintaining regulation, but the decentralized implementation of reform meant that each provincial association fought its own battles on its own territory. That placed the provincial associations in potential conflict with each other, since each could be expected to help protect its members from extra-provincial outsiders.

Shippers pooled their resources to deal with regulators and the trucking associations. Regulatory decisions directly affected the terms of transport supply, making shippers interested parties in proceedings and providing an incentive for common positions. The National Industrial Transportation League (NITL) in the United States and the Canadian Industrial Transportation League (CITL) in Canada organized trucking's thousands of clients. Both the NITL and the CITL supported deregulation, although on the Canadian side, as will be seen in Chapter 5, that determination was not immediately made. When the CITL did decide to support deregulation, its large and national organization made it possible to focus pressure on the federal government and so make deregulation a political priority. The CTL subsequently became the Canadian Industrial Transportation Association. Compared to the decentralized array of trucking associations, the shippers' greater degree of integration was a significant comparative advantage; although, as Chapter 5 will show, the truckers and provinces had the residual powers of delay.

The Teamsters

The Teamsters Union's goal of winning high wages for its members gave it a stake in regulation because protected market shares meant stable and profitable employers. Collective rate making was especially favourable because it enabled the Teamsters to bargain for generous settlements, whose costs could then be collectively shifted to shippers.

In the United States, the union was a loose affiliation of regional power centres until the 1950s, when Presidents Dave Beck and Jimmy Hoffa centralized the organization. In 1969 the Teamsters won the power to negotiate Master Freight Agreements covering all unionized carriers. Those agreements established uniform pay rates and enabled the Teamsters to call nationwide strikes. Dealing with the Teamsters was another reason for carriers to be well organized. Unionized carriers negotiated collectively with the Teamsters as Trucking Management, Inc., whose member firms employed about 65 percent of the 170,000 Teamsters working in motor carriage.

Master Freight Agreements suited both sides. They allowed carriers and a powerful union to bargain from positions of collective strength and to achieve uniform outcomes. The union's interest in raising costs in a key category made it an adversary, but it depended on regulation as much as did the carriers. The ATA and the Teamsters joined forces to preserve regulation over the years and made a desperate cooperative effort to thwart the Motor Carrier Act, 1980. The Teamsters' ability to integrate all labour in trucking was incomplete, however, since its domain is common carriers. Private and contract carriers, as well as owner-operators, are non-union.

The Teamsters had less centralized power in Canada than they did in the United States because regulation was provincially based. As with the trucking associations, the provinces' varying kinds of rate regulation and levels of price competition limited the basis for an integrated national organization. There are also many regional and local non-union firms, although contract settlements with large unionized carriers do establish wage comparisons. The Canadian Teamsters opposed deregulation for the same reasons as did the American Teamsters, but Canada's decentralized precincts diffused activity. At the federal level the Canadian Labour Congress (CLC) was the main opponent. Its stance, however, was part of the its strong opposition to the Canada-United States Free Trade Agreement (FTA). The two issues converged when the FTA was negotiated – just as the Motor Vehicle Transport Act was receiving parliamentary attention. The CLC regarded deregulation and free trade as twin evils and put Canadian truckers on their list of free trade's victims. Five years earlier, when the Trucking War had placed American and Canadian carriers directly at odds, the Teamsters union on both sides of the border avoided involvement. The opposed interests threatened division within the union.

Conclusion

Assumptions about the role of government and the characteristics of particular industries can support pervasive long-term government interventions. Railways, it was originally believed, could not withstand competition from trucking; and trucking, it was believed, was inherently prone to instability. It was thought that the regulatory regime that was in force on the railways was also the proper one to apply to trucking. Consequently, regulatory assumptions were uncritically shifted from the former to the latter, and this resulted in an elaborately structured arrangement of rules, partitions, and standard prices. Institutional persistence lay in the trucking industry's stability, the achievement of which had been the purpose of both governments in the 1930s.

The practical expression of those assumptions was entry, route, and commodity controls. These controls entrenched a particular sectoral organization, as we saw with common, private, and contract carriage, and produced parallel and complementary industries in Canada and the United States. Because these were artificial partitions in a naturally diverse and flexible industry, deregulation opened the way not only to competition, but also to reorganization. For that to occur, however, regulation's supporting assumptions had to change. By the 1970s there were points of argument. As economic research began to reveal a naturally efficient and competitive industry beneath the elaborate structure of rules, the public's true interest in regulation began to be questioned. This critique is taken up in the next chapter. Here we have seen the regulatory assumptions in practice.

3

The State Withdraws: Critique and Reform in the United States

Motor carrier deregulation in the United States was spread over three years, but the results were decisive. This outcome is striking because the ATA and the International Brotherhood of Teamsters had a long political track record of rebuffing reform initiatives, and they were regarded as powerful special interests. In the face of their determined opposition, one would expect regulatory reform to be, at best, a half measure involving political compromise and adjustment; instead, deregulation was thoroughgoing and radical, and the results for the ATA and the Teamsters were drastic. To understand why, we must consider the Interstate Commerce Commission's latitude to act.

This level of latitude is present when authority is centred in a single agency whose influence in a particular sector is determinate.[1] An agency's position is strongest when it has a clear role conception, political support, and legal authority. A clear role conception focuses the agency's purpose for both its members and its sectoral constituency and fosters decisiveness. Political support, bolstered by legal authority, enables an agency to act independently of its constituency's wishes. "Individual bureaus," in the words of Atkinson and Coleman, "will be more autonomous when they administer a corpus of law and regulation that defines their responsibilities and those of societal groups. These rules will not be subject to negotiation, either in their interpretation or their implementation."[2] Comprehensive regulation provides many such occasions.

As we saw in Chapter 2, the Motor Carrier Act, 1935, invested the ICC with control over entry into the industry, zones of operation, pricing, competition, conditions of service, and the terms of dealing with both shippers and regulators. As was also seen, the ICC performed these functions under a mandate that was stable and durable enough to qualify as an institutionalized set of assumptions. As long as the ICC's decisions suited the interests of its motor carrier constituents, it operated relatively free of conflict. The assets of political support and legal authority, however, also supported the ICC in the very different pursuit of deregulation. With the backing of an accumulated economic critique and encouragement from the White House, the ICC proceeded, in the face of protests and alarm from the industry, to re-interpret its legal authority. Instead of restricting entry and competition, the ICC induced them.

Congress, which *is* sensitive to diverse representations, became involved partly in order to avoid having its own emerging interest in reform being overtaken by the ICC. The resulting legislation, reflecting trucking's remaining political power, was a compromise that stopped short of complete deregulation. In interpreting and administering its new mandate, however, the ICC simply proceeded with its purpose of complete deregulation, which it quickly achieved. Respective to Congress, the ICC's performance was possible for three reasons. First, the ICC's ability to dominate relations within the trucking sector was undiminished; second, Congress's own inclination to restrain the ICC was lukewarm; and third, Congress's behaviour reflected a major shift in institutionalized assumptions, allowing the passage of reform legislation and administrative latitude for the ICC. The supporting assumptions subsequently reconfigured around competition. The results of this were structural and basic: the relationships between carriers and shippers shifted from being guided by administered rules to being guided by direct interaction.

Critique and Change

Ideas matter. That is the implication of the concept of policy-oriented learning, in which the transformation of policy preferences is a key condition for major policy change. The central actors are members of policy coalitions composed of individuals both inside and outside of government.[3] To account for change, policy-oriented learning does not require interest group realignment – the core of traditional pluralist explanations of public policy; rather, people in a position to influence or administer policy are persuaded by the proponents of change to accept new definitions of key problems and solutions. The focus is "on the ways in which the policy preferences of extant actors are transformed."[4] For that reason, individuals outside the usual constellations of interest groups and government bodies are important participants.[5] In the case of deregulation, academic economists were prominent and influential. In order for change to actually transpire, ideas and research must be linked to external developments that cast doubt on existing policies, and a plausible alternative must be available. Officials who support change and can implement the alternative must be in place.[6]

As we will see, academic critiques of trucking regulation reach back to the late 1930s and gained sophistication during the 1960s and 1970s. The crucial external development was the energy and stagflation crises of the mid-1970s, which academic economists were able to link to regulatory waste. A concurrent development was the weakening of regulation's legal footings, which was brought on by unprecedented federal court challenges of ICC decisions. Pro-reform commissioners were appointed to the ICC by the Ford and Carter administrations, who were persuaded to do this by the economic critique and by the energy crisis and stagflation. With the Carter administration's support, the ICC began in-house reform in 1977 and, in a series of administrative rulings, had changed the basis of entry and competition by 1979. Congress's intervention with the Motor Carrier Act, 1980, simply affirmed the ICC's actions. A similar pattern characterized American airline deregulation, although Congress was involved at an earlier stage.[7]

From an institutional perspective, the economists' critique attacked regulation's supporting assumptions. From the original audience of academics, the critique gained enough credibility over the next twenty-five years to displace those assumptions and to remove a set of institutionalized norms that had been in place for almost half a century. The supporting assumptions, rooted in the Depression, held trucking to be a naturally unstable industry and regulation to be requisite for dependable transportation. Two factors favoured their continuation.

First, the trucking industry had been regulated since the 1920s (if state-level measures preceding the Motor Carrier Act, 1935, are considered) and had grown and developed under tight controls. It was difficult to imagine the industry under any other conditions. Moreover, as an unregulated infant industry, trucking was turbulent and unstable, making for a plausible post hoc argument that regulation was instrumentally rational.[8] That attribution persisted even though the regulatory model imposed in 1935, as was seen in Chapter 2, was designed for railways and not motor carriers and addressed a completely different problem: monopolistic abuse by a powerful industry. Second, regulated trucking was stable and profitable. Aside from Teamster strikes, this crucial service operated dependably year after year. In the absence of obvious or impending problems, a prudent case could be made for simply leaving it alone. The economists' contribution as members of the advocacy coalition was to build a compelling case that the regulatory model did not fit the trucking industry and that the results of this model were inefficiency and waste. Despite the impressive academic case, however, deregulation was still merely an experiment. Without the energy crisis and stagflation, and without reform-minded ICC commissioners, change probably would not have been as thorough as it was. Congress was content with liberalization.

Deregulation left carriers and shippers to reach their own accommodations and opened the way for Canadian carriers to operate in the United States. That development will be seen in the next chapter. The purpose now is to review the economic critique; the role of the White House and the ICC; the passage of the Motor Carrier Act, 1980; and deregulation's effects on the industry through the 1980s and 1990s. Chapter 3 concludes with the elimination of state-level controls in 1995, which represented deregulation across the board.

The Critique

Motor carrier regulation, with its barriers to entry and collaborative pricing, invited scrutiny. According to economist James C. Nelson, who was one of the main contributors to the literature on trucking regulation, criticism began appearing as early as 1938.[9] He published a paper advocating competition in transportation in 1942,[10] and he credited a report he prepared in 1944 for the Board of Investigation and Research (an independent federal agency) with setting the points of reference for later critiques in the 1950s and 1960s.[11] Dudley Pegrum, professor of economics at the University of California, elaborated the basic case in 1952. Trucking, he argued, is a naturally competitive industry. Entry, route, and commodity controls cause inefficiency, and rate controls set needlessly high prices. Competition would reward efficient carriers and benefit shippers. The loss of inefficient carriers, who would be driven out by competition, would not open the way for survivors to raise prices because the prospect of good earnings would attract competitors, either as new firms or as existing ones redeploying their equipment – a tribute to trucking's natural flexibility. With regulation crippling that flexibility, and with collective rate making compensating carriers for sub-optimal utilization, shippers and the general public bear excess transport costs.[12]

In 1957 the governors of the New England states, concerned about carrier prices and regional development, authorized an extensive investigation of motor carriage in the region. The report, which became a standard reference in the motor carrier regulatory literature, pointedly addressed rates and competition, connecting the economic critique to practical policy issues. One of the report's principal findings was that operating costs of the region's motor carriers showed little relationship to the size of the carrier firms. Removing controls would not lead to large carriers becoming dominant and predatory; rather, removing controls would enable all carriers to increase their efficiency through better equipment utilization.[13] Economies of scale became a major research focus in the 1970s, as we will see presently.

In 1965 Pegrum drew out the regulatory implications of trucking's flexible technology. Trucking, he argued, is highly adaptable to changes in transportation demand, and firms have ample incentives to compete for new business arising from those changes. By making route and commodity authorities rigid, regulation restricts trucking's ability to respond to opportunity, benefiting neither the public nor competition-minded carriers.[14] To the objection that lifting controls would replicate the conditions of the 1930s by attracting too many carriers, producing cut-throat competition and leading to high rates of failure and instability, the economists' rejoinder was that the industry is inherently flexible.[15] Capacity in trucking, wrote John Lansing, is short-term, both because of the comparatively brief operating life of trucks and the ease of altering fleet size. Those conditions make it possible for truckers to tailor their operations to traffic demands, working against long-term oversupply.[16] This flexibility is an inherent feature of trucking's basic technology and would not change under deregulation.

Political Inertia

These ideas had no immediate political success, and until the 1970s the record is one of abortive or defeated efforts at trucking reform. President Truman vetoed the Reed-Bulwinkle Act, 1948, which gave antitrust immunity to collective rate making, but the law was passed by a Congressional override. The Eisenhower administration's interest in allowing more room for market forces was reflected in the report of the Presidential Advisory Committee on Transportation Policy and Organization, issued in 1955.[17] To promote price competition, the Transportation Act, 1958, included a provision to prevent the ICC from denying rate reductions. A legislative change of wording, however, placed the act's terms of reference in the preamble of the Interstate Commerce Act, thus removing its practical effect. In 1962 President Kennedy also proposed ending the ICC's power to deny rate decreases, but that initiative died in Congress. In 1971 the Nixon administration put forward the Transportation Regulatory Modernizaton Act. It would reduce the ICC's power to restrict motor carrier entry and limit routes and commodities, and it would establish a "zone of reasonableness" within which carriers could raise or lower rates without ICC approval. That legislation also was not passed, although it did get to the stage of Congressional hearings.[18]

In every instance the ATA and the Teamsters put up vigorous opposition, and their success contributed to their reputations as formidable special interest lobbies. In their favour was the fact that interstate motor carriers were doing very well. Although the economic arguments just seen attributed those results to protected territories and profits, the ATA and the Teamsters maintained that the purpose of the Motor Carrier Act was a healthy industry. Regulation worked. As the economic critique grew in refinement and visibility, however, the ATA was required to refine its own case. The new elements appeared in the ATA's testimony during the House of Representatives hearings on the Transportation Act, 1972. One point of refinement concerned creamskimming – a concept in theories of regulation.[19] The ATA argued that, under deregulation, new entrants would concentrate on the most desirable traffic, leaving less profitable remains for the older firms. The ATA also adduced economies of scale, asserting that they existed in trucking and required continuing regulation. Efficiency, the argument went, increases with carrier size. Inequity appears because only well-capitalized firms could invest in terminals and profitably operate extensive and dense route structures. Firms with less capitalization would have greater amounts of empty vehicle movement because of their inability to rationalize traffic. These operations would lower the overall efficiency of road transport and impose unnecessary costs on the public. As will be seen shortly, economists investigating economies of scale in trucking later in the 1970s obtained very diverse results. Concluding on a more familiar note, the ATA asserted that relaxing controls would endanger the balanced and profitable firms and lead to destructive competition.[20] Again legislation was forestalled.

The Critique Elaborated

In 1968, reflecting on the difficulty of challenging regulation's institutionalized assumptions, Pegrum lamented the lack of a foundation in economic theory. "All of the reports since 1954," he wrote, "have placed considerable emphasis on the desirability of reducing governmental restraint on transport and of affording greater opportunity for the play of competitive forces. However, none of them has developed the economic premises upon which such an approach must be founded."[21] An "authoritative formulation" for a "comprehensive and progressive program for Congressional action ... is lacking at the present time."[22] He may have been too pessimistic. In the previous year the Brookings Institution received $1.8 million from the Ford Foundation for an eight-year research program on regulation. The yield from that grant was 22 books, 65 journal articles, and 38 doctoral dissertations, which, taken together, represented a major advance in the knowledge and publicity necessary for successful political change.[23] The American Enterprise Institute also took up deregulation as a research priority, further increasing publicity and, with its conservative imprimatur, making the issue genuinely bipartisan.

Work and elaboration continued to focus on the notion that motor carriage is a naturally competitive industry. A key research question concerned whether or not trucking has economies of scale. The answer bore directly on whether or not lifting regulatory controls was a good idea, for the existence of economies of scale would give large carriers lower cost structures and, hence, would support predatory discounting, enabling them to drive out smaller competitors and to use their market power to raise prices and earn excess profits. The 1970s produced a variety of findings. Some researchers found indications of increasing returns to scale,[24] along with economies of scale in the production of high-quality service, with larger fleets of vehicles making it possible to assemble and dispatch shipments more rapidly.[25] Other researchers found only very weak evidence of economies of scale[26] or no evidence at all.[27]

Some who did find economies of scale discovered that these derived from conditions not related to the firm's size,[28] while others found that large route networks, although not directly related to lower costs, did enable carriers to assemble enough loads to achieve high levels of vehicle utilization.[29] Still others found diseconomies of scale in large carriers.[30] Other economists held that economies of scale, if they did exist, were not of sufficient magnitude to enable large carriers to exploit lower costs and to earn monopoly profits.[31] A related view held that the entry of new carriers on a particular route would not require others to exit. They would simply share traffic more widely. Instead of leading to a plague of bankruptcies and an increase of concentration, reform would, in fact, lessen concentration.[32]

Ann Friedlaender and Elizabeth Bailey advanced understanding with the argument that trucking is a multiproduct industry. LTL carriers, we saw, offer different services than do TL firms, and TL carriage itself is available on a for-hire, contract, or private basis. Within those broad divisions are a multitude of individually distinctive services based on commodities, route density and extensiveness, equipment, cargo handling, and the ability to meet highly specific shipper requirements. The products of any of these combinations, although all involve vehicles and the movement of goods, differ significantly in quality. That view lent a diverse and qualified perspective to economies of scale. When trucking is regarded as a multiproduct industry, Friedlaender and Bailey found, scale economies vary according to the carrier's level of output and the mix of its transport products, with economies appearing in some combinations and diseconomies in others. That being the case, concentration may occur in some particular sectors in trucking with the lifting of regulatory norms, but, given the industry's diversity and the ease with which shippers can shift traffic among carriers and sectors, competition should be workable.[33]

Since 1984, six of the nine studies conducted have found no significant economies of scale in American trucking. Three of those studies used pre-deregulation data,[34] one used post-deregulation data,[35] and two used data from both periods.[36] Two of the three studies that did find scale economies used pre- and post-deregulation data as well,[37] and one used only post-deregulation data.[38] Commenting on these findings, University of British Columbia transport economist Garland Chow said that one of the studies showing economies of scale did so by using a controversial methodology and that another was flawed in how it measured carrier output. In general, Chow believes, recent research is strongly in agreement that returns to scale in trucking are constant, although he notes that the issue is still contentious and is tied to political differences over deregulation.[39]

The conclusion that predatory pricing would not occur under deregulation was also supported by an analysis of the trucking industry's structure. Predatory pricing requires firms with enough resources to cut rates below variable costs long enough to drive out competitors but without injuring themselves. Successful predation also requires high enough barriers to entry to enable the predatory firm to gain back the losses from discounting and enjoy a lack of competition long enough to make its efforts worthwhile.[40] The low capital cost entry barriers and the ease with which existing firms can redeploy resources, however, make it possible for new competitors to take advantage of opportunities created by successful predation. In such situations, new competitors could offer prices below those a successful predator had just raised. The higher the predator hiked prices, the greater the latitude for a newcomer to realize earnings over costs.[41]

A variant of destructive competition involves novice firms with an incomplete knowledge of their costs entering and charging unsustainably discounted rates in order to attract shippers. Although doing this would guarantee the newcomers a short career in trucking, they would succeed in disrupting orderly relationships among carriers and shippers and weaken established competitors, who would be forced to keep pace. Preventing this was one of the ATA's arguments for regulation. The counter argument, however, was that businesspeople do not set out to have their enterprises fail and that "ill-advised entry is not a frequent and persistent danger."[42] A final theme of destructive competition – and one widely used in regulatory proceedings – was that the entry of new firms of any sort might drive existing carriers into bankruptcy. To that was posed the rejoinder that such competition was not predation but the normal efforts of carriers to attract business by offering more attractive services and rates than their rivals. The firms most threatened by such behaviour are those who had been made "so fat and complacent" by regulation that they could not cope with normal business activity.[43] Carriers that were overpaid and inefficient to that extent were of no benefit to the public interest.

A related structural issue was concentration. Supporters of deregulation saw relatively little concentration of carrier firms and regarded this as another index of a naturally competitive industry. Even in situations where there was only one carrier on a particular route, the removal of entry controls would make it possible for other carriers to redeploy their equipment and provide competition. The efficiencies of carriers enjoying high levels of vehicle utilization would not be sufficient to deter the entry of rivals if prevailing rates were high enough to make competitive discounting worthwhile.[44] Trucking's flexible technology and capital cost structure were also used to argue against administered prices. High minimum rates might be justified if motor carriage were characterized by high fixed costs. The costs in trucking, as many transport economists pointed out, are predominantly variable and are accounted for by such factors as labour and fuel. In addition, the freight-carrying capacity is spread over a number of relatively small vehicles that are relatively cheap to buy or lease and that may be added or deleted as demand requires. Those features make fixed costs in trucking very unlike those of railroads or utilities, whose capital equipment is concentrated in large units that are expensive and difficult to adjust in the short run. To meet peak periods of demand, railroads and utilities must carry extra capacity through normal times and charge rates that compensate for that expense. Since trucking technology allows easy adjustment to levels of demand, motor carriers do not require fixed rates.[45]

Studies of exempt carriers challenged the trucking lobby's argument that an unregulated industry would produce unreliable service. Exempt carriers, often owner-operators, handled commodities – primarily unprocessed agricultural products – that were not regulated by the ICC. In 1935 farmers insisted that agricultural commodities not be included in the new Motor Carrier Act and strenuously opposed ICC efforts in subsequent years to apply a narrow interpretation to agricultural exemption. That episode was often pointed out as an index of shippers' true preferences. According to one study of exempt haulers, which found them to have lower costs and revenues than regulated carriers, the "data suggest that the farmers were right ... the effect of regulation is to raise, not lower average rates in the trucking industry."[46] This same study also found that exempt carriers did not fit the image of unstable and short-lived operations that were part of the institutionalized historical depiction – a finding made more impressive by the open price competition among exempt carriers. Whenever regulated carriers or regulators had suggested bringing exempt carriers under ICC control, agricultural shippers had been "prompt to protest, arguing that exempt carriers are more flexible, cheaper, and offer substantially better alternatives than the regulated firms."[47] Senate and House hearings in 1972 on the Nixon administration's reform legislation found not one complaint concerning service from exempt carriers but a litany concerning regulated carriers.[48]

Finally, reformers attacked restrictive route and commodity authorities as well as private carrier restrictions on the grounds of waste – an argument that became particularly pertinent after the energy crisis of 1973. Forcing carriers to travel needlessly roundabout routes, allowing them to haul approved commodities in only one direction, and to pass up available loads on return trips all meant vehicle capacity being under-utilized, raising the operating costs of motor carriers overall, and – tellingly – wasting fuel.[49] One of hundreds of examples of such restrictions was the case of a carrier serving Harrisburg, Pennsylvania. When hauling packaged goods south to Florida, the carrier was required first to travel 198 miles northeast through New York City. Returning from Florida, the carrier was permitted to haul only clothing or fresh vegetables.[50] Similarly, a 1980 survey of private carriers found that the respondents' fleets were empty for 27 percent of their mileage because of the regulatory restriction forbidding them from hauling for-hire freight. With, at that time, private carriage accounting for 44 percent more intercity freight than regulated truckers, waste of that magnitude was a significant consideration.[51]

The only serious deficiency in the economists' critique was that statistical and modelling techniques did not allow them to reach uniform estimates on the overall costs of regulation to the American economy. Pointing to a range of estimates of those costs from "a few hundred million dollars to $20 billion," Roger Noll, speaking to a conference on regulatory reform in 1978, asserted that "members of Congress and politicians in general respond to such a range of estimates by believing that economists have nothing to say."[52] Even so, against the accumulation of serious economic research depicting a structurally competitive industry, the ATA and the Teamsters had nothing of comparable development and sophistication.

The policy implications of the critiques pointed to an institutional role reversal for regulators. Instead of restricting competition among firms, they should ensure that there is a "pool of potential competitors who can respond to profit opportunities by entering the market."[53] Once such a pool exists, tight controls over rate authority can be loosened. The proper role of regulators, therefore, is to award authority – even for routes and commodities the applicant may not use. Doing so enables the new carriers to be potential competitors – competitors who are able to contest excessive prices charged by the firms occupying those niches.[54] In other words, the institutional role would change from restriction to admission.

The economic critiques were a good successor to the institutionalized assumptions that had supported regulation. Congress's behaviour after passage of the Motor Carrier Act can be seen as reflecting a fundamental shift in its view of regulation. At the annual oversight hearings on the act's implementation, the ATA and Teamsters displayed an industry reeling under the combined effects of deregulation and recession, resembling the dire conditions of which they had always warned. Congress, as will be seen shortly, showed no willingness to intervene, even though the industry's distress was unmistakable. Free entry and exit were becoming the regular condition.

Regulation in Crisis: Energy Shortages, Stagflation, and Institutional Legitimacy

Critiques and alternatives, regardless of their merit and appeal, are themselves not sufficient to alter policy preferences to the point of producing major change. The instigating factor is external developments that call existing policy into serious question and allow reform advocates to show how their alternative would provide a remedy. In the words of Sabatier and Jenkins-Smith, "The core [basic attributes]of a governmental action program is unlikely to be changed in the absence of significant perturbations external to the subsystem, that is, changes in socio-economic conditions, system-wide governing coalitions, or policy outputs from other subsystems."[55] Undeniable evidence of trouble with existing policy, in other words, has to exist before critiques and solutions will be considered seriously enough to prompt change.

By 1971 there was a strong feeling among economists and regulators themselves that "much of regulation in the United States is in deep trouble." That assessment emerged from a conference of thirty-two experts on regulation, representing a diversity of perspectives and experience, convened by the Brookings Institution to consider the Ash council's recommendations for reforming American regulation. "Former commissioners appointed during both Republican and Democratic administrations, academic experts from three disciplines, and individuals who had held high staff positions in regulatory agencies in both the 1950s and 1960s, while often differing in their assessment of the causes and possible cures of regulatory failures, nevertheless recognized the critical state of affairs in regulation."[56]

The experts identified two principal failures: (1) creating and preserving economic inefficiency and (2) favouring the interests of the regulated firms over the interests of the general public.[57] In the economic climate of the 1970s, as inflation and soaring fuel costs threatened economic stability, the normal means of economic policy seemed incapable of producing – or even finding – remedies. The economic critiques of regulation, however, pointed to easily understood waste, and the trucking industry's presence on the public roads made waste particularly easy to visualize. As regulatory reform became associated with energy savings and inflation-fighting efficiency, academic ideas were transformed into serious policy alternatives, and defending the institutional status quo meant opposing a defined public interest.[58]

The distance between academic economists and administrators was not wide. The number of "formally trained economists in policy-making positions," according to Gary Seevers, a member of the Council of Economic Advisers (CEA), was "certainly at a record level" in the executive branch, where deregulation enjoyed strong support.[59] As a result of the CEA's advocacy of deregulation, wrote Seevers in 1975, "the idea no longer frightens as many people as it did at one time."[60] Professional consensus was an indicative outcome of President Ford's Summit Conference on Inflation, which was convened in the fall of 1974 and deliberately included economists "from every faction of the discipline."[61] Although the economists were unable to agree on measures to combat inflation itself, they were united in the view that some areas of economic regulation were imposing needless inefficiency. Their recommendations for trucking amounted to complete deregulation: removal of all entry barriers and route and commodity restrictions, loosening of rate regulation to allow more price competition, and repeal of the Reed-Bulwinkle Act, which had granted antitrust immunity to collective rate making among motor carriers. When President Ford indicated to Congress that regulatory reform was to be a priority of his administration, he moved deregulation into the wider political arena.[62]

The Ford administration formulated comprehensive legislation to liberalize entry controls on interstate trucking. Introduced in Congress as the Motor Carrier Reform Act, 1975, on 13 November, the legislation provided for a greater reliance on competitive forces, more flexible pricing, and easier and faster awarding of operating authorities. The legislation also called for removing arbitrary restrictions on private and contract carriers, removing "wasteful and inefficient" route restrictions in existing authorities, and liberalizing backhauling of regulated commodities.[63] Again the ATA and the Teamsters applied lobbying pressure, and Congress did no more with the legislation than call for comments.[64] This time, however, Congress did appoint a National Transportation Study Commission, whose report, issued in 1979, recommended dropping public convenience and necessity and giving increased emphasis to improved competition, service innovation, and energy efficiency. The report also recommended allowing more route and rate flexibility, leaving individual carriers to decide which routes to serve and what rates to charge. Under these changes the ICC's previously restrictive role would become "residual."[65] To show its serious intentions, the report included a legislative action plan.

Court Challenges and New Appointments
Actual movement towards deregulation was prompted by federal court challenges and presidential appointments. The first court challenge came well before the energy crisis. In 1964 a New Hampshire court, in *Nashua Motor Express, Inc.* v. *United States*, ruled in support of a carrier in a substantive challenge of an ICC denial of application. Questioning the basis of public convenience and necessity – the institutional cornerstone of restrictive entry – the court argued that the ICC should specifically consider the desirability of competition and greater variety of service. Although the ICC and other courts did not adopt the views of the *Nashua* decision, it did cause considerable discussion in the commission. Gradually, in the late 1960s and early 1970s, the ICC began to hold that adequacy of existing service was not the determining factor in considering applications. Also taken into account was the public's interest in improved transportation and protection from monopoly conditions.[66]

In a 1969 policy statement, *Motor Service on Interstate Highways: Passengers,* the ICC weakened the *Pan American* standard – public convenience and necessity's operational formula – by asserting that existing carriers "have no inherent right to be protected from merely new, as opposed to destructive, competition."[67] In 1974, in a case that had been pending for ten years, the Supreme Court ruled, in *Bowman Transportation, Inc.* v. *Arkansas-Best Freight System, Inc.*, that the ICC has no special obligation to protect certificated carriers from competition.[68]

As early as 1972 the commission had taken an interest in rate bureaus. In a major change in rate regulation, the ICC instructed rate bureaus not to forbid individual member carriers from setting and filing their own independent rates.[69] In the absence of independent rates, collectively set ones had the force of a cartel, exactly the collusive outcome protected by the Reed-Bulwinkle Act, which exempted collective rate making from antitrust prosecution. With the new provision for carriers to set independent rates, the ICC introduced new latitude for price competition and curtailed the rate bureaus' power to suppress it.[70]

Both President Ford and President Carter appointed pro-reform commissioners to the independent regulatory agencies and eventually created a majority of ICC commissioners who would favour less regulation in agency decisions and rule makings.[71] The Carter administration benefited from the "significant political momentum" continuing from the Ford administration and from the prominence of consumer and environmental concerns about regulation, a result of interest group successes and heavy media coverage.[72] The Carter administration also favoured internal reform over congressional intervention.[73] Propelled by those appointments and by the implications of the *Bowman* decision of 1974, the ICC began reconsidering and then reversing its long-standing policies. With the strong endorsement of the Carter administration, the ICC undertook an in-house review of regulation in 1977. One major recommendation in the review report was to give weight in entry proceedings to determinations that granting an application would promote efficiency, improve service, and lower rates. A powerful push towards deregulation came in another substantive court challenge of an ICC decision. In 1977 the Federal Court of Appeals ruled, in *P.C. White Truck Lines, Inc.* v. *ICC,* that the commission had acted improperly in denying the White application because it had not assigned enough merit to the applicant's likelihood of improving competition. To the ICC the decision meant that the protective *Pan American* norm had become legally vulnerable. In its statement granting the White application, the ICC referred specifically to the anticipated effect of increased competition.[74] Commenting on a similar transition at the Civil Aeronautics Board in those years, Roger Noll and Bruce Owen write: "Since the mid-1960s there were critics within the agency itself who believed that the protectionist policies of the CAB were unwarranted. When the agency itself began to be severely criticized by academic scholars, the courts, and Congress, it turned to these internal dissidents to produce a report about the problems of the agency and their solutions. The result was a blueprint for turning around the policies of the agency."[75]

Noll and Owen also apply that characterization to the ICC and the Federal Communications Commission, crediting them for "taking the lead in reforming regulatory policies."[76] An observer of the ICC added the note of political survival: "While the ICC is under heavy pressure from motor carriers to 'step back' from its newly adopted entry policy, it simply cannot afford to do so and remain viable in the public eye."[77]

That same year, in *Policy Statement on Motor Carrier Regulation*,[78] the ICC abandoned the *Pan American* provision that required an applicant to show that existing carriers could not provide the service being sought. The ICC also limited opportunities for protest by granting that privilege only to carriers whose traffic was affected. Previously it was possible for other certificated carriers to file protests, allowing them to exercise not only their individual interests in protecting their own territories but their collective interest in managing the industry. In 1979, in *Liberty Trucking Co., Extension: General Commodities*, the ICC further reduced the ability of certificated carriers to protest new applications.[79] The *Pan American* standard had allowed carriers to protest new applications by proving prospective harm to their own traffic and revenues. Equating competition with the public interest, however, the *Liberty* decision reversed the onus from the applicant to the protestant, who now had to show that the general public would suffer from the entry of a new carrier.[80] Under the new presumption, carriers arguing harm to the public from the entry of a new competitor had very discouraging prospects. Furthermore, showing harm to one's own traffic and revenues, even to the extent of going out of business, was no longer valid grounds for having an applicant denied entry.[81] And, providing applicants with yet another benefit, the ICC began considering lower rates as positive evidence.

Under those much more generous provisions the ICC began approving nearly all entry applications. In *MC-No. 135* the ICC initiated changes to expedite the approval process. *MC-No. 135* also introduced a new kind of operating authority, a master certificate, to cover expanded areas of service. Previously, operating authorities contained numerous route, commodity, and directional restrictions, usually the result of compromises reached with the protesting carriers during entry proceedings. The ICC's new master certificate would authorize much broader areas of activity. The agency also lifted the prohibition against private carriers hauling cargoes for hire. Finally, the rule restricting contract carriers to serving no more than eight shippers was lifted, enabling those firms to expand their operations.

Using its discretionary authority to interpret legislative mandates, the ICC changed the basis of trucking regulation from protecting certificated carriers from new competitors to encouraging price and service competition and inviting newcomers. For truckers with interests to protect, that was bad enough. More starkly, however, the ICC showed its ability to act, instituting immediate and drastic effects by changing important rules. Just as the commission had used its administrative discretion to ordain four decades of order and comfort for regulated carriers, it now used that same discretion to overturn their whole basis of doing business. For carriers left out of the old arrangement, principally regional and intrastate operators, the ICC was creating great opportunity, and they began applying for authorities in unprecedented numbers.

Congress Enters

The ICC's legislative mandate, the Motor Carrier Act, 1935, still contained the basic norm of public convenience and necessity, and changing that would require new legislation from Congress. By 1978 congressional politicians had become concerned that the ICC's actions threatened to pre-empt their own beginning involvement, acknowledging that the practical source of reform had been administrative and not legislative. The ICC agreed not to implement further changes until Congress had passed a new Motor Carrier Act.[82] New fundamental assumptions favouring competition were increasingly apparent in the ICC's policy changes, but the changes were internal and not publicly debated. At that point the new assumptions were administrative and not institutional. Now that legislative change was a prospect, the challenge to regulation's institutionalized assumptions came into the open, and the congressional debate over the new Motor Carrier Act, 1980, was their last stand.

Senator Edward Kennedy took the initiative by arranging for his judiciary committee to hold a series of public hearings on competition in the airlines and, subsequently, turned the committee's attention to trucking. According to Alan Altshuler and Roger Teal, there were important political reasons for dealing with airlines first. The public pays airfares directly, while it pays freight rates indirectly (in consumer prices) and is, therefore, more attentive to arguments that airfares are artificially high. The airline industry was also much less politically powerful than were motor carriers because there were far fewer airlines than there were trucking firms. The airlines were concentrated in a few congressional districts, while trucking companies were everywhere. Airlines also had a much smaller workforce than did motor carriers.[83] The appearance of complaisant regulation and static institutionalized assumptions, however, invited political intervention in both industries. In the words of Roger Noll and Bruce Owen, "A fully captured regulatory agency is vulnerable to attack by political entrepreneurs who owe no political debt to the special interests that seek to use an agency for their own purposes. To the extent that an agency becomes moribund and passively responds to special interests in a way that injures another segment of the citizenry, the way is opened for a politician to expand his own support by exposing it."[84] Although that characterization can account for politicians' motives, it should be remembered that, by the time Congress became involved, the ICC was actively pursuing reform and antagonizing special interests and, by that measure, was not at all moribund.

Senator Kennedy's hearings attracted considerable public attention and were instrumental in advancing the legislative fortunes of deregulation. He introduced a far-reaching trucking bill calling for complete deregulation. Increasingly frightened by the ICC's reforms and Senator Kennedy's proposals, the ATA and the Teamsters began an intensive lobbying campaign to thwart the legislation. Senator Howard Cannon's commerce committee sponsored a more moderate bill, retaining the public convenience-and-necessity entry standard as well as rate controls, but including the ICC's recently revised principle of presuming competition to be in the public interest. That provision, as was seen, would require those opposing granting new operating authorities to prove that doing so would harm the public interest. The ICC made its own preferences clear. During Senate hearings on the Motor Carrier Act, 1980, ICC witnesses testified that the bill did not do enough to promote competition. The ICC also provided analysis and comments on the committee reports and drafts of the legislation.[85] The Teamsters and the ATA, increasingly desperate, saw the legislation as at least preferable to Senator Kennedy's more comprehensive reforms and as a means of restraining the ICC from further reforms of its own.

Favouring reform legislation were shippers who testified to the commerce committee about the improved services and lower rates they anticipated. Two principal groups of motor carriers also supported deregulation, and their defection removed the ATA's ability to claim opposition by all sectors of its membership, thus illustrating the difficulties of trade associations that represent complex industries. Contract carriers liked the ICC's recent abandonment of the "rule of eight." They could now serve any number of shippers and operate nationwide. The Contract Carrier Conference broke ranks with the ATA and openly sided with pro-deregulation forces in Congress. So also did private carriers, who were enjoying their new permission to handle cargoes for hire and were keen to see it protected in legislation. Consumer advocates such as Ralph Nader spoke in favour of lower retail prices for the public.

This support, however, was less intense than was the ATA's and the Teamsters' opposition, and it was not the dominant force in Congress. While showing that reform would benefit important constituencies, the shippers and manufacturers were politically subordinate to the executive branch's advocacy, the force of the economists' arguments, the bipartisan appeal of deregulation, and the momentum of the ICC's initial reforms.[86] Reluctantly, the ATA and the Teamsters eventually supported Senator Cannon's bill, the Motor Carrier Act, 1980. Even so, there was enough manoeuvring and conflict to provide political scientist Dorothy Robyn with ample material for a legislative case study.[87]

The Motor Carrier Act, 1980, confirmed the ICC's new policy of equating competition with the public interest in entry proceedings.[88] Although the act stopped short of ending rate regulation, it established a "zone of reasonableness" for common carriers, making it possible for individual carriers to raise or lower rates 10 percent without ICC approval. The act also limited the power of rate bureaus to set fixed rates. Finally, the act instructed the ICC to remove route, commodity, and directional restrictions in existing operating authorities. These changes reflected institutionalized assumptions that were seriously weakened but not destroyed. Because of the ICC's own reforms, which were already in effect as the act went into force, entry was virtually open, rates were competitive, and restrictions on routes and commodities were being lifted. Congress, however, kept provision for entry and rate regulation in the act, reflecting a legislative compromise between far-reaching reforms and the status quo. In that way, the act approved ICC policy changes that deeply undermined regulation's institutionalized norms and assumptions while preserving their formal referents.

The ICC Presses Ahead

The new legislation did not contain the ICC. Requiring carriers protesting new entries to show harm to the public interest made public convenience and necessity vestigial, and the ICC began to base its entry decisions on the remaining norm of fitness. In previous commission practice, proving that one was "fit, willing, and able" to provide service had required evidence of insurance and responsibility. Under "responsibility," the commission could consider the applicant's record of safety and regulatory violations and the quality of its record keeping. Although denying an application on the grounds of fitness was not as frequent was denying it on grounds of public convenience and necessity, "fit, willing, and able" did have a practical meaning to both regulators and carriers. An entrance policy based only on fitness could still be used to screen out applicants.[89] After passage of the Motor Carrier Act, however, the ICC took a much more generous view of fitness. In the words of ICC chairman Reese Taylor, "Before I arrived they issued a certificate [of operating authority] to a guy that was in the county jail in L.A."[90]

Following the Motor Carrier Act's instructions, the ICC also encouraged holders of existing authorities to apply for route expansions and the removal of restrictions, thus opening up vast new domains. Where previously

84 percent of the operating authority applications contained one-way restrictions, the ICC processed no applications in 1981 containing directional conditions. The reform also applied to authorities in force. Between 1980 and June 1982, some 5,000 carriers got directional, route, and commodity restrictions removed from their authorities.[91] Before 1980 no trucking firm had operating authority for all forty-eight contiguous states. Soon fifty carriers had national domains. To open the market even further, the ICC awarded new applicants much broader route and commodity authorities than they had requested and made acceptance of these unsought expansions a condition of granting authorities, acting literally on Friedlaender's and Bailey's prescription that the task of regulators is to ensure an ample supply of potential competitors.[92] In the first year of the Motor Carrier Act, the ICC processed 28,700 applications for new or expanded authorities. To put that figure into perspective, there were approximately 18,045 carriers holding ICC authorities at the time of the Motor Carrier Act's passage. These changes completed the ICC's institutional transition. Previously, its role had been to manage the industry's membership and structure of services. The ICC's role now was to encourage carriers to enter, to be flexible, and to actively compete. The new rules were direct and simple. In compelling carriers to enlarge their domains, however, the ICC's purpose openly exceeded that of Congress, and its actions were eventually rebuked by a federal court.

The ATA was soon aware that keeping entry and rate controls in the Motor Carrier Act was not restraining the ICC. Several months after the act's passage, the ATA's general counsel announced that the association would counter the ICC in the congressional oversight hearings (provided for in the act for the first five years) and in court challenges of the ICC's interpretations.[93] The test case, *American Trucking Associations, Inc.* v. *ICC*, contested the ICC's insistence on awarding broader route and commodity authority than applicants had sought. At the end of a series of rulings and appeals, the US Federal Court of Appeals held that the ICC had indeed exceeded the intention of the Motor Carrier Act by removing restrictions in existing authorities and refusing to impose restrictions on new ones. Taking up other issues, the court held that the ICC had acted improperly in allowing private carriers to haul cargoes for hire and in giving insufficient attention to fitness norms in deciding new applications. The ICC appealed to the Supreme Court to overturn the rulings, and it requested the Court to indicate the interpretive boundaries of the new Motor Carrier Act. The Supreme Court refused to hear the appeal.[94] The ICC, however, simply modified its decisions enough to limit the grounds for future challenges. The ICC had already won its point anyway, for, by the time the appeals were completed in 1983, its policies had achieved their purpose. The results were so thorough, in fact, that ICC commissioners had begun suggesting sunsetting the agency and transferring the non-economic regulatory functions still remaining to the Department of Transportation. The proposal represented a complete dismantling of regulation's administrative apparatus. What remained to be confirmed was the durability of the new assumptions of competition.

A New Congressional Status Quo

The ATA and the Teamsters had hoped to use the annual congressional oversight hearings on implementation of the Motor Carrier Act to show how destructive deregulation was. They presented an alarming picture. Testifying on 14 December 1982 before the Subcommittee on Surface Transportation of the Senate Committee on Commerce, Science and Transportation, the ATA showed that, of the 288 carriers in the National Financial Data Base in 1979, sixty-three had gone bankrupt by November 1982. Average return on net investment for those carriers was 4.67 percent. Of the ten largest carriers, five had operated at a loss in 1981 and one had gone bankrupt. Since 1979 carriers representing 14 percent of total motor carrier capacity had gone out of business.[95] As new carriers continued to pour into the market, and as the recession shrank traffic, carriers offered deeply discounted rates in order to survive. The result was record levels of carrier bankruptcies and marginal conditions for the rest.

The ATA and the Teamsters blamed these effects on the end of protected domains and prices, and they reminded Congress that these were the very effects they had warned of during deliberations on the Motor Carrier Act.[96] The ICC disagreed. Testifying before the same hearings, ICC chairman Taylor blamed the industry's problems on the recession. He supported his argument with a General Accounting Office study on Teamster job losses in trucking, which found the cause to be general economic conditions rather than deregulation.[97] Members of the congressional committees expressed concern for the truckers, but Congress made no attempt to change the Motor Carrier Act or to interfere with the ICC's interpretation of it. Direct ATA and Teamster appeals to President Reagan produced no relief either.

These results are evidence that the institutionalized assumptions had completed their shift from regulation to deregulation. The Motor Carrier Act had modified and limited these assumptions but had not overturned them. That was accomplished by the ICC's regulatory faits accompli. When Congress took no action upon being provided with clear evidence that its legislation was being exceeded and that the industry was suffering, it signified that the transition to the new assumptions concerning deregulation was complete. As change accumulated, deregulation became the new state of affairs. Institutionalization begins when people begin to accept rules and assumptions as normal.[98] In passing over five annual occasions to challenge the ICC, Congress acknowledged this transition.

Deregulation and the Industry: Transition and Trouble

Deregulation quickly created excess capacity. At the time of deregulation in 1980, there were 18,045 carriers with ICC authorities. In the first year of deregulation, as we saw, the ICC processed 28,700 applications for new or expanded authorities. By the end of 1991 the number of carriers with ICC authorities stood at 47,890.[99] Another source of excess capacity was lifting of route and commodity restrictions.[100] When those restrictions were in place, carriers had to operate more equipment for given traffic levels than would be necessary if there were no barriers to full utilization. Collective rate making had reimbursed carriers for those inefficiencies, but there was a pool of extra equipment that was on hand when the restrictions came off and carriers could operate freely. Increasing capacity even more were five new groups of carriers that had been allowed into the interstate market. Common carriers expanding from intrastate operations or from limited commodity authorities added their equipment. As did contract carriers, who had become a freelance element. TL carriers capitalized on their new ability to offer low-cost, direct, and nationwide service. Private carriers, allowed to handle extra cargoes for hire, contributed their trucks. A final source of additional capacity was leased vehicles, which became a factor when the ICC relaxed a rule that had prevented equipment-leasing firms from also supplying drivers. That enabled shippers to become private carriers and allowed small operators to expand quickly. All sought business from the same pool of traffic.

As these new carriers began streaming into the market, however, the 1981 recession shrank freight volume. Competition became acute as carriers slashed rates to stay in business. Discounts of 70 percent off quoted prices were not uncommon. LTL carriers had particular exposure to discounting. With their technology centred on terminals for consolidating small consignments into full-trailer loads, LTL carrier services involved shipment delays. Under regulation, when no separate TL sector existed to offer prompt service, shippers had to wait. With direct service now available from TL carriers, LTL carriers had to compensate for slower service by offering generous discounts.[101] Used to protected margins under regulation, many carriers were not ready for the degree of cost controls necessary for survival. Adaptive carriers struggled to find savings and efficiencies before it was too late, but those that did not were quickly in serious trouble. The major difference between the survivors and the failures was the ability to adapt quickly. That involved anticipating deregulation, being well managed, positioning adeptly in the market, and adjusting to overcapacity.[102]

Small firms in general, according to an analysis by Dun and Bradstreet, did badly. In 1981 they accounted for 60 percent of American motor carrier revenues but earned only 20 percent of the motor carrier profits, for a return on equity of 1.55 percent.[103] Many of these smaller firms had expanded from family businesses and were still managed by the original owners. Also vulnerable were owner-operators, who were often cheaper to use than were company equipment and drivers, but who were also easier to let go in order to reduce capacity. Even when still driving, owner-operators, who divide revenues with their carrier and pay their own operating costs, had their shares cut by discounting.

Because of the latitude for discounting from filed collective rates, price information among carriers was no longer standardized. Shippers negotiated discounts privately, and with carriers unaware of what their rivals were charging, shippers could apply pressure for more cuts, with both sides knowing that there were other carriers desperate for business. Savage undercutting replaced the united front of collective rate making, and confidential bargains replaced posted prices. The struggle to stay in business showed in aggregate form in operating ratios – the percentage of revenues claimed by expenses. Before deregulation, as we saw earlier, the ICC had approved rate increases to keep carriers' operating ratios at ninety-three. A ratio of ninety-eight is the "boiling point," and a ratio over 100 shows net loss. In the first nine months of 1982 the average ratio for all but the ten largest carriers was 98.7.[104] Thirty-eight percent of all the regulated carriers in 1982 had operating ratios over 100. Nineteen eighty-two was a peak year with regard to the percentage of carriers operating at a loss, but in 1984 the percentage of regulated carriers with operating ratios over 100 was still twice that of pre-deregulation 1978.[105] Another index was business failures. Trucking firms went bankrupt by the hundreds. In the first five years after deregulation 6,470 carriers closed. In 1985, well after the end of the recession, 1,533 carriers went out of business, a rate averaging six firms per working day. These failures, according to the ATA's director of statistical research, affected all sectors and were 9.5 times greater than were the failures of pre-deregulation in 1978.[106]

The turbulence continued throughout the decade, with 1986 recording the highest number of failures in a single year – 1,553 firms – between deregulation in 1980 and the recession in 1991. The failure rate in trucking, at 137.5 per 10,000, was nearly twice the failure rate for all American businesses.[107] Conditions began deteriorating again in 1989. An ATA analysis of ICC data showed that carrier net profit margin fell to 1.87 percent from 2.59 percent a year earlier.[108] By 1991, only six of the fifty largest common carriers that were in business in 1965 had survived. Among the next rank damage was equally heavy. From the top 241 common carriers of 1981 there were only eighty-five left by 1991; twenty of those had failed in

1990.[109] The recession of 1991 began increasing carrier casualties again with 1,155 going under in the first half of the year alone.[110]

Those exiting left opportunities for the survivors. In 1979, the five largest LTL carriers earned about 35 percent of the total carrier revenues. By 1989 the top five's share had climbed to 44 percent.[111] Were the process not hindered by absorbing excess capacity and by shippers shopping for discounts through the 1980s, the top carriers probably could have expanded even more.[112] Even with those impediments, the interstate LTL carriers' rate of concentration under deregulation was "without parallel in American business history."[113] These gains did not produce greater profitability, and the long-haul LTL carriers have probably exhausted their technological advantages. Nor did the LTL carriers' gains produce conclusive evidence of predatory pricing, according to a report prepared by the United States General Accounting Office. That report was requested by the House Public Works Committee and the House Judicial Committee following filing of a $344 million antitrust suit in 1987 by a New York carrier, Lifschutz Fast Freight, against Yellow Freight, Roadway Express, and Consolidated Freightways for conspiracy to use predatory pricing to drive smaller carriers out of business.[114] The three carriers were cleared of the charge on 6 July 1993, when the fourth US Circuit Court of Appeals upheld a lower court dismissal of the case.[115] The pricing pattern, said the president of ABF Freight System, is interactive. In other words, carriers base their discounts on other carriers' actions. Thus discounting is intramural and not part of an "overall strategy of predatory pricing."[116]

This turbulence was reflected in the stock market. Between 1979 and 1988, 33 of the 45 trucking stocks – representing the largest carriers – dropped from the listings, but 19 new stocks appeared, including 11 carriers expanding from private to public ownership. Nineteen public trucking firms were bought out during the 1980s, and many of the buyers were railroads and foreign investors. In all, said one investment banker, "With the exception of the high technology industry, I don't think I've ever seen an industry where there has been such an incredible turnover of players going out of business, being sold, going public, being created."[117]

Rate bureaus continued to operate, and rates were still filed. Instead of binding all member carriers, as in the past, collective rates became marker prices and served as reference points for shippers and carriers in their individual rate transactions. That, too, began to end. In early 1992, Roadway Express, one of the firms that survived deregulation in a strong position, announced its intention to withdraw from rate bureaus. That followed the exit of the other top LTL carriers, Yellow Freight Lines, Consolidated Freightways, Overnite Transportation, ABF Freight System, and Carolina Freight Carriers. Industry observers believed those major abandonments would lead to the gradual end of collective rates.[118] The withdrawal of these carriers brought two changes. First, their market share enabled them to lead rate bureau pricing by going along with or rejecting collective price increases;[119] second, their ability to make increases hold reflected their relationships with their shippers and not with other carriers. Rate bureaus are no longer needed, said the president of Carolina Freight Carriers, because "freight rates are essentially negotiated with shippers."[120] As pricing became a "reaction by carriers to what their competitors [were] doing,"[121] and as discounting became pervasive, rate bureaus were no longer able to play their integrative roles of standardizing prices, and that key function became atomized. The new quality of interaction introduced a social element into the industry, with carriers watching each other's behaviour for guidelines to their own actions and viewing prices as indicators of their competitors' positions and capabilities.[122] From the universal prices and administered domains that prevailed under regulation, relations among carriers and shippers became atomized and directly interactive, based on mutual perceptions and comparisons.[123] As a further departure from standardized prices and services, and demonstrating a further atomizing of the relationships between carriers and shippers, pricing negotiations were a blend of rates and service. Both sides knew that lifting controls made conditions of service flexible and that varying levels of service entailed varying costs. The result was a "market situation in which a trade-off bargaining process is now permitted where negotiated rates reflect the service mix provided."[124]

A sophisticated way of matching prices to particular shippers appeared in the TL sector. J.B. Hunt Transport, the second largest TL carrier, initiated a differential rate system in 1991. It did so to calibrate charges more accurately to particular shippers, and it based its rates on the exact time spent loading and unloading shipments and "other specifics of each delivery." That, coupled to a shipper's payment record, was to be the basis for the "class-assigned" rate charged. The system would be similar to that used by insurers to rate customers for particular premium levels. Individual ratings are made possible by onboard computers, which are located in each of the fleet's cabs and which enter delivery data. The system would closely match actual costs with particular shippers and would help in planning equipment movements, thus leading to more efficient utilization. The most important advantage of this system involves price competition. Accurately based individual prices reduce the need to make across-the-board rate increases. Avoiding flat increases makes it possible to combat rate discounting by other carriers, who are given an opening whenever a major carrier seeks a general rate hike from its shippers.[125] Hunt's system represents a further individualization of carrier-shipper relations.

These developments illustrated the fragmentation of administered rules, territories, and prices. With the ICC freely granting new authorities and inviting existing carriers to expand and to be mobile, territories were no longer protected and clearly marked. The same was true of the sectoral divisions that had been so carefully maintained. The boundaries between LTL, contract, and private carriers quickly broke down, and a large new sector of TL carriers emerged. Complex patterns of competition resulted as firms within the sectors vied for traffic and as the sectors themselves became rivals, differentiated by their technologies and their abilities to meet special requirements. In pricing, posted rates became initial reference points for individual bargaining. Periodic collective rate increases, a still-legal vestige of regulation, sought to raise returns but were vulnerable to being discounted away. The rate levels that emerged were the aggregate results of a decentralized and continuously interactive process. For regulatory reformers, highly mobile firms able to offer transport without regulatory restriction and to compete freely over prices were exactly what they had wanted. For the ATA and the Teamsters, this was exactly what they had feared.

The American Trucking Associations: Disorientation and Reconciliation

The ATA, having fought and lost the battle of its life and seeing its membership struggling, found the early 1980s to be extremely discouraging times. The old institutionalized assumptions of protection and control were finished politically, and the ICC was bent on disruption. The ATA's own member conferences of common, private, and contract carriers, who had stayed within their sectoral boundaries under regulation, had publicly broken unity over the Motor Carrier Act's passage and were now seeking inroads against one another. That, according to one assessment, "had a profound effect on the ATA's interconference relationships ... In effect deregulation ... turned what was formerly a well-defined, compartmentalized 'family' into a pack of squabbling relatives."[126]

That raised the prospect of the ATA itself fragmenting, always a possibility with trade associations that seek to represent diverse industries. Their "internal homogeneity is always precarious, being heavily dependent upon external conditions sustaining it."[127] The danger to cohesion becomes particularly strong when external changes exert differential effects on the membership, exacerbating their divergences. With rules, territories, and rates disintegrating, with varieties of services proliferating, and with its own members in determined rivalry for market shares and survival, the protector of truckers could only stand aside, disarmed, and watch the process continue.

Some of the larger common carrier members, whose dues in the ATA reflected their size, questioned the organization's usefulness. Their attitudes reflected continuing unhappiness over the ATA's recent failure, but they also reflected the industry's condition. Some members struggled and failed, but others, after intense efforts, began to find more secure positions. Both could wonder what benefits the defeated lobby could provide. For the failing firms, turning back the clock was something the ATA could not do. The surviving firms owed success to their own efforts and not to lobbying. In response, the ATA appointed a new president, Thomas Donohue, whose aims recognized the diversity and competition in the ATA's ranks. Instead of providing a common front, as had previously been the case, he believed, more modestly, that the ATA should work for cooperation among the member sectors and focus on new issues facing the industry under deregulation (e.g., safety, insurance, and environmental rules).

As part of that policy, the ATA convened a Blue Ribbon Task Force of thirty-seven of the most prominent individuals in trucking to propose a new policy to reflect the views of its member firms. The task force's report, issued on 13 January 1987, showed a pervasive change among the ATA's membership. In striking contrast with the ATA's long stand against deregulation, the report recommended ending all economic barriers to entry. The only regulations remaining should concern carriers' responsibility for safety and finances. As practical businesspeople, the members of the task force recognized the new prevailing state of affairs. At the fundamental, working, day-to-day level, deregulation was the new institution. The state had withdrawn and was not expected to return. Carriers, in their dealings with shippers and each other, were on their own.

With regard to rates, the task force recommended retaining antitrust immunity for collective rate making, defending it as providing a "needed repository of market information" but recognizing the diversity of the actual prices prevailing among member carriers and shippers and, thereby, acknowledging that collective rates had indeed become reference numbers.[128] These were more than grudging adjustments. The recommendations showed that the carriers themselves had pragmatically adopted new business expectations based on competition and flexibility – the very result the economists had advocated in eliminating regulation. Building those new conditions into their own planning and operations probably reflected the practical view that deregulation was here to stay rather than any warm espousal of the economists' values. The recommendations may also have reflected the fact that many of the members who were most injured by deregulation and who had the greatest reason to object were bankrupt. For the surviving membership, deregulation was the reality for the foreseeable future. The task force exercise did not prevent fragmentation. The Private Carrier Conference, believing that complete deregulation was in its members' best interests, left the ATA in 1987.

The ATA's largest members had been busy adjusting their operations. Roadway Express, for example, expanded into the Pacific Northwest under deregulation and made its presence known with 50 percent discounts on shipments of over 5,000 pounds leaving the region. The large carriers also

devoted unprecedented attention to marketing, identifying which opportunities suited their resources and which were desirable gains. Accepting
the reality that the old structures and protections were gone for good and
seeking survival and advantage in the new order, carriers such as Roadway
furthered the process of change as they competitively adapted. As senior
voices in the ATA, moreover, they directed the association to recognize
those facts. Senator Robert Packwood, a proponent of complete deregulation, saw promising flexibility in the task force's report: "I think we have an
atmosphere now where it would be possible to sit down with the leadership
of all components of the trucking industry and talk about what does make
sense and whether we can agree on a legislative package."[129]

The industry's diversity showed clearly in 1992 in the ATA's inability to
take a common position on the Bush administration's proposal to reduce
state-based controls on trucking. Such initiatives issued occasionally from
the White House through the 1980s, and, like previous ones, the latest was
not expected to get far in Congress. While other interested parties were
making their case in congressional hearings, however, the ATA stood on the
sidelines, unable to reconcile the opposition of most of its members to further deregulation with the desire of some of its large TL members for total
deregulation.[130] As we will see shortly, the ATA did not resolve its position
until state-level deregulation picked up surprising political momentum in
spring 1994. As a final reflection of the changes following deregulation, by
1995 the majority of ATA members were TL carriers. As to whether power
within the ATA has shifted from LTL carriers as a result of deregulation, Lana
Batts, president of the Interstate Truckload Carriers Conference, one of the
ATA's member conferences, reported "that recognition is taking place." One
index is that more TL carriers are serving as ATA officers.[131]

The Teamsters: Shrinking Pay, Thinning Ranks

Deregulation produced even more discouraging outcomes for the Teamsters
than it did for the ATA. The union had benefited from regulation and collective rate making. Having won the ability to negotiate a nationwide Master Freight Agreement with all unionized carriers in 1964, the Teamsters
could bargain for generous settlements, knowing that the carriers would
pass the increased costs along to shippers as new collective rates. Negotiating uniform agreements gave the union a centralized position in the industry. The carriers negotiated collectively as Trucking Management Inc. (TMI),
which formed in 1978 from a merger of employer groups. The Teamsters'
position changed drastically after deregulation. The old convenience of
passing on increased labour costs ended when collective rates lost their
force and shippers, enjoying freely available discounts, no longer had to
accept regular rate increases. Rate discounting affected unionized and non-
union carriers alike, forcing all to operate with less revenue. That, in turn,

put severe pressure on wages. With sectoral boundaries down, unionized carriers faced aggressive and mobile non-union TL and contract carriers. The results showed clearly. In 1983 carriers that accounted for 28 percent of motor carrier revenue were either on the verge of failing or were bankrupt.[132] As unionized LTL carriers struggled and failed, growth shifted to the non-union sectors. In defence, many LTL carriers began establishing their own non-union subsidiaries, which enabled them to pay wages 25 percent to 30 percent below union scale.[133] Other carriers struggled to streamline their operations and cut costs. All of these developments meant layoffs and thinning ranks for the union. According to Teamster president Ron Carey, in 1992 testimony before the House Public Works and Transportation Committee's Subcommittee on Surface Transportation, 166,739 Teamster jobs had been lost since 1980.[134] Faced with these pressures, amidst much opposition from the rank and file, the union agreed to wage reductions.[135] In the settlement that ended a national strike against LTL carriers in April 1994, the union also agreed to changes that allowed carriers to divert more freight to rail and to hire part-time dock workers – again to much unhappiness from some of the locals.[136]

The Teamsters also saw the Master Freight Agreement unravel. Between 1982 and 1984 TMI, the bargaining agent for unionized carriers, had its membership decline from 286 to 29 carriers. Fifty of those departures were due to bankruptcy. The others, believing that they could not afford wage and benefit settlements agreeable to the larger and stronger carriers, decided to break ranks and form a coalition of smaller carriers in order to negotiate their own agreement with the Teamsters.[137] Another reason for opting out was to accommodate regional differences that emerged under deregulation. In the western states, for example, the number of carriers signing the Master Freight Agreement dropped from 300 in 1964 to 30 in 1982. In dealing with the union separately, many carriers sought exemptions from standards in the national agreement, and many locals made informal wage and rule concessions to strapped employers.[138] Fragmentation of the Master Freight Agreement has reduced the union's power to strike because fewer members are covered under one contract. The carriers with the most to lose are the surviving national LTL carriers, which lost considerable traffic in the strike of 1994. Later in the decade some of the major national carriers undertook separate negotiations, further diminishing the union's ability to coordinate a strike.

Just before the April 1994 Teamsters strike, Carolina Freight Carriers withdrew from TMI and reached a separate agreement, leaving TMI with only twenty-two members. At the end of the strike, the president of TNT Freightways placed an advertisement in the *Wall Street Journal* assuring shippers that TNT would "take an independent course in future negotiations" so that customers "will never again endure the hardships brought about by this strike."[139] For other TMI members, the lesson of the strike was to quickly diversify into non-union operations – principally regional carriers and package freight. Before spinning off their unionized LTL carriers, in 1996 Consolidated Freightways and Roadway Express, the parent firms, were earning half of their revenue from non-union operations – primarily regional LTLs. According to a senior motor carrier industry analyst at Merrill Lynch, both Consolidated Freightways and Roadway could "eventually replace [their] unionized national freight network with a nonunion carrier network. It's happening now. The seeds are planted."[140]

These pressures have told on the union itself. The highly centralized power structure gave way to internal factionalizing, weakening the union's ability for concerted action. That weakness prompted militancy in some of the locals, which, in 1983, rejected a set of concessions negotiated by Teamster president Jackie Presser. Membership losses have seriously weakened the union's finances. In 1992 the union's income was $78 million, but its expenditures were $135.6 million. One of the largest increases in spending occurred in the area of unemployment benefits. Without changes in spending, according to the 1993 Teamsters financial report, the union's funds would be gone by 1994.[141] In 1994, *Traffic World* reported that the union's net worth had declined by half in the previous year.[142] The union's power revived in 1997 when it struck United Parcel Service (UPS), its largest employer. One of the union's well-publicized issues was UPS's increasing use of part-time staff. The cause of preserving good-quality jobs resonated well with the general public, and the conclusion of the strike left the Teamsters' stature and self-confidence higher than they had been since deregulation, although finances remained a problem.

Deregulation across the Board

As we saw, the Motor Carrier Act, 1980, did not provide for complete deregulation. The conditions just seen resulted from the act's aggressive implementation by the ICC. Congress took almost no interest in legislating complete deregulation until 1994, when it surprised the industry with the Trucking Regulatory Reform Act, which pre-empted remaining state controls. The conditions leading to that development will be seen presently. In the meantime, a brief review of Congress's behaviour in the intervening fourteen years shows a new and stable status quo, with competition and turbulence accepted as the industry's condition. That attitude was matched by perfunctory interest from the Reagan and Bush administrations.

There were occasional initiatives. Senator Robert Packwood introduced the Trucking Competition Act, 1983, which would have ended all economic regulation of trucking within sixty days, abolished collective rate-making immunity by 1 July 1984 (the Reed-Bulwinkle Act was still in effect), required the ICC to show cause to Congress by 1986 for any remaining regulation of trucking, and terminated the ICC's trucking jurisdiction in 1987. The Reagan administration was not particularly interested, and there were few supporters in Congress. In 1986 Packwood, still an advocate of complete deregulation, blamed Transportation Secretary Elizabeth Dole's lack of support for limiting any chances legislation might have.[143]

The Reagan administration did introduce a bill on 19 May 1987. The Trucking Productivity Act would have taken trucking responsibility away from the ICC, repealed antitrust immunity for collective rate making, and eliminated any remaining regulation on entry and rates. It would also have prohibited the states, which still had authority over intrastate trucking, from passing or enforcing any measures that would impinge on interstate trucking. To make these measures more palatable in Congress, the bill made no mention of sunsetting the ICC, something the administration had sought to do by budgetary means in 1986 and had reversed in Congress.[144] The bill died at the end of Congress in 1988.

The eventually successful initiative to deregulate intrastate trucking came from air package carrier Federal Express. Federal uses trucks to consolidate freight consignments for movement by air and for local pickup and delivery. Much of that trucking takes place within state boundaries, raising the question of whether it is under state regulatory jurisdiction. The Airline Deregulation Act, 1978, forbade states from regulating the activities of air cargo carriers, but there were diverse state controls on trucking. The resulting disparities interfered with national operations. Federal Express called on the National Industrial Transportation League, an association of shippers, to join in lobbying Congress for legislation to override state controls. Doing so would remove a century-old distinction between federal and state jurisdiction over transport and remove the last sectors of control.

As in the earlier move to deregulation in the 1970s, federal courts provided crucial support. In 1991 the 9th US Circuit Court of Appeals, ruling against California, held that Federal Express is a deregulated air carrier whose intrastate trucking operations were outside state jurisdiction.[145] That decision was upheld a year later by the US Supreme Court. Encouraged, Federal Express, joined by UPS, which had expanded into air cargo operations, began a two-year lobbying campaign to have the federal government override state controls. The White House was sympathetic. Transportation secretary Samuel Skinner stated the Bush administration's interest in completing deregulation at the state level,[146] seconded in 1992 by his successor, Transportation Secretary Andrew Card.[147]

Following House hearings in 1990 on the issue, four separate House bills to deregulate at the state level were introduced in 1992, but none was acted upon.[148] Momentum picked up when Senator Wendell Ford, acting on behalf of UPS, attached an amendment to the Senate Federal Aviation Authorization Act of, 1993, to exempt interstate air cargo carriers from state regulation.[149] Several states had been moving towards deregulation on their own. In 1992 Maryland officially ended entry and rate controls, and Michigan ended rate controls and liberalized entry. The most important change came when Texas, long one of the most closely regulated states, deregulated truckload carriers in 1993. Kentucky began deregulating in 1994.

Three of the largest LTL carriers – Roadway Express, Overnite Transportation, and Consolidated Freightways – lent their support. Roadway and Consolidated did so because they both had air-freight and package operations at the time. All hoped to extend the measure to other kinds of trucking, and on that basis Yellow Freight joined forces. The ATA, previously opposed, decided to lend support on the basis of equal treatment for all sectors.[150] The ATA's opposition had been based on division in its ranks; some of its smaller members, those with primarily intrastate operations, would be badly hurt by the new legislation. The dilemma of presenting a common position for a diverse trade association was illustrated by ATA president Donohue's remarks to the House committee considering the measure: "Donohue didn't flinch when asked for the ATA's position. 'Well, congressmen, some of my friends are strongly against the bill and some of my friends are strongly in favor of it. So on this particular issue, I'm sticking with my friends.'"[151]

The Senate and House decided simply to expand the provisions to include all motor carriers. Household carriers retained their exemption. This amendment passed with no debate, and, on 23 August the aviation funding bill was signed into law by President Clinton. Section 601 of the bill eliminated the states' power to impose entry, rate, and service controls on motor carriers. States were allowed to keep their powers over safety, vehicle dimensions, taxation, and hazardous materials.[152] The provisions went into effect on 1 January 1995. The result of withdrawing controls at both levels of government was a seamless field for carriers and shippers. American deregulation was complete.

Sunset

This activity began the final round for the ICC. On 16 June 1994 the House had voted to end the commission's funding. As a result of the rate undercharge crisis the ICC had come to be regarded as not just vestigial but incompetent. The crisis had developed because liquidators of defunct carriers dunned shippers for the difference between discounted freight rates and those filed with the ICC. Because the ICC could not resolve the problem, Congress intervened with the Negotiated Rates Act, 1993, which gave the ICC responsibility for monitoring rates and mediating disputes between carriers and shippers. The new act also made terminating the ICC illogical because doing so would remove the means of its own enforcement.[153] The problem was solved by the Trucking Industry Regulatory Reform Act, which eliminated federal rate filing and removed all but insurance and safety provisions from entry requirements, reducing the ICC's responsibilities even further. Both houses passed the act without debate, and President Clinton signed it on 26 August 1994.[154] Pressure to eliminate the ICC resumed in Congress almost immediately. By this time the ICC was trimming its staff, which was already a fraction of its pre-1980 size. The final initiative came as part of the Republican Congress's efforts to eliminate federal departments, notably Commerce, Energy, and Education. Failing on those fronts, Congress was able to claim the ICC.[155] In November 1995 both the House and the Senate, supported by the Clinton administration, voted to terminate the ICC, and on 31 December 1995, after 108 years of operation, it closed its doors. Its building, a Constitution Avenue edifice, was taken over by the Internal Revenue Service for extra office space.

Conclusion

Assisted by a sophisticated and eventually persuasive economic critique and aided by more general concerns about energy, inflation, and the effectiveness of regulation, reformers succeeded in bringing about institutional change. In a demonstration of its autonomy from both the trucking industry and from Congress, the ICC dismantled the structure of regulation that had been its raison d'être, acting first to expand the interpretation of the Motor Carrier Act, 1935, and then to expand the terms set by Congress in the Motor Carrier Act, 1980. By generously admitting new carriers and handing out broad grants of authority, the ICC opened territories it had previously protected and encouraged carriers to make the most of their new opportunities.

The result left carriers and shippers to determine relationships on their own during their daily transactions. The ICC systematically eliminated its central role and, finally, the commission itself was gone.

Although American deregulation was motivated and executed as a domestic reform, its international dimension soon appeared. In 1981, when deregulation's effects were in full progress and the outlook for carriers was at its most troubled and uncertain, the ICC began granting operating authorities to Canadian applicants on the same generous terms as it did to American ones, adding foreign competitors to the turmoil and raising perplexing diplomatic problems. The Trucking War that ensued is the subject of the next chapter.

4

Deregulation, Discrimination, and Diplomacy: The Trucking War

Aggressive reciprocity involves imposing trade barriers in order to equalize terms of access with a country whose barriers are higher than one's own. Unlike trade negotiations, which seek to balance future restrictions, aggressive reciprocity operates against barriers that are already in place. And, unlike the World Trade Organization's procedures under international agreements for identifying inequities, aggressive reciprocity is bilateral: one country judges its trading partner.[1] Simply continuing with existing protective policies can activate aggressive reciprocity if the trading partner deems them to be more protective than its own. As a defensive measure, aggressive reciprocity can be used to end the free ride of protecting a home market while taking advantage of an open one. As a liberalizing measure, threatening the use of aggressive reciprocity can reduce barriers and open up markets, although failure of the threat results in greater protection.[2]

The Trucking War seems to be a plausible example of aggressive reciprocity.[3] The United States adopted a radical reform of trucking regulation, which included granting free entry into the American interstate market to Canadian carriers. American carriers soon complained that continuing regulatory barriers in Canada denied them equal access and gave Canadian carriers unfair advantages in transborder freight markets. The conflict developed in 1980-1 and became a serious bilateral problem in 1982. It featured an escalating diplomatic dispute and a congressionally backed Interstate Commerce Commission moratorium on granting new authorities to Canadian carriers. It ended with a bilateral agreement assuring both sides' carriers "full, fair and equitable" treatment. Canada subsequently deregulated its own trucking, creating a symmetrical arrangement on its side of the border. All this would suggest a straightforward case of aggressive reciprocity, although the moratorium actually carried out the threat of raising barriers to Canadians. It would also suggest a coercive origin to Canadian deregulation, in which the federal government complied with the bilateral agreement by adopting mirror legislation. Left to its own choices, it follows, Canada would have kept its controls.

To see why this interpretation does not fit, it is necessary first to look at the issues involved. These were a blend of domestic regulation and international trade. As a regulatory issue the point of conflict was discrimination: Canadian regulators were held to be more exclusionary to American applicants than to Canadian ones. Challenging the imbalance on a regulatory basis raised the question of administrative propriety under Canada's own domestic law and, more broadly, the question of Canada's sovereign right to regulate its transportation.[4] As a trade issue the point of conflict was reciprocity: Canada would not return concessions granted by the United States. Both diffuse and specific reciprocity were at issue.[5] Diffuse reciprocity entails a generalized expectation of equity through common standards of behaviour, such as those embodied in the World Trade Organization (WTO), and its effectiveness depends on a collectively understood obligation.[6] It is compatible with unconditional Most Favoured Nation (MFN) treatment, whose purpose is a broad liberalization of trading conditions among many states. Specific reciprocity, on the other hand, involves "situations in which specified partners exchange items of equivalent value in a strictly delimited sequence." Explicit obligations cover particular exchanges.[7]

As a matter of diffuse reciprocity, Canada's treatment of trucking could be seen as exploiting a trade concession made by the United States, thus acting against the normative *spirit* of the General Agreement on Tariffs and Trade (GATT) – the WTO's precursor – and justifying American dissatisfaction. With, at the time, practical action under GATT precluded by the absence of provisions on trade in trucking services, the remedy for the imbalance would be specific reciprocity – negotiating an agreement for trucking. An agreement could designate exactly the terms of fair and equitable treatment of the two countries' carriers in each others' jurisdictions. Practical action under specific reciprocity would involve direct changes to Canada's regulatory norms and the surrender of sovereignty over a major domestic regulatory area. Canada had made such concessions under GATT's diffuse reciprocity in the expectation of trade gains, but making concessions under unilateral pressure from the United States as specific reciprocity – and in a traditionally domestic sphere of regulation – presented the prospect of losing sovereignty and gaining nothing.[8]

Regulatory reformers, of course, could argue that Canada would gain under a common liberalized regime because of improved carrier service and lower prices. That argument, however, came after the Trucking War, as the effects of deregulation in the American market became established and widespread and as Canadian shippers compared transport costs (as will be seen in the next chapter). In the Trucking War, the Canadian government's purpose was not improving efficiency but defending sovereignty and avoiding precedents of successful foreign intrusion into domestic policy areas. Deregulation, particularly in harmony with the United States, also did not fit the Trudeau government's nationalist policy agenda; instead, the government had embarked on two major initiatives – the National Energy Program (NEP) and the Foreign Investment Review Agency (FIRA) – whose purpose was to provide greater control over the economy and to reduce American economic influence.

The attitude of both sides can be understood in light of reciprocity's more general standing as a social norm. Defined as a "mutually contingent exchange of benefits," reciprocity has been regarded as a universal property of social relations. Its key provision is that recipients of benefits are obliged to reciprocate.[9] Failing to perform that obligation fosters a sense of inequity and injury. Although the obligation is limited by the recipient's ability to reciprocate, differing assessments of that ability may be a source of conflict.[10] Canada's failure to perform its reciprocal obligation underlay the complaints on the American side; Canada's ability to reciprocate underlay the sense of imposition felt on the Canadian side. It was not reasonable for the US to expect Canada to surrender sovereignty after American unilateral action and the disruption of an established and symmetrical arrangement.

Grounds for disagreement over the ability to reciprocate can be narrowed by international or bilateral agreements that apply common principles to particular areas of exchange. Joining such agreements acknowledges the principles' potential application to particular areas, narrowing differences about the ability to reciprocate and facilitating resolution. Agreements that state specific areas of exchange and specific mutual commitments narrow the grounds even further. At the time of the Trucking War, however, the pertinent standards and provisions, including those of fairness and equity, were all contained in domestic regulatory rules and enforced by domestic agencies. Because both countries' entry standards had been exclusionary, trucking had no precedent as a bilateral problem. With no international or bilateral agreements covering trucking, the conflict hinged on an asymmetry between domestic policies.

One remedy for the United States was to restore the symmetry by restricting entry of Canadian carriers. The ICC, however, had abandoned the *Pan American* standard, which recognized prospective harm from new entrants as grounds for denying applications. The same purpose could be served by using a *Pan American* replica or a mirror Canadian standard, but such special provisions would violate the ICC's own regulatory principle of nondiscrimination, as the Canadian government was quick to point out. More fundamentally, the matter was a question of structural asymmetry. In the United States, regulatory rules had given way to prices and competition; in Canada, regulatory rules were still fully present.

The overlapping of the regulatory issue of discrimination and the trade issue of reciprocity affected the actions of both sides. Those actions shed additional light on the question of whether or not the Trucking War was a case of aggressive reciprocity. The Interstate Commerce Commission, to which the initial American carrier complaints were directed, clearly understood the difference between discrimination and reciprocity. The ICC regarded any charge of discrimination as a matter for Canadian regulators. It also saw that any efforts on its part to achieve balanced entry norms would involve specific reciprocity. On both grounds it was extremely reluctant to become involved. It saw no jurisdictional basis for questioning Canadian practices, no regulatory mandate to consider reciprocity in entry decisions, and no diplomatic mandate for seeking a settlement. When Congress finally pressured the ICC to conduct an investigation, the agency found no evidence of Canadian discrimination, carefully avoided the central question of reciprocity, and withheld its report as long as possible. Congress, on the other hand, did not clearly distinguish between discrimination and reciprocity. When Congress backed the moratorium on new grants of authority to Canadian carriers, supporters spoke more generally of American applicants being unfairly treated in Canada.

Ambivalence in the American executive branch reflected the same conundrum. The Department of Transportation and the Office of the United States Trade Representative (USTR) were initially sympathetic to American carrier complaints and saw Canadian entry as a potentially serious problem. In light of Canada's flat unwillingness to negotiate, however, both agencies saw regulation as the preferable solution, and both sought to persuade the ICC to consider reciprocity as a standard in deciding Canadian applications. The USTR's office also preferred a regulatory solution because it saw trucking as one of the least promising areas for services trade agreements – a recognition, in part, of the industry's structural complexity and, in part, of specific reciprocity's tendency to produce difficult and intricate negotiations and to complicate trade relationships.[11] At the same time, none of the executive branch departments supported the congressional moratorium, which mandated regulatory action and put direct pressure on Canada. For its part, the State Department was concerned less with trucking than with a bilateral relationship that was already disturbed by NEP and FIRA. The USTR's office would have preferred to stay out of the dispute but ended up with the task of seeking a resolution. It came away with a document that papered over Canada's resolve to change nothing on its side. The executive branch was willing to let the matter drop and persuaded Congress to accept the agreement, even though Ontario conspicuously turned down two major US carrier applications shortly afterwards.

Structurally, the American position was weak. As we saw in the last chapter, the ability to take decisive action increases with the concentration of authority in a single agency. That autonomy enabled the ICC to execute peremptory reform. The converse applies here. A state is weak in a particular policy area or sector when "authority is dispersed and no one group of officials can take the lead in formulating policy."[12] When that condition prevails, a variety of actors is able to exercise some influence on policy and decisions. Even when the actors' purposes are the same, the diversity complicates the process. When the actors' purposes diverge, or when the actors perceive different solutions to a problem, the process becomes further complicated and the chances of resolute action diminish. That is particularly so if one powerful actor prefers a drastically divergent solution. This was true even though the United States, compared to Canada, enjoyed the advantage of a centralized jurisdiction, which located trucking regulation in Washington and enabled the diplomatic, trade, and regulatory sides of the dispute to be coordinated at the federal level. A dispersion of interests, solutions, and authority neutralized that advantage.

On the Canadian side regulation is decentralized among ten provincial boards, and managing the dispute required the federal government to coordinate with the provincial governments – a situation that always contains the possibility of conflict. Canada's structural diversity, which heralds weakness, was offset in the Trucking War by a unity of purpose, which heralds strength. The federal government agencies and the provincial governments were unanimous on resolutely opposing the ICC moratorium. Canada's motor carriers, happy with the domestic status quo and pleased with the opportunities the ICC was offering them, were strong allies. Midway in the dispute the federal and provincial governments did discover that they were not unanimous about the regulatory procedures of FIRA, some of whose applicants were American carriers. This difference emerged as a surprise during a key encounter with the Americans, when it was important to show collective resolve; instead, provincial officials turned with surprise and anger on their federal colleagues. Diplomatic resistance, however, succeeded in the end. Because all of the domestic actors supported resistance, and because the task was clearly diplomatic, External Affairs was able to take charge of Canada's actions. External Affairs' uncompromised purpose was to keep matters in diplomatic channels and to combat what it regarded as a troubling intrusion into domestic policy. The Canadian side thus had the benefit of a centralized and simplified structure of decision making and a single, unwavering position. There was also the advantage of public support. Canada's history of economic nationalism, and the Trudeau government's evocation of it in promoting major policies, made it possible to frame American pressures for market access and harmonized policies as threats to national identity. That gave a narrowly sectoral issue, like trucking, a broad resonance and provided Canada with a basis of support that was absent on the American side. Even more favourably, the divisions and conflicting solutions on the American side handed tactical advantages to Canada.

Congress's failure to distinguish clearly between discrimination and reciprocity in some of its statements allowed the Canadian government to frame the issue as regulation rather than trade and to assume the position of defending existing domestic policy. By denying that its highway transport boards treated American applicants any differently than they did Canadian ones, it easily rebutted charges of regulatory impropriety. By insisting that its regulation was being administered as usual, it refuted charges of creating new inequities. By keeping the terms of the dispute clearly domestic, it treated solutions based on specific reciprocity as unwarranted and extreme. Any idea that Canada could end the imbalance by adopting parallel changes to its regulatory norms, the Canadian government maintained, was an unacceptable infringement on its regulatory sovereignty. Fault for the imbalance, the Canadian government emphasized from the outset, lay completely with the United States. By responding to American actions as they occurred, Canada could take the position of repelling threats to its sovereignty and keep the onus for resolving the question focused on Washington. This position also avoided the less convenient question of not returning favours.

Because of the close interplay of bilateral and domestic factors, management of the dispute would seem to fit the two-level game model. That model contains two negotiating tables – one international and one domestic. The possibility of conflict occurs at both tables because bargains acceptable at one may be vetoed at the other. The negotiators' task at the international table is to construct a "win-set" of agreements that will be acceptable at their respective domestic tables. The ways in which negotiations at one table may affect negotiations at the other provide participants with wide latitude for tactical calculation and scholars with analytical complexity.[13] The Trucking War, however, was not a two-level game. Canada's unwavering insistence that the issue was non-negotiable foreclosed the construction of a win-set of gains and concessions. There was no need for domestic persuasion on the Canadian side because the provinces and the CTA supported the federal government's position. *Had* there been an agreement that included Canadian concessions, a second stage of negotiation may have been involved. There was also no manoeuvring of domestic groups on the Canadian side. In fact, to eliminate the possibility of any inadvertently compromising contact between Canadian domestic agencies and the American side, the Department of External Affairs took charge of all communication once the dispute became serious. On the American side, the persuasion of domestic constituencies had occurred before the bilateral negotiations, when the executive branch got the congressional supporters of the moratorium to relax its provisions enough to allow an early conclusion.

These considerations notwithstanding, Canada *did* subsequently deregulate, leaving aggressive reciprocity as an explanation – if not of process, at least of outcome. The act containing the new regulatory standards, however, was passed five years after the Trucking War, and the forces prompting it were a mixture of the domestic and the international. Domestically, reform had roots extending back to federal provincial differences over railway rates and the National Transportation Act, 1967, which partially deregulated them. Political pressure for reform of trucking materialized when the effects of American deregulation began to appear as sharply lower carrier prices, representing cost disadvantages for Canadian shippers. Such disadvantages melded transport into a larger set of concerns about economic management and international competitiveness. The process of Canadian deregulation, with its resonance in both international relations and public policy, will be seen in the next chapter.

For people interested in the way governments treat complicated sectoral problems with major trading partners, the Trucking War is a gem. Access for motor carriers would not seem to have the makings of international conflict, but the ingredients were all there: a high level of trade, extensive commercial ties, politically articulate domestic interests, an important industrial sector, a blend of domestic and bilateral policy issues, and generous rations of perceived injury and indignation.[14] Treating the events in sequence makes it easy to understand how the various government agencies became involved and how conflict escalated. Given the roster of participants, that is an important consideration. A sequential treatment also shows how, at every stage, questions of discrimination overlapped with questions of reciprocity. The episode's broader implications will be considered at the end.

Transborder Trucking before Deregulation

Regulators in both countries did not generally award very large domains to foreign carriers. As transborder operations expanded over the years, regulators granted operating authorities to allow cargo to be interchanged at designated places just inside the border, and that proved to be a stable arrangement. On the eve of the Trucking War, over 80 percent of the motor freight moving between the United States and Canada was interlined between American and Canadian carriers.[15] Single-line service is more attractive because one carrier is responsible from origin to destination. Shippers appreciate the convenience and better service; carriers appreciate not having to depend on other carriers. There are also revenue considerations. In joint-line arrangements carriers divide revenue on whatever terms they negotiate, but single-line carriers can keep it all for themselves. At the time of the Trucking War, transborder trucking generated about $1 billion annually, an impressive block of revenue. Converting to a single-line operation requires a more extensive territory to replace the interline carrier's, and this, in turn, expands the number of shippers who can be served. Operationally, single-line service between the United States and Canada is very feasible because Canada's major population and traffic centres are close to the American border and have direct highway connections. The obstacle was high entry barriers in both countries – until deregulation.

The ICC granted few operating authorities to Canadians before 1976. Responding to complaints that the ICC was discriminating against Canadian applicants, regulators from British Columbia, Alberta, and Saskatchewan met with ICC officials in San Francisco in 1974. The discussions showed that Canadian applicants were subjected to frivolous protests, and the ICC agreed to modify its procedure to limit protests to carriers actually possessing authority to operate on the same route. The Canadian officials were persuaded, however, that the ICC did not discriminate against Canadian applicants and that difficulty in getting large grants of authority from the ICC was equally common for American and Canadian carriers.[16]

Recognizing the growing demand for single-line service between the two countries, in 1979 the ICC met in Banff, Alberta, with Canadian provincial regulators and the Canadian Conference of Motor Transport Administrators – an interprovincial regulatory coordinating body. The ICC proposed setting up joint hearings for international single-line applications. A working group of ICC and provincial officials had found that their legislation and application procedures were similar enough to make such proceedings possible. The ICC also helpfully explained to the Canadian regulators the new policies it was adopting to encourage entry and competition, unaware, perhaps, of the problems Canadian entry would cause the ICC two years later. Passage of the Motor Carrier Act, 1980, eliminated the need for joint proceedings because there were no longer application hearings at the ICC.

Canadian practice with regard to admitting American carriers was not uniform because motor carrier regulation was dispersed among ten separate provincial boards. Some provinces, particularly the western ones, were believed to have admitted a larger portion of American-owned carriers than Ontario and to have granted larger territories. Canadian Freightways was prominent in Alberta and British Columbia and operated international freight service in connection with its American parent company, Consolidated Freightways. This still constituted interline service between parent and subsidiary firms, however, and the transfers were made inside the Canadian border.[17] Ontario's entry policies were the crucial ones. Almost half of Canada's motor carriage is based there. Detroit-Windsor and Buffalo-Fort Erie are the two main gateways to the United States, and traffic between the United States and Ontario accounts for approximately half of the transborder volume.[18] As we will see momentarily, Ontario's entry policy was not liberal.

How many American carriers were licensed in the ten provinces was not known for certain. The Canadian boards' records showed a carrier's foreign nationality only if that carrier had no Canadian place of business.[19] That made it impossible to know how many American-owned carriers were actually operating single-line service into Canada. That information could only be found by inspecting each individual operating authority ever granted, a job that would involve going through the thousands of authorities lodged away in provincial files. Thus, when discrimination became an issue in the Trucking War, the raw data were not available to make a convincing case either way.

Even though provincial practice on admitting American carriers may have been variable, the norm of public convenience and necessity supported restrictive entry policies in all of the Canadian jurisdictions. Data from British Columbia, Quebec, and Ontario showed that while the provincial boards did award operating authorities, the great majority of applications came from existing firms. As a result, those firms also received by far the largest share of favourable decisions, amounting in Quebec to 85 percent.[20] Furthermore, the number of licensed motor carriers in Ontario actually declined between 1965 and 1975 in about half of the motor carrier categories. In the important general commodities sector, the number of Ontario-certificated carriers had increased by only thirty firms between 1928 and 1975 (from 325 carriers to 355), enabling those firms to grow along with traffic. One index of that growth is fleet size: Ontario vehicles licensed for general commodities increased from 945 in 1928 to 13,544 in 1975.[21] Between 1975 and 1982 Ontario awarded no new LTL common carrier authorities for general commodities to either Canadian or American applicants.[22] These practices created no bilateral difficulties as long as the ICC also operated under public convenience and necessity. The two countries were served, by and large, by domestic carriers.

Opening the Gates
When the ICC began granting operating authorities freely, it handed Canadian carriers the opportunity to open single-line service into the United States and to develop business there. Previously restricted to terminals at the border and in closely neighbouring cities, Canadian carriers could expand far into the American market. There were only two legal limitations. The first was on purely intrastate services, which almost all states continued to regulate; the second was on cabotage, which is transportation by a foreign carrier between domestic points. Cabotage in both countries is governed by customs rules concerning equipment and immigration rules concerning drivers. Canadian vehicles and drivers may pick up and deliver domestic loads in the United States as long as their direction of travel is generally from, or back to, the border and as long as the cargoes are incidental to the purpose

of the trip.[23] Those determinations are usually made at the roadside by state highway police. Canadian carriers can avoid cabotage restrictions by opening American subsidiaries with American drivers and trucks.

The territories unfolding were huge. One early grant of authority went to Motorways, a large Winnipeg-based LTL carrier, which received eighteen-state authority for general commodities – the most lucrative cargo category. Its authority included entry points on the international boundary in Washington, Idaho, Montana, North Dakota, Minnesota, Michigan, and New York as well as pickup and delivery points in Idaho, Illinois, Indiana, Iowa, Michigan, Minnesota, Missouri, Montana, Nebraska, North Dakota, New York, Ohio, Oregon, Pennsylvania, South Dakota, Washington, Wisconsin, and Wyoming. To encourage the development of nationwide services, particularly in the TL sector, the ICC subsequently began granting forty-eight-state authorities. For Canadian carriers used to plodding through years of regulatory proceedings for the most incremental expansions, the ICC's new policy was handsomely generous. These same grants were also expanding the territories of American carriers. With the old relationships changing under deregulation, and with the recession creating desperate competitors, there was unusual attentiveness to new entrants. The Canadians were quickly noticed, particularly by American carriers whose territories they affected.

These were the American carriers with Canadian interline agreements. With new operating authority, Canadian carriers could now proceed straight through the border gateways to their destinations, bypassing their former American interline partners and diverting the joint traffic to themselves. Once in the United States, Canadian carriers could capture traffic in the reverse direction by soliciting backhaul cargoes to Canada, thus bypassing their interline partners once again. Their advantage was being able to offer expedited transborder service. Approximately half of the populations of both countries live within a day's drive of the Buffalo and Detroit gateways, and Canadian carriers could begin claiming that traffic for themselves. The business potential was impressive.

There was another reason for American carriers to be annoyed. In 1978 Yellow Freight sought a major grant of authority in Ontario. Yellow argued public convenience and necessity on the grounds of delays with its Canadian interline carriers. As with all LTL common carrier general commodities applications in Ontario, Yellow Freight's application was strongly protested. Yellow Freight's opponents persuaded the Ontario Highway Transport Board that any delays were the applicant's fault and not theirs. Having spent $193,000 in Canadian legal fees, Yellow Freight had its application turned down. Both Canadians and Americans close to the proceedings believed that Canadian lawyers had charged Yellow a high figure for a poor application. Worse, Yellow Freight had its speed and dependability – the most basic points of a carrier's reputation – held as deficient before shippers and other carriers, adding embarrassment to failure. Yellow Freight's experience in Ontario was not forgotten two years later when the ATA began hearing about the number of Canadian applications being filed under the new Motor Carrier Act.

The Complaint

The basic note was sounded in 1978 by Washington lawyer William Shawn, an expert on transborder trucking and an adviser to a number of carriers. He warned that in deregulating trucking the United States would be "unilaterally disarming" itself against foreign carriers.[24] Two months after enactment of the Motor Carrier Act, 1980, as Canadian carriers began applying for ICC authorities, ATA president Bennett Whitlock took up the issue. On 10 September 1980, he wrote to ICC chairman Darius Gaskins warning him that unequal access between the United States and Canada would become an increasingly serious problem, as more Canadian carriers took advantage of easy entry.[25] Shortly afterwards, Shawn issued a similar statement: without Canadian reciprocity, American international carriers would eventually find themselves in the position of the American merchant marine, with a major share of their traffic lost to foreign carriers. Whitlock's preferred remedy was regulatory. "Our objective," he wrote to Gaskins, "is to seek parity in the treatment of American carriers in securing operating authority." The ICC, Whitlock made clear, could solve the problem by applying stricter entry standards to all international carrier applications. To avoid antagonizing the CTA and prompting retaliation by the Canadian government, Whitlock advocated applying strict standards to both American and Canadian carriers.[26] Shawn also advocated regulatory relief. As a longer-term measure he proposed a trade solution – a North American transportation compact.

Gaskins promised that Canadian entry would be looked into. This occurred at a closed meeting on 9 and 10 December 1980 with members of the Canadian provincial highway transport boards and the Canadian Council of Motor Transport Administrators. When told of the ICC's concerns about unequal rates of entry, the Canadian officials denied that Canada discriminated against American applicants. Canada, they maintained, was simply following its long-standing rules.[27] Raising the issue of Canadian sovereignty, the officials rejected reciprocity and pointedly asserted that bringing American concerns to them about entry imbalances suggested a desire to pressure Canada into adopting parallel policies. According to a Canadian official who was present, the ICC agreed that Canada did not treat American applicants differently than Canadian ones.[28] With that conclusion in mind, the ICC continued to approve Canadian applications. That behaviour became a key part of the ATA's complaint.

As the ICC's meeting with the Canadians clearly showed, both reciprocity and discrimination were at issue. The difference needs to be noted again. Discrimination involves applying differential norms or procedures to a particular class of individuals. Ensuring standardized and non-discriminatory treatment of customers has been a prime concern of regulators. Securing such treatment was an original rationale for rate regulation. Discrimination also pertains to the regulators' own behaviour. In order to prevent differential or unfair treatment, regulators were required to follow formal procedures and due process. Alleging discrimination against Canadian provincial regulatory boards, therefore, would mean that American applicants being treated more stringently than Canadian ones. Addressed to a foreign government, the charge of discrimination also becomes a matter of trade. Under GATT, both foreign and domestic firms come under the principle of national treatment, which holds that laws and regulations "designed to achieve domestic regulatory objectives be applied equally to both domestically produced and imported services."[29] Discrimination violates that principle and constitutes a non-tariff barrier. At the same time, seeking non-discrimination does not itself constitute effort to harmonize other governments' domestic regulations.[30]

Reciprocity is a cooperative exchange of favours involving trade and the conditions of doing business. Such bilateral cooperation may be arranged by a negotiated agreement in which all parties agree to adopt equally favourable terms towards the others. Reciprocity may also occur sequentially, when one trading partner liberalizes its conditions and the other partner follows suit. In either form, reciprocity increases mutual access, while non-reciprocity creates one-sided advantages. Retaliation against such deliberate imbalances can also be reciprocal, with one government adopting restrictions similar to another's. Directed to provincial regulatory boards, a charge of non-reciprocity would mean failing to lift restrictive norms after the ICC had done so and preserving unequally favourable positions for Canadian carriers. Concerns in Canada that the United States might be seeking to export deregulation focused on expected reciprocity.

The ATA

For the ATA, large-scale Canadian entry was an unprecedented problem. As long as both countries had applied strict entry rules and the ICC had governed the American half of international trucking, the ATA required no expertise on foreign issues. The ATA's lawyers were specialists in the domestic law of regulation, not in the international law of trade or in the regulatory and business law of Canada. The Canadian issue arrived just after the ATA had lost the legislative battle of its life. Powerless before an ICC bent on aggressive interpretation of the Motor Carrier Act, and beset by members reeling under deregulation, the ATA confronted a problem for which it had almost no preparation. Seeking help where it could, the ATA tackled the problem as both a regulatory and a trade issue. It was not always clear, as will be seen, whether the ATA fully appreciated the implications of the two approaches.

Among the ATA's 17,000 members, views on Canadian entry varied. In one group were firms such as Yellow Freight, which had experienced problems with Canadian regulators, or anticipated difficulties in expanding into Canada, or feared Canadian inroads into the United States. Other American carriers had satisfactory dealings with Canadian regulators and no complaints about the conditions of doing business there. Several of those firms disapproved of the ATA's making an issue of Canadian entry. Initially reluctant to object, these carriers, as will be seen later, ended up publicly opposing the ATA and Congress. Most of the other ATA members were not immediately threatened. Canadians accounted for less than 5 percent of the 1981 applications to the ICC – an index of the size of the American market and the flood of carriers seeking authorities under the new rules. What was important to one segment of ATA members was of secondary or no interest to the majority. Those differences in the ATA's ranks reflected the diversity of its membership and the tasks of trade associations who represent complex industries. When the ATA decided to take a strong stand on Canadian entry, it attended to one particular set of interests. Those differences in the ranks were also reflected in the low-keyed and judicious treatment of the matter in *Transport Topics*, a weekly newspaper published by the ATA. The main story at the time was the struggle in all sectors to cope with deregulation.

Data gathered by the ATA showed that the carriers most hurt by deregulation and the recession were small firms with annual revenues of under $5 million and medium firms with annual revenues of $5 to $25 million. On average, small and medium carriers lost money in 1981 and 1982 in the New England states; the Mid-Atlantic states of New York, Pennsylvania, New Jersey, Delaware, Maryland, and West Virginia; and the Central states of Illinois, Indiana, Michigan, and Ohio.[31] According to an analysis prepared for the ATA by Chase Manhattan Bank, in 1981 two of those regions showed the largest declines in net carrier operating income in the country, with Mid-Atlantic down 76.4 percent and Central down 94.4 percent.[32] For the Central region that represented the second year of losses.

The major gateways to Canada are located in the Mid-Atlantic and Central regions. Small and medium LTL carriers generally have regional territories, and carriers serving Canadian gateways would be directly vulnerable to losses of joint-line business. Regional territories also lack the diversity of potential traffic that is available in large ones, magnifying the effects of traffic losses for small and medium carriers and limiting their alternatives. Worse, poor earnings for those carriers made it more difficult for them to compensate for joint-line losses by redeploying their resources, particularly if those resources involved terminal facilities. As we will see in Chapter 6, regional LTL carriers began to benefit dramatically in the early 1990s from their structural and service advantages, and some opened interline services across the border. Those advantages, however, were by no means apparent in the deregulatory turmoil ten years earlier.

Taking up the carriers' cause posed trouble with the CTA. The ATA firmly maintained that it had no quarrel with Canadian regulators and carriers and no desire to see Canada pressured into deregulation. At a meeting of the CTA in Toronto on 25 June 1981, ATA chairman Eugene Kane said he opposed the export of deregulation to Canada. "We fully understand where the fault lies," he said. "It lies on our side of the border, not yours."[33] He denied that the ATA was seeking action against Canadian carriers and repeated that his association's objective was obtaining stricter ICC treatment of both American and Canadian international carriers. That position was consistent with the ATA's effort in the early months of deregulation, as was seen in the last chapter, to find a test court case to combat the ICC's aggressive interpretation of the Motor Carrier Act.

There had been no previous occasion for conflict with the CTA. Under regulation, the task of both associations was protecting their members. The ATA had now lost that ability, and its members were busy coping with free-ranging competition. For some the new competitors were foreign. The ATA's mission would direct it to seek relief for them, just as it had done against new competitors under regulation. The CTA's position was less straightforward. On the one hand, it, too, was committed to protecting its members and was opposed to deregulation in Canada. The CTA had also foreseen the conflict with the United States and had drawn the correct implications. In autumn 1979, as deregulation began gaining political momentum in Congress, CTA executive director Ken Maclaren wrote to the ATA forecasting a regulatory imbalance between the two countries and the likelihood of political pressure on the American government to correct it. On the other hand, many of the CTA's largest members were responding gladly to the new opportunities south of the border. Taking their side against American complaints would put the CTA directly at odds with the ATA and leave the former in the awkward position of defending Canadian carriers taking advantage of an opened American market while seeking to preserve a restricted Canadian one.

The Teamsters Union faced similar division. For the Teamsters, however, the conflict was not between organizations, as it was with the ATA and the CTA, but within the union itself. The Teamsters leadership was initially very sympathetic to the complaints of the ATA and favoured the same solution of applying tighter entry standards to Canadian applicants. The union's Canadian locals, whose members stood to gain by increased operations into the United States, objected strenuously. To prevent serious rifts from developing between the American and Canadian membership, and to avoid the charge frequently made in Canada that international unions represent only American interests, the Teamsters leadership decided to take a neutral position on Canadian entry and avoided further public involvement.

Finding Help: The Executive Branch

With the ICC showing no apparent concern about the steady stream of Canadian entries, the ATA's executive committee in early February 1981 voted unanimously to use its political resources to get aid from other agencies in the federal government. The first opportunity involved trade. The USTR's office was preparing a presidential report for Congress on the desirability of free trade with Canada and Mexico and was conducting hearings on the experiences of firms in various sectors. In testimony on 12 February 1981, the ATA general counsel argued that the Motor Carrier Act had disrupted a previously harmonious arrangement for international trucking. He cited the September 1980 exchange of letters between ATA president Whitlock and ICC chairman Gaskins and remarked: "This correspondence will indicate that the Commission is more interested in exporting its deregulation philosophy than in utilizing its authority to correct the impending imbalance."[34] The reference to exporting deregulation showed the ATA still seeking to avoid provoking the CTA. The ATA's remedy was the same one it had advocated with ICC chairman Gaskins: the tightening of entry controls for international carriers from both countries.

The USTR's report to Congress raised the trucking problem and directly implicated Canada. In doing so it went beyond the ATA's requests for remedy on the American side of the border. Disadvantages for American carriers in Canada, said the report, were based in the Canadian regulatory system, which required applying separately to each province and produced longer delays, higher legal expenses, and more occasions for denial than was the case in the United States. The report also noted that, in contrast to the United States, few commodities are exempt from regulation in Canada, giving Canadian carriers in the United States unrestricted access to a much greater variety of freight than is available in their own country. Taking up the ATA's complaint, the report also stated that American carriers had lost business as Canadian carriers acquired single-line operations into the United States.[35] These points found receptive listeners in Congress, which later became the principal source of action in the dispute.

The ATA also turned to the Department of Transportation (DOT), hoping to circumvent the ICC's jurisdiction by casting the problem in the broader terms of national transportation policy. In 1981 DOT was not an immediately obvious source of sympathy. During the legislative battle over the Motor Carrier Act just a year earlier, DOT had been a strong opponent of the ATA. Now, however, unbalanced foreign competition was the issue, and there was a desire to see what could be done to help.[36] DOT officials responsible for international transportation saw a new and potentially serious problem, and they were concerned that there was no clear policy to deal with it. To find the basis for one they set about informally gathering information about Canadian entry. Two sets of considerations were present. The first was the pro-deregulation climate in DOT, the Reagan executive branch generally, and the ICC, and this was matched by the Reagan administration's disinclination to resort to trade barriers. The second was the prospect that the Canadian problem could become quite serious. This DOT officials began discovering first-hand.

Transportation Secretary Drew Lewis met with the Canadian minister of transport Jean-Luc Pépin on 17 July 1981 and formally identified transborder trucking as a major problem. Pépin expressed similar concern, while making it clear that solutions were not his to offer. Officials from DOT met with Ministry of Transport officials in Ottawa again on 12 November 1981. There were no Canadian officials present who would speak authoritatively, but the strained tenor of the meeting convinced DOT members that the Canadians were not prepared to yield. When DOT officials returned to Washington they began consulting closely with the Departments of State and Commerce, and the USTR's office, to find a common position.

Finding Help: Congress

In June 1981 the ATA testified to the first of five annual House and Senate oversight hearings on the Motor Carrier Act. The ATA, as we saw in Chapter 3, had hoped to use those hearings to persuade Congress that deregulation was proceeding far beyond Congress's intent and was having severe effects. One of those effects was foreign entry. Testifying on behalf of the ATA was Stephen Flott, a director of the CTA and executive director of the Ontario Trucking Association. "While the Motor Carrier Act of 1980 did not remove the test of public necessity and convenience," Flott said, "the Interstate Commerce Commission clearly decided to make a mockery of the concept of entry control."[37] Expressing apparent sympathy with the ATA, Flott said that the ICC had created a "one-way street" for Canadian carriers.

Such statements from an official of the CTA might appear incongruous, but the CTA still had reason for common cause with the ATA. Now that deregulation was a fact in the United States, CTA officials were worried that its effects would reach over into their own bailiwicks. The CTA was aware that regulatory reform had already emerged as a prospect in Canada, as will be seen in the next chapter, and it feared the consequences. With the ATA's plight to contemplate, those consequences were easy to imagine. Transborder controversy would also put pressure on Canada to deregulate. For the CTA, therefore, it was quite consistent to join the ATA in seeking to get Congress to reconsider how the Motor Carrier Act was being implemented.[38]

If the CTA's purpose in siding with the ATA was to protect itself, then it got the opposite results. The House Oversight Committee was nominally sympathetic to the ATA's demonstrations of hardship but did not intervene. Complaints about *foreign* competition, however, did produce action, even though some members of Congress suspected the ATA of using the issue to roll back deregulation.[39] Legislation on foreign entry followed.

In fall 1981 the House Committee on Public Works and Transportation was drafting HR 3663, the Bus Regulatory Reform Act, 1981, which completed the deregulation of interstate transportation. On 20 November 1981 Representative Donald Albosta of Michigan introduced a bill, HR 5064, that would require the ICC to apply the public convenience and necessity standard in entry applications for single-line service between the United States and any points in Mexico or Canada. Addressing the question of discrimination, the bill would also instruct the ICC to deny operating authority to any foreign motor carrier whose government does not admit American-domiciled carriers on the same terms as apply to its own domestic carriers. Albosta had been a member of the House Oversight Committee during the trucking hearings in June, and his district was close to the Detroit/Windsor gateway, and, following the hearings, several American carrier representatives had contacted him. The anti-discrimination provision from Albosta's bill was added in subcommittee as an amendment to the bus bill.

The amendment gave the ICC the discretion to deny a bus or motor carrier application from a Canadian or Mexican firm if the ICC determined that American carriers were not being treated "at least as favourably" as were the nationals in those two jurisdictions. The amendment also authorized the ICC to consider aspects of treatment beyond the two governments' granting of applications.[40] In remarks to the House about the amendment, Congressman Glenn Anderson of California, chairman of the House Public Works Subcommittee on Surface Transportation, sounded themes of both discrimination and reciprocity: "If foreign carriers wish to be treated in the United States on the same basis as our domestic carriers, then our carriers must be treated the same in their home country." Congressman Albosta was specific that the issue was not just discrimination: "The language [in the amendment] makes it very clear that the Congress believes reciprocity is a vital factor to be considered when the ICC makes a decision on granting operating authority to a Mexican or Canadian-owned or controlled trucking company."[41] The House passed the bill.

Finding Help: The Regulatory Process

Several carriers decided to protest the Canadian applications at the ICC. The *Pan American* standard had allowed protests on the grounds of prospective harm from new competitors and had been very effective in restricting entry. The ICC had abandoned the *Pan American* standard and was no longer listening to arguments about competitive harm, and it had already shown its disinclination to pursue regulatory differences with the Canadian government. Formal protests concerning particular Canadian applications, however, had not been tried. In September 1981 Yellow Freight, Wheaton Van Lines, Ryder Truck Lines, Associated Truck Lines, and Central Transport (and its affiliates C.T. Transport of Michigan and McKinley Transport Ltd. of Ontario) protested the ICC application of the large Canadian carrier Dominion Consolidated Ltd. for authority to serve points in nine states. Loss of business was the principal objection, while another was the difficulty of obtaining comparable authorities in Canada. On the free-trade side of the issue was Buffalo-area congressman Jack Kemp, who wrote to the new ICC chairman, Reese Taylor, supporting the Dominion-Consolidated application as good for Buffalo and the United States.[42]

The involvement of Yellow Freight and Dominion-Consolidated showed the repercussions of terminated interdependence. Interlining makes carriers interdependent through pooled traffic and coordinated truck movements. One side's wish to discontinue the relationship causes conflict because it gains all of the previously shared benefits for itself. Conflict between Yellow Freight and Dominion-Consolidated went both ways because each had sought to end interlining and each was resisted by the other. In the first instance Yellow Freight was the terminating party. Dominion-Consolidated had been Yellow Freight's interline partner in Ontario, and when Yellow Freight had applied for Ontario operating authority in 1978, Dominion-Consolidated's own opposing argument included the issue of traffic diversion. One index of the degree of conflict was Yellow management's belief, according to two attorneys familiar with the case, that Dominion had orchestrated the failure of its application.[43] On the other side, Yellow Freight and several other of the protestants had been Dominion-Consolidated's American interline carriers, and now, at the ICC, the interests, arguments, and prospective losses were exactly reversed.

The ATA joined a second protest. This was from three Michigan-based carriers and it was launched against the Canadian carrier Overland Western International's application for expanded operating authority. This protest specifically asked the ICC to consider Canadian reciprocity. The ATA then joined Yellow Freight in requesting the consolidation of seven Canadian applications into a single proceeding, and, on 1 December 1981, the ATA asked for consolidation of twelve Canadian carrier applications. These consolidations were to allow reciprocity to be addressed as a common issue. Raising reciprocity in specific applications brought Canadian regulation directly into American proceedings and escalated the conflict with both the CTA and the Canadian government. By joining the protest the ATA could be seen by the CTA as denying its earlier assurance that it had no quarrel with Canadian practices and carriers and no desire to apply pressure. By labelling the issue as one of reciprocity, the ATA took the conflict to the Canadian provincial and federal governments, which saw the implications of exported deregulation and were very concerned.

DOT was also interested in reciprocity, but its desire was to see the ICC take action. As Secretary Lewis had discovered first-hand, Canada viewed the problem as entirely of the United States' own making and maintained that there was nothing to negotiate. In the face of that position the ICC was the most direct and convenient means of dealing with the problem. Question of whether the ICC had the authority to consider reciprocity had been raised by counsel for three Mexican applicants. Aware that Mexico's completely exclusionary policy on foreign carriers might arise in proceedings, the three Mexican carriers had challenged the ICC's authority to consider it, arguing that there is no mention of reciprocity in the Motor Carrier Act. If that view were to prevail, then the ICC would have no basis for considering foreign regulatory practices. For its part, the ATA hoped that the Mexican cases – obvious, unqualified instances of non-reciprocity and discrimination – could be used to establish broad principles to deal with the more complicated situation with Canada.

The legal reasoning is worth noting for the way it ties reciprocity to regulation. DOT's Deputy General Counsel, in a brief on 13 November, allowed that the act does not specifically mention reciprocity but asserted, "we believe that the consideration of reciprocal commercial opportunities for United States carriers in foreign markets is implied in section 10101(a)(7) which directs the Commission to 'promote competitive and efficient transportation services.'" Noting that it had long been the policy of the American government to exchange opportunities for US industries abroad for commercial opportunities for foreign enterprises in the United States, the department urged the commission to "consider reciprocity, as well as the basic goals of competition and efficiency, in determining whether to grant operating authority to any applicant."[44]

The USTR also favoured a regulatory solution. Like DOT, the USTR's Office was well aware of Canada's position on negotiations. That option, however, conflicted broadly with the USTR's opposition to sectoral approaches to reciprocity. That left regulation. William Brock, the US trade representative, decided to advocate regulatory reciprocity directly to the ICC after a visit from a Yellow Freight representative, who complained that the ICC was not giving due weight to the international implications of the Motor Carrier Act.[45] The USTR's immediate reaction was to acknowledge that there were indeed differences in the way the two countries treated applications and that carriers had reason to be concerned. On 17 July 1981, the same day of DOT secretary Lewis's meeting with Transport Minister Pépin in Ottawa,

USTR Brock wrote to ICC chairman Gaskins expressing concern about Canadian regulatory procedures. Brock also raised the exclusionary effects of Canada's FIRA. FIRA, whose mandate to subject only foreign firms to controls made it openly discriminatory, was to figure importantly in the issue later on. As did Brock's letter, which became a point of Canadian complaint.

The ICC flatly refused to entertain reciprocity. In turning down the objection against Dominion-Consolidated, the ICC stated: "We believe the protestants' complaints about Canadian law and policy should be addressed to the proper Canadian authorities."[46] In its 7 December ruling on the appeals to consolidate applications, the commission replied that "allegations concerning reciprocity lie outside the present record and thus constitute unverifiable hearsay." Addressing the question of discrimination, the ICC held that the protestants had failed to establish that Canadian regulators applied different standards to American carriers.[47] On 14 December the ICC granted operating authority to Kingsway Transports Ltd., one of Canada's three largest carriers, having denied a request from three American carriers to present oral arguments regarding Canadian discrimination.

Further Escalation

The Canadian entry issue received senior-level attention on 11 January 1982 when DOT secretary Lewis brought it to the president's Trade Policy Committee. The focus of Lewis's concerns was the growing political seriousness of the problem and the lack of a clear policy. The committee considered the problem in light of the administration's broader concerns on trade and reciprocity and of the position of the Canadian government. With the problem escalating in the United States, Canada's position heralded diplomatic trouble, and at that point the State Department became involved. The section of the State Department responsible for the issue was the Office of Transportation and Telecommunications. The problem had gone first to the Office of Maritime Affairs, since that office had long experience in international transportation and in dealing with a regulatory agency – the Federal Maritime Commission. Transportation and Telecommunications received the assignment in late 1981, when it became clear that trucking was too complex for the Canada desk to handle and that managing it would require cooperation with other departments. Favouring that office taking on the assignment was the background of the new assistant secretary of state for Transportation and Telecommunication Affairs, Matthew Scocozza, who assumed that post in February 1982. Before that he had been chief counsel of the Senate Commerce Committee and had helped draft the Motor Carrier Act, 1980, an experience that gave him a thorough knowledge of trucking and regulation. His view of the problem with Canada was that it was quickly becoming a "mess." When the ATA learned that Transportation and Telecommunications would be managing trucking diplomacy, it contacted the office and asked that it do what it could to foster a smooth long-term relationship with Canada.[48]

Congress Prods the ICC

The idea of an ICC moratorium on Canadian applications was first aired in the June 1981 House Oversight Hearings. Representative Henry Nowak of New York, whose district was the Buffalo/Fort Erie gateway, broached the idea officially with the ICC on 6 January 1982. In a letter to ICC chairman Taylor, Nowak cited a Buffalo Teamsters Union estimate that 600 jobs in the area had been lost to Canadian carriers. That, Nowak asserted, was evidence that the ICC's policy was causing injury. Noting also reports that the reciprocity question was dividing the ICC commissioners themselves, Nowak asked Taylor to suspend action on new Canadian and Mexican applications until Congress could take legislative action.[49]

The ICC, still unmoved, replied to Nowak that it had no legal authority to detain applications without legislation specifically dealing with reciprocity. Replying to the question of discrimination, the ICC also refused to take issue with Canada's regulatory boards, maintaining that the Canadian application process is open to American carriers and that provincial boards administer restrictive standards regardless of the nationality of applicants. The ICC did not completely close the door. Mentioning that there were several pending applications involving Canadian reciprocity and petitions to detain them, the ICC assured Representative Nowak that it was "actively considering" reciprocity and would "carefully weigh all of the evidence."[50]

The Senate was also becoming involved. Republican members asked Wisconsin senator Robert Kasten, a member of the Commerce, Science and Transportation Committee (the same committee that drafted the Senate version of the Motor Carrier Act, 1980) to sponsor a bill addressing the Canadian question. The Republicans knew that Democratic senator Howard Cannon of Nevada was preparing a measure of his own, and they felt that sponsorship of their bill by a senator from a state near Canada would be fitting. Some Wisconsin carriers had also discussed the matter with Kasten. The bill, S. 2057, was introduced on 3 February 1982. As did the Albosta bill and the Bus Regulatory Reform Act just passed by the House, the Kasten bill would instruct the ICC to deny applications to Canadian- or Mexican-domiciled carriers if those governments did not apply "substantially the same licensing standards" to their own nationals. Kasten's bill also instructed the ICC to begin a rule-making proceeding to determine whether the Canadian and Mexican governments in fact practised such discrimination against American carriers. In addition, the Senate bill would also apply the public convenience and necessity standard to applicants for single-line international service, restoring the symmetry with Canadian practice. That was precisely the remedy the ATA had been advocating.

More immediate action was in the offing. Senator Cannon, chairman of the committee and sponsor of the Motor Carrier Act, 1980, had received complaints from carriers and promised to take action.[51] On 10 February Senator Cannon introduced a resolution asking the ICC to place a moratorium on the approval of operating authorities to Canadian and Mexican carriers until Congress could consider the issue fully. Cannon said that his purpose in requesting the moratorium was to prevent further injury to American carriers. The move was necessary, he told the Senate, because the ICC's legal mandate had never distinguished between foreign and domestic truckers. Granting authorities to foreigners in a non-discriminatory way was not the problem. "The problem is that U.S. carriers are being denied the same rights by Canada and Mexico that nationals of those countries enjoy in the United States" – a question of reciprocity. During the time the ICC had been making such grants to Canadians, Cannon knew of no American carrier receiving a major grant of authority in Canada: "The issue is not one of regulation vs. deregulation, but rather a question of basic fairness to American carriers." In a 10 February letter to ICC chairman Taylor, Cannon said, "It seems to me that the ICC could be of great assistance to Congress if it could conduct an investigation itself of the many issues involved. I urge you to do so."[52] Twenty-two Senators co-sponsored Cannon's resolution.

ICC: Reluctant Investigator

Developments on the Canadian entry issue had put into question the extent of ICC's jurisdiction and its interpretation of the Motor Carrier Act. On the one hand, the ICC's mandate under the new legislation was to promote competition and to improve service to the public. By that criterion, approving new international single-line service furthered both purposes. Harm to existing carriers had ceased to be grounds for protest. On the other hand, there was a stream of pressure from the trucking industry, the executive branch, and Congress to consider reciprocity and discrimination. All three of the ICC's most important constituencies – the executive branch, Congress, and the trucking industry – were expressing displeasure with its behaviour. The ICC is an agency of the executive branch, and although it is structurally independent, it is nonetheless sensitive to concerns and priorities in the executive branch, as its increasingly decisive shift to deregulation showed in the 1970s. Statements from DOT and the USTR urging the ICC to consider reciprocity could not be ignored. Similarly, the ICC is responsible for interpreting the intent of Congress in administering regulatory legislation. Expressions of congressional intent were undeniably pertinent. That was particularly so with the amendment to the Bus Regulatory Reform Act, legislation that, when law, would constitute part of the ICC's mandate. Finally, the American interstate carriers under the ICC's jurisdiction were protesting Canadian applications individually and through their trade association.

The ICC's position was made more difficult because many in the commission believed that, while it had the authority under existing legislation to consider reciprocity, it did not have the authority as a domestic regulatory agency to challenge other countries' rules and procedures. That being so, it would be inappropriate for the ICC to take issue with Canada.[53] There was also some feeling that Canadian regulators, the ICC's organizational counterparts, were merely continuing to administer the same rules as had the ICC until 1978 and were acting properly under their own legislative mandates. More pragmatically, there was no appetite among ICC officials for becoming involved in a complex and inflammatory international dispute. Improving business opportunities for American carriers in Canada was a matter for trade and diplomatic officials, not regulators. The ICC staff did believe that it could take action in cases of proven foreign discrimination against American carriers.

A factor favouring the continued granting of entry was the strongly pro-deregulation outlook of the ICC commissioners. Not everyone regarded the commissioners' devotion to principle as a positive thing. According to a lawyer involved in the Canadian question, ICC commissioners before the late 1970s had been "regulatory hacks" who dutifully implemented tight controls. Now, with the exception of Chairman Taylor, they were "deregulatory hacks" who just as dutifully kept the gates open to applicants.[54] Canadian applications continued to arrive, and by February 1982 the number of authorities granted to Canadian carriers since 1980 stood at 312.

Following the Senate resolution's strong suggestion, the ICC, on 22 February, 1982 began Ex Parte MC No. 157, Investigation into Canadian Law and Policy Regarding Applications of American Motor Carriers for Canadian Operating Authority. In its announcement of the proceeding, the ICC said it shared the Senate's and American carriers' concerns. Conceived as a "purely fact-finding procedure," the inquiry sought to establish "whether existing Canadian law and policy effectively discriminate against United States motor carriers, precluding their participation in the single-line transportation of international general commodity freight."[55] The ICC defined discrimination broadly as including "the effect or impact of particular policies and laws" and not merely the question of "disparate treatment." The announcement also mentioned reciprocity, which it defined as "a general concept of fair competitive opportunities for American motor carriers in foreign countries."[56]

MC-157 would focus on four issues: whether the ICC could legally take into account Canadian regulatory treatment of American carriers when considering applications from Canadian carriers; whether FIRA had any effect on American motor carriers; whether the provincial boards apply different standards to American applicants than they do to Canadian applicants; and what the ICC's options were if the results showed discrimination. The proceeding was to begin in a month, a promptness caused, in part, by Congress's interest in the issue and, in part, by a group of 100 pending Canadian applications, ten of which were for forty-eight-state authority or for very large territories. After announcing the investigation, the ICC flagged the applications of a number of Canadian carriers and suspended action on them until the MC-157 proceedings were completed. It also reopened the files on several granted Canadian applications for reconsideration in light of MC-157 findings.

Canadian carriers with pending applications or recently granted authorities were vexed, and several with suspended applications filed suit with the ICC charging denial of due process. Others made more fundamental objections. Soon after the announcement of MC-157 three Canadian firms – Provost Cartage, Inc., Transx, Ltd., and Frederick Transport Ltd. – filed motions seeking a dismissal of the investigation on the grounds that the ICC had no jurisdiction to consider reciprocity. They based that position on the absence of the word "reciprocity" in the Motor Carrier Act, 1980, which contrasted to the International Air Transportation Competition Act's specific authorization to the Civil Aeronautics Board to take corrective measures when the actions of a foreign government injure the competitive position of an American air carrier. The motion also held that, under the Trade Agreements Act, 1979, the area of trade reciprocity was reserved for the president.[57]

The scope of the ICC's intentions was not altogether clear. On the one hand, it emphasized that Canadian practices would be considered "only as they affect or relate to transportation services and competition on the United states side of the International Boundary Line," presumably in order to avoid giving the impression of conducting an investigation in Canada. At the same time, the ICC held that it had much broader authority under public convenience and necessity, which the Motor Carrier Act authorized the ICC to continue considering – a major reason, as was seen in the last chapter, that the act stopped well short of complete deregulation. Although the ICC had set that standard aside in its proceedings, the Motor Carrier Act did confer the power, the ICC noted, to exercise wide-reaching discretion in matters relating to motor carrier service – a discretion "sufficiently broad to enable the Commission to consider whether law or policies of the Canadian government have an anti-competitive or discriminatory impact on the United States motor carrier industry." And although the ICC had stopped considering harm to existing carriers in domestic applications when it dropped the *Pan American* standard, the authority was still there to do so. Finally, the commission cited legal precedent for considering the "transportation situation" in another country and in the foreign portion of international carrier movements in determining need for service.[58] Notwithstanding these interpretive footings, the ICC's own legal specialist believed the commission lacked the authority to conduct the investigation. Reportedly, the response from the ICC's chairperson was to find legal means to proceed.[59] For a Canadian government seeking to anticipate what to expect, MC 157's terms of reference gave much latitude for speculation.

Regulators and Diplomatic Channels

In undertaking the investigation as it did, the ICC dismayed the State Department. For the Canadian government, the ICC prepared a list of thirty questions on provincial regulatory practices and thirty questions on the workings of FIRA. The ICC sent those questions to the State Department to be vetted, and after doing so the State Department in turn sent them to the Canadian Embassy. In the meantime, however, one of the legal proceedings to quash the investigation resulted in the ICC's releasing the questions to the public. That embarrassed both the State Department and the Canadian Embassy. More extra-diplomatic action followed. The ICC drafted a covering note to Canadian provincial regulatory boards and to FIRA, dated 30 March, requesting that answers to the questions and expert provincial and FIRA witnesses be made available for cross-examination in the investigation's oral hearings. The note, however, was not directed to the State Department and the Canadian Embassy, the proper diplomatic channels. To make matters even worse, the ICC allowed the contents of that note to become public as well. In the end, the note never did reach any officials in Canada, although they did manage to learn the contents. The clumsy handling of the note annoyed officials in the State Department, one of whom wryly characterized the ICC's actions as a "segmented procedure."

In dealing with each other over the years, ICC officials and Canadian regulators had developed their own communication channels and regarded their relationship as collegial. They had never had to deal, however, with such a divisive and basic matter of policy. Now that transborder trucking was politicized and contentious, the ICC's direct communication with the Canadian government crossed from regulation to diplomacy, the State Department's domain. In acting before receiving the department's advice, the ICC ignored the latter's expertise in handling contentious matters with foreign governments. For the State Department, the ICC's action came at a particularly troublesome time.

The Reagan administration's free-market ideology and the Trudeau government's economic nationalism, coinciding as they did, strained Canadian-American relations badly. One of the sorest points was FIRA. While Canadian economic nationalists saw it as an assertion of sovereignty, many businesspeople in the United States (and, less vocally, in Europe) saw it as an unfriendly tribunal. Another irritant was the National Energy Program, which was implemented in order to regain Canadian ownership in a sector dominated by foreign corporations. American oil interests in Canada regarded the program's treatment of foreign oil firms as discriminatory, and Canadian nationalists regarded that view as arrogant.[60] Overhanging these economic issues was conflict over acid rain, with most Canadians believing that the Reagan administration was deliberately obstructing measures to improve air quality. These issues gained much public attention in Canada. With the bilateral relationship already querulous, the State Department feared, the ICC's direct requests for information would appear presumptuous and invasive. Adding a judicial imperative, the ICC issued subpoenas to the American carriers that had dealt with FIRA, having got the list of carriers from the Canadian Department of External Affairs.

Canada: Providing Facts, Minding the Boundary

The Canadian government released that list because it believed the facts in the dispute were on its side. At the same time, the procedural aspects required careful handling because of the domestic agencies involved, the implications for sovereignty, and the precedents that might be set. Concerns about domestic agency involvement were the first to emerge. At the beginning of the dispute in December 1980, when the ICC chairperson had first invited provincial regulators to the commission to discuss Canadian entry, the federal government was worried that these officials, attending the meeting on their own, might be "ambushed." At the same time, the federal government was reluctant to send along a representative. As we saw in Chapter 2, the provinces' unwillingness to surrender their exclusive authority to regulate trucking had decentralized Canadian trucking regulation, and the provinces were vigilant about any federal efforts to reclaim jurisdiction. After that meeting the provincial officials were reluctant to make any further trips to the ICC. The ATA blamed the ICC's unchanged views on granting Canadian applications on the fact that the meeting had been closed, making the Canadian regulators feel that they were being charged with collusion.[61]

Subsequently concerned about the dispute's escalation, federal transport and foreign policy officials persuaded the provincial regulators to agree to a public meeting with the ICC set for April 1982. Just then, however, the ICC announced MC-157, unilaterally suspending consultation and surprising the Canadian regulators. That the people they had known and dealt with at the ICC had given them no prior notice before launching a formal investigation, Canadian regulators felt, was an indignity. More practically, what the ICC had requested would be nearly impossible to provide. The ICC was apparently unaware that the provincial boards did not have special sections or categories in their records for foreign carriers. To supply information about respective rates of approval and denial for American and Canadian applicants, and thus address the issue of discrimination, the provincial regulators would have to go through each individual operating authority and application in their files, and this amounted to examining thousands of documents.

Responding to the ICC's requests for information raised the questions of sovereignty and precedent. Although the federal government believed that providing facts would be to Canada's advantage, it would also set a precedent for cooperating with American domestic governmental agencies asking for information from Canadian domestic governmental agencies. If that precedent became established, then a regulatory agency could bypass diplomatic channels and make formal requests to its counterpart. The Canadian government wanted to refute charges of discrimination and so did prepare a response. To protect its agencies from extraterritorial gestures, the Canadian government sent its response not to the ICC but to the State Department, as a diplomatic note.

In exercising that vigilance, the Department of External Affairs was involved in the trucking issue at the very early stage of the December 1980 meeting at the ICC.[62] Following that, the Canadian Embassy in Washington kept closely informed of all the aspects of the dispute: the contested Canadian applications at the ICC (particularly the legally intricate Dominion-Consolidated case), the political activity of the ATA, the Bus Regulatory Reform Act amendment in the House, and the Cannon resolution in the Senate. The embassy was also well informed about the internal deliberations at the ICC over the Canadian applications and the origins of the MC-157 investigation.

In contrast, the State Department did not become a direct participant in the issue until the passage of the Cannon resolution in the Senate, although it was visited by a Yellow Freight representative over a year earlier and was aware of the issue's development. Its involvement followed the standard practice of taking interest in legislation that will affect a foreign government.[63] Since the dispute was already serious, the State Department's comparatively later involvement reflects the low priority of such issues in American foreign policy. The two governments' differing concentration on bilateral issues shows in another way. The Canadian government's greater focus on the bilateral relationship is usually matched by media coverage, so that when bilateral issues become contentious, the diplomatic asset of mobilized opinion is often present. That asset came into play later in the dispute.

Whitewashing Reciprocity

The ICC investigation did not please the ATA. Remarking on the ICC's handling of complaints about Canadian carriers and the way it launched MC-157, an ATA official likened events to a "rugby game of bureaucratic confusion and incoherence," showing no consistent policy or pattern.[64] The ATA was suspicious that the investigation was proceeding only under political duress and that the ICC would minimize exposure to itself and conflict with Canada. That would mean carefully avoiding the contentious issue of reciprocity and focusing on the safely limited one of discrimination. In its written submission to MC-157, the ATA noted that when ICC chairman Gaskins responded to the ATA's original written complaint about Canadian entry in 1980, he had construed the issue as discrimination. The ATA president, greatly disturbed, had replied that the issue is the "different entry controls which exist."[65] Charging that the ICC had "ignored the reciprocity issues or dismissed them as hearsay" in awarding operating authorities to Canadian carriers since then, the ATA claimed "serious misgivings" about MC-157. Although the ICC's announcement of the investigation, the ATA acknowledged, referred to "different licensing standards," the "underlying tone of the notice indicates that discrimination ... is the sole issue." The ATA also complained that the ICC's early deadline for submission of statements of March 23 "smacks of a *pro forma* investigation aimed at getting it over and done with."[66] A member of Congressman Albosta's staff expressed the same view, believing the investigation would be a "whitewash."[67]

The ATA also had relations with the CTA in mind. In a response to Canadian news media seeking clarification of the ATA's position, Whitlock stated that the ICC's "unfortunate misdirection of effort" away from the issue of reciprocity "can only inflame the sensitivities of Canadian carriers, the provincial transport boards, and federal officials in Ottawa." Had the ICC dealt with the reciprocity issue at the outset, stated Whitlock, "both American and Canadian applicants would have been treated more fairly." The ATA did say that it would participate in MC-157 "in an effort to get the agency back on track," and it left open the possibility that MC-157 actually would find evidence of discrimination and impeded investment.[68]

MC-157, the USTR, and Trade in Services
The USTR believed that differential trucking access was a legitimate trade issue and supported the ICC's efforts to gather information. Even so, a USTR official familiar with Canada believed that MC-157 was too occupied with discrimination. He, too, believed the ICC had adopted that focus in order to avoid contentious trade areas and had been given a pretext for doing so by a misplaced use of the term "discrimination" in one of the original protests filed against Canadian applicants – a small but noteworthy index of the ATA's lack of familiarity with trade law. At the same time the USTR's office did not favour a negotiated solution. One of the reasons USTR Brock had sought earlier to persuade the ICC to consider reciprocity was his

opposition to sectoral approaches to freer trade. That was not a unified view in the executive branch, but even without that obstacle, several practical factors made a bilateral trucking agreement an unlikely negotiating project: the thousands of motor carrier firms in the United States and Canada, the complex network of transborder traffic lanes joining points in the two countries, the vast array of commodities shipped by truck, and the decentralized jurisdictional arrangement of regulation in Canada. These would probably make it impossible to negotiate a bilateral agreement to give motor carriers commercial access in Canada. International civil aviation, in contrast, had the advantages of small numbers of air carrier firms, a limited number of air corridors and traffic centres, and centralized jurisdictions governing access.

In the early 1980s the USTR's office was advocating that services be taken up as a major task in the next round of GATT negotiations, and in December 1983 it submitted to GATT a 300-page study on trade in services.[69] Because services were so novel and difficult to negotiate, the Office of the USTR saw the best strategy as tackling the easy industries first. As an unusually difficult industry, trucking was very low on the USTR's list of negotiating priorities. The European Economic Community's subsequent problems in getting agreement on road transport among its members for 1992 showed the USTR's assessment to be accurate.[70] The USTR sent no submissions to the MC-157 inquiry

The Ottawa Meeting: Federal-Provincial Disarray

Concerned that the trucking issue was beginning to cause major difficulties in overall Canadian-American relations, the State Department organized a trip to Ottawa for March 4. The purpose of the trip was to brief Canadian officials on the recent legislative and regulatory developments affecting Canadian firms; ascertain the position of the Canadian government; and gather information about FIRA, provincial entry practices, and the amount of harm to American carriers caused by the regulatory imbalance. Before the trip the department's Office of Maritime and Land Transportation consulted extensively with the ATA and with officials in major carrier firms, seeking information both about problems with Canadian authorities and successful dealings with them.[71]

The roster of participants at the Ottawa meeting shows how far the trucking issue had moved up the bilateral agenda. Representing the United States were officials from the State Department, DOT, and the Department of Commerce. Heading the delegation was Matthew Scocozza, deputy assistant secretary of state for Transportation and Telecommunications. Showing the Canadian government's greater ability to focus resources on bilateral issues, its delegation was more senior. It was headed by Edward

Lee, assistant under-secretary for US affairs in the Department of External Affairs. Also present were senior officials from Transport Canada, FIRA, the Ministry of Trade and Commerce, the Treasury Board, the Canadian Council of Motor Transport Administrators, and nine of the provincial regulatory boards. The tone was serious.

The American delegation emphasized that it was not there to negotiate about any of the outstanding issues but was simply interested in gathering information on American motor carrier operations in Canada, provincial trucking regulation, federal trucking policies, and the role of FIRA in motor carrier acquisitions. Information gathered, Scocozza indicated, would be shared with the ICC for its investigation. The delegation urged the Canadian officials to cooperate with the ICC in MC-157 and indicated that it would be willing to convey information from the Canadian government if the latter were diffident about dealing directly with the ICC. Scocozza briefly outlined the origin and current status of the Bus Deregulatory Reform Bill, the Kasten Bill, and Senator Cannon's resolution. Taking no official position on those initiatives, Scocozza indicated that the Reagan administration took them seriously and expected the bus bill, amended to include a provision on granting operating authorities to Canadian truckers, to be enacted by summer. Addressing the ICC investigation, the delegation emphasized that the process was directed only to the issue of discrimination and was not an effort to pressure Canada into adopting parallel regulatory norms. The delegation also indicated, however, that an ICC finding of no discrimination would not rule out action by Congress.[72]

The attitude of the Canadian delegation was "cool and defensive, assuming the role of a misunderstood, wronged party." Referring to USTR William Brock's 12 November 1981 letter urging the ICC to consider reciprocity, the Department of External Affairs' assistant under-secretary criticized the action as badly timed, as prejudicial to the applications of Canadian carriers, and as blowing the issue out of proportion. Several Canadian officials, taking a position that the Department of External Affairs would subsequently emphasize, denied that Canadian carriers constituted a competitive threat in the United States. That position, characterized by a member of the American delegation as "poor little us," emphasized the disparate size of the two markets and the two motor carrier industries. Without presenting data, the Canadian officials asserted that it is American carriers with Canadian subsidiaries that actually dominate transborder single-line trucking. Those carriers' large existing route networks in the United Sates place them in advantageous positions to command international traffic. Operating from a smaller national base, Canadian carriers would have to spend proportionately far more to achieve similar coverage in the United States. For those reasons, the Canadian delegates insisted, American carriers should not be overly concerned about Canadian carriers coming to do business.

The chairman of the Canadian Council of Motor Transport Administrators (CCMTA), asserting that "Canada would not put itself in the position of apologizing for having a system different than the U.S.," presented data gathered from each of the provinces on the approval and denial rates for American carriers. The samples were variable, with one going back only five months and another sixteen years, and with some covering all classes of authority and others only international ones. There was no information on the crucial question of the territorial scope of the authorities and the size of the domains involved. In a somewhat hopeful vein the CCMTA chairman noted that several provinces were reviewing their trucking statutes and that there was the prospect of regulation in Canada eventually moving in the same direction as that in the United States.

The American delegation expressed appreciation at the work involved in gathering the information from record files but said that the information was too disparate to enable any conclusions to be drawn about Canadian entry practices. In addition, the delegation indicated that without more systematic and detailed information they could not promise that allegations about Canadian discrimination would be set aside. The tart Canadian reply was that the burden of proof of discrimination rested with the United States and that Canada would make no further efforts to survey motor carrier application files, although it would be willing to respond to individual complaints.[73] The *New York Times* characterized the Ottawa meeting as evoking "anger and some frustration" from Canadian officials.[74]

To that point of the meeting the conflict was between the American and Canadian federal governments, with the American government questioning and the Canadian federal government defending its regulatory practices. The FIRA representative's presentation, however, evoked incredulity from the provincial representatives, who provided embarrassingly public evidence of jurisdictional and political discord on the Canadian side. To the American delegates, who watched with quiet fascination, it was apparent that many of the provincial officials did not fully understand FIRA's purpose and procedures. When these were made clear in the presentation, several of the provincial officials voiced strong objections. A particular point of criticism was FIRA's policy of conducting its deliberations in secret and giving only general explanations of denied applications, prompting a number of sharp questions about FIRA's regulatory principles and its fairness to applicants. Some provincial officials also asked why FIRA had reviewed only twenty-eight of the hundreds of applications the provincial boards had received from American firms, and they expressed surprise on learning for the first time that several of the carriers among those twenty-eight were already American-owned. Because the provincial regulators' work acquaints them with hundreds of trucking firms, their surprise provided unintentional but supporting evidence of non-discrimination.

All the same, their open criticism of FIRA embarrassed the federal gov-ernment. In the presence of a foreign delegation inquiring about restrictive entry practices, a key set of officials objected to an institution intended to scrutinize foreign entry. The point at issue was structural. The Canadian Constitution grants the provinces jurisdiction over natural resources and over property and civil rights. The importance of natural resources in Cana-dian foreign policy has implicated provincial interests, especially over energy prices and exports, and the jurisdiction over property and civil rights gives the provinces broad regulatory powers and the ability to create non-tariff barriers. For these reasons, a fractured diplomatic facade is always a possibility whenever foreign policy issues involve issues of provincial jurisdiction.[75] Somewhat defensively the Canadian federal representatives emphasized to both the provincial and American delegates that FIRA had no special mandate for trucking and only becomes involved if a foreign carrier wishes to acquire a Canadian firm or establish a new firm in Canada. On the more fundamental question of whether FIRA's mandate in directing its reviews only to foreign firms made it inherently discriminatory, the fed-eral delegation was adamant that FIRA's aims and practices would not be changed because of questions over its operations – from either provincial or foreign representatives.

The American delegation left believing that FIRA's mandate and involve-ment in motor carrier acquisitions complicated the otherwise straightfor-ward issue of provincial entry restrictions, particularly in light of the provincial regulators' latitude to require prior FIRA clearance before consid-ering an American application.[76] At the same time there was doubt that, given the small number of instances of its involvement, FIRA constituted an entry barrier for motor carriers. That consideration did not diminish DOT's continuing preference for a regulatory solution. The ICC should simply consider FIRA as well as provincial regulatory practices in granting authori-ties to Canadian carriers. Regulation's case-by-case procedure would also provide desirable latitude. DOT recognized that there would be times when an overriding public interest would be served by approving Canadian appli-cations. It would therefore be best, in DOT's view, for the ICC to maintain the flexibility to consider Canadian applications on their individual merits and to take Canadian regulatory practices into account as circumstances might warrant. For that reason, DOT opposed any moratorium on granting authority to Canadians or – as the ATA would prefer and the Kasten bill would require – reapplication of the *Pan American* standard to international carriers or the creation of a similar new standard.[77] Reciprocity, however, had not gone away. On 10 March, shortly after the meeting, the State Department testified to the Senate Foreign Relations Committee that dif-fering entry policies in Canada may create problems for American motor carriers, once again acknowledging reciprocity as the underlying issue.

MC-157: Doubts about Discrimination

The ICC set a schedule of regional hearings in Seattle, Minneapolis, Detroit, and Buffalo. The hearings began in Washington, DC, and ended there on 4 May 1982. Forty-six American and Canadian carriers testified, as did the Buffalo local of the Teamsters Union, the Ontario Trucking Association, the Canadian Highway Transport Lawyers Association, and the North Atlantic Ports Association. Senators Donald Riegle of Michigan and Slade Gorton of Washington as well as Congressmen John LaFalce and Henry Nowak of New York submitted statements, as did Stephen Flott for the CTA and the provincial trucking associations. The Buffalo Teamsters local appeared independently, with the International Brotherhood of Teamsters itself continuing to take no public stand on the issue. In comments filed for the hearing, the ATA emphasized that unequal access left the door open to eventual domination of bilateral trade by Canadian carriers. The ATA also pointed out that the ICC was looking only at discrimination and urged it to look at reciprocity as well.[78]

The largest American carriers before the inquiry were Yellow Freight, IU International (then owner of Ryder Truck Lines and now-bankrupt Pacific Intermountain Express), Matlack Inc., Schneider Transport Inc., Central Transport, and Leaseway Transportation Corp. Their testimony tended to focus more on expected than actual experience. Under cross-examination by lawyers representing Canadian carriers, many American witnesses admitted that they were not personally familiar with specific FIRA procedures and that their firms' entry into Canada would not require FIRA approval. American carrier representatives admitted also that some of the opposition to denied American applications before provincial boards came from other American carriers already operating in Canada. Cross-examination showed, in addition, that American carriers reporting difficulties with Canadian boards could not demonstrate that those experiences resulted from discriminatory treatment. Finally, American carriers citing revenue losses because of interline traffic diverted to Canadian carries allowed, under cross-examination, that economic recession had also injured their earnings. Canadian carrier representatives strongly denied that they had ever seen instances of discrimination against American carriers by provincial boards. Their brief argued that no discrimination against American carriers had been shown and that FIRA, while discriminatory, represented no "serious obstacle" to American carriers' ability to expand into Canada.[79] The ICC's final report on MC-157, issued on 8 October 1982, upheld those positions.

MC-157: Friendly Fire

On behalf of the Canadian trucking associations, Stephen Flott began by taking up the argument, made by Canadian officials at the Ottawa meeting, that the structural differences between the two national markets favour American carriers by making it more difficult for Canadian carriers to enter far enough to generate profitably long average lengths of haul. But then Flott began acknowledging the American carriers' case. The predominantly northward flow of general commodities LTL traffic, he argued, made Canadian carriers highly dependent on inbound LTL traffic from American interline partners. American carriers incorporating northbound traffic into new single-line service into Canada would damage Canadian carriers. That mirrored the argument of American carriers protesting diversion of interline traffic on their side of the border.

Worse, Flott recommended an ICC moratorium on all new applications from both American and Canadian carriers for international service.[80] He did so in the spirit of heading off serious escalation of the conflict and preserving some area for negotiation. Instead that did not help the CTA, as many of its largest member firms were already certificated in the United States. Supporting a moratorium put the CTA in the position of blocking access to similar gains for its other members. Much more seriously, Flott's proposal contradicted the Canadian government's position. Insisting that any restriction on Canadian entry was unfair under the ICC's new easy entry rules, the Canadian government regarded the ICC's partial moratorium on Canadian applications, implemented just before the MC-157 investigation got under way, as its principal grievance. Flott's proposal also undercut the lawsuits launched by several Canadian carriers against the ICC, who had suspended their applications.[81]

MC-157: Canada Charges Discrimination

Increasing the pressure and turning the tables of accusation, Canada sent a diplomatic note charging the ICC with discrimination in postponing the Canadian applications and in reopening the files of recently granted applications. The investigation itself, the note asserted, in light of the Canadian government's willingness to provide information, its agreement to attend the cancelled April public meeting at the ICC, and its gathering of provincial entry data for the Ottawa meeting with the American delegation, was unnecessary. The Canadian government also strongly objected to the ICC's subpoenaing the records of American carriers that had dealt with FIRA. The documents of those carriers' subsidiaries might well be located within Canadian jurisdiction, giving the subpoena extraterritorial force. The note regretted that the ICC had given no prior notification, holding that such action "reflects insensitivity to the implications of a U.S. regulatory agency purporting to investigate the affairs of a sovereign state by methods presumably designed for very different types of investigation in the U.S. domestic context." Even though Ottawa acknowledged never receiving the ICC's request for information and expert witnesses, the note stated sharply that it was not the practice of Canadian officials to testify at foreign regulatory tribunals.

By refusing to entertain any thought of reciprocity, Canada could keep the issue focused on discrimination. The ICC's unwillingness to consider reciprocity greatly aided that purpose, and the terms of its investigation had given it the burden of proof. Now, with the investigation failing to show evidence of discrimination, Canada could fortify its position by emphasizing wrongful accusation and treatment. Any regulatory measures against Canadian carriers could then be held as evidence of further misconduct, placing Canada in a position to retaliate. The final item in the diplomatic note made that connection: the ICC was endangering "previously harmonious relations between Canadian federal and provincial agencies and the US-based interests with whom they may deal on a regular basis."[82] That threat would become more explicit as the conflict escalated. To document its own position of non-discrimination, Canada sent a sixty-five-page diplomatic note. The note provided information about each province's regulatory statutes and practices, emphasizing that there was no provision in any of them for the discriminatory treatment of foreign applicants.

Public Convenience and Necessity at FIRA

The note also sought to clear up questions about FIRA, whose role of investigating only foreign business takeovers was discriminatory. FIRA's 1980 denial of IU International's bid to acquire Canadian Motorways Ltd. was the episode that had come to light in the MC-157 hearings as the most detailed instance of an American carrier's rejected takeover application. To put the case in a more positive context, the diplomatic note included a FIRA memorandum that stated that trucking is not a key industrial sector requiring special treatment. To put concerns further at ease, the memo also included an explanation of the reason motor carriers might experience greater hindrance than other kinds of firms in getting FIRA approval: "It may be more difficult for investors in the trucking industry to show that their proposals are likely to yield real benefits [to Canada] because, by and large, Canada has a well-developed trucking network that appears to be adequately meeting the demand for such services. Moreover, unlike the situation in some other industry sectors, foreign investors were unlikely to bring unique or distinctive capabilities to the trucking sector."[83]

By including that statement, however, External Affairs revealed that FIRA applied its own public convenience and necessity standard, in which applicants must show that their services will not duplicate existing ones. Since public convenience and necessity had come to be treated by the ICC as a restrictive doctrine, submitting such a statement to the MC-157 investigation did not cast FIRA's activities in a very liberal light. In the end, however, the ICC remained unwilling to challenge Canada's regulation of foreign investment. More concerning to the Canadian federal government, however, was "certain proposed legislation under discussion in the Congress of the United States which would address allegations of unfair treatment of US truckers in Canada, or an alleged serious imbalance in the two regulatory systems, by measures discriminatory against Canadian motor carriers generally."[84]

That apprehension was not misplaced.

Congress Forces the Issue

Senator John Danforth of Missouri added an amendment to the Senate's version of the Bus Regulatory Reform Act that instructed the ICC to cease issuing operating authorities to foreign motor carriers whose governments discriminate against American carriers until a bilateral agreement assuring "full, fair and equitable treatment" of US motor common carriers had been achieved. The negotiations were to be conducted in consultation with the Departments of State and Transportation and the USTR. Once an agreement was achieved, the ICC would be authorized to resume granting operating authorities to carriers from the country involved. Should the ICC find a foreign carrier's government to be violating such an agreement, the amendment also gave the ICC the authority to deny, limit, or cancel existing authorities to those carriers, subject to a sixty-day presidential review.[85] The amendment passed committee with a vote of fifteen to one. The views of the Canadian government were well known on the Commerce Committee. A member of the committee staff had been in regular contact with an official at the Canadian Embassy since before the Ottawa meeting and was directly aware of the Canadian government's views as the Danforth amendment was being developed.

During the MC-157 hearings ICC chairman Taylor had told Senator Kasten that "even if the worst kind of discrimination were discovered," the ICC would not have the power to withhold certification. The purpose of the amendment, according to Kasten, was to "provide the ICC that power unambiguously."[86] During the markup of the bus bill, Senator Kasten had withdrawn his own bill, S. 2057, and supported the Danforth Amendment. According to several American and Canadian officials, representatives from Yellow Freight had asked Danforth to do something about Canadian entry after it became known that the MC-157 investigation would show no Canadian discrimination.

Opposing Danforth: The Executive Branch Joins Ottawa

The Canadian Department of External Affairs took strong exception to the Danforth Amendment. In its diplomatic note of 19 May 1982, issued eight days after the amendment's presentation to the full Senate, the Department of External Affairs repeated its charge of discrimination, calling the amendment a "clear violation of the principle of national treatment." The note complained that the amendment had been attached despite efforts by the Canadian government to show American carriers already being accorded full, fair, and equitable treatment, and in the absence of proof from MC-157 of discriminatory treatment by Canada.

The Department of State, DOT, and the USTR opposed the Danforth amendment as well. DOT secretary Lewis wrote to Senator Danforth threatening to recommend a veto of the bus bill if the trucking amendment were not changed. That was the position also, Lewis wrote, of USTR William Brock and Deputy Assistant Secretary of State Matthew Scocozza. DOT's position showed how the dispute had evolved by that point. DOT did not oppose the House amendment when it was passed, but it preferred that there not be a Senate version. The reasoning was diplomatic. MC-157 was getting under way as the Senate version of the bus bill was being developed. If MC-157 did show discrimination, then the House amendment would provide the legislative means for dealing with it; but if no discrimination were found, then the matter would be easier to drop if only one version of the bill contained the amendment. From DOT's point of view, the worst outcome would be a conference committee version containing the Danforth amendment, which would lock the executive branch into very specific ways of dealing with the problem.

In the view of DOT officials, the amendment's provision to suspend grants of authority until an agreement could be negotiated was problematic for three reasons. The first involved discrimination. With the ICC investigation finding no evidence of provincial discrimination or serious difficulties with FIRA, it would be difficult to justify any cut-off of grants to Canadians. The other two reasons involved negotiations and reciprocity. DOT worried that the Canadian federal government's lack of jurisdiction over provincial entry norms and practices would leave the United States having to seek ten separate agreements. In addition, the amendment could require congressional certification of the results, and Canada's position darkened the prospect of achieving satisfactory ones. The Danforth amendment was also unwelcome for a purely domestic reason. DOT officials were eager to finish the department's legislative program of deregulation, and buses were the final interstate transport industry on the list. In light of that eagerness, Lewis's threat of a veto was a strong index of DOT's concern about the Danforth amendment. "I am certain," Lewis stated in his letter to Danforth, "you can appreciate the difficult position in which we in the Administration find ourselves."[87]

Trying Trade Remedy

To solve the dilemma, Lewis cooperated on a joint effort with the USTR to get compromise language into the bus bill. On 25 May, Secretary Lewis met with representatives of the trucking industry and suggested that they seek relief under Sections 301 and 305 of the Trade Act, 1974, which allows American firms to obtain remedies for demonstrated injury from foreign firms. The USTR's office had indicated that it would be willing to help American carriers learn how to take action under Sections 301 and 305. Danforth accepted the idea. Officials in the USTR's office consulted with American motor carrier representatives on the problem. After examining the issue, however, "strict constructionists" in the USTR's office read the Trade Act's terms –"unreasonable, unjustifiable and discriminatory" – as referring to existing trade agreements. Since there was no bilateral agreement on trucking with Canada, and since there were not even GATT legal frameworks covering trucking service, Canadian regulatory practices were not unreasonable or unjustifiable in ways that would qualify as a grievance under the Trade Act. The USTR's office informed Senator Danforth of that conclusion. Negotiated settlement, Danforth replied, would be the acceptable compromise on his moratorium.[88]

The USTR: Reluctant Negotiator

The USTR's office regarded some form of moratorium as politically inevitable and knew that USTR officials would be the negotiators both with Senator Danforth and, later, with Canada. Although there were individuals in the USTR's office who would have liked to use the moratorium to extract concessions from Canada, several important considerations made the USTR's office the moratorium's strongest executive branch opponent. First was the view that acting to redress a particular disadvantage may bring into play a wider and unintended set of problems, particularly if the sector involved is structurally complex and the other side brings up its own disadvantages. One set of structural complexities was Canada's regulatory system and the beginnings of regulatory review in several provincial governments. Since these were not moving coherently to the kind of uniform national rules that would favour a bilateral trucking agreement, there was concern that Canada could exploit such disunity to hobble negotiations.

Second was the view that unilateral remedies such as moratoriums invite retaliation from the other side. For the USTR's office, entering into negotiations after such an exchange would further complicate the chances of reaching a settlement. The Canadian government, which was beginning to indicate unspecified measures against American carriers in Canada as possibilities it might consider, did nothing to discourage that perception. More generally, the USTR's office, looking forward to multilateral services negotiations at the next round of GATT, had little enthusiasm to spend its resources in the highly difficult sector of trucking.[89] A final factor was USTR Brock's own views. According to officials in both the Canadian Embassy in Washington and the Ministry of Transport in Ottawa, Brock had come to feel personally embarrassed, as evidence accumulated that provincial boards did not discriminate against American carriers, about his letter to the ICC in 1981 asking the commission to consider Canadian entry standards.[90] By the time the moratorium was added to the Senate bus bill, Brock had become opposed to restrictions on Canadian truckers.

Such a response to an entrenched Canadian position, in the view of Charles Doran, was more broadly characteristic of relations between the two countries. The Canadian government's ability to focus on single bilateral issues enabled it to take advantage of the American government's reluctance to escalate conflicts on non-strategic issues.[91] Trucking was a quintessential non-strategic issue, and with the conclusion of the MC 157 investigation and the introduction of the Danforth amendment, there was no appetite in the executive branch for raising the stakes. The task of the USTR's office was simply to "get out from under" the ICC's existing moratorium and Danforth's proposed one.[92]

The issue needed to be resolved quickly. The set of delayed Canadian applications at the ICC was due to be decided in June, and there was apprehension among American truckers that the MC-157 investigation would result in granting the entire lot. Officials at the ICC, whose involvement in the Canadian issue had been reluctant from the start, were delighted to see matters shift to the area of trade and legislation and were in no hurry to issue their report. The Danforth amendment's provision lifting the moratorium only on the conclusion of a bilateral agreement by the USTR also promised to free the ICC from the unwelcome task of assessing discrimination and reciprocity in its entry decisions. Because the bus legislation was still pending when the suspension of the Canadian applications was due to end, on June 16 the ICC delayed making a decision on them for another thirty days.

Meanwhile, officials from DOT, the USTR's office, and the State Department debated with the Senate Commerce Committee on the final language of the trucking amendment. With Danforth unwilling to abandon the idea of a moratorium, the objective of the executive branch departments was to secure compromise language that would leave the moratorium open-ended until the USTR's office could negotiate a settlement with Canada. The compromise, drafted jointly by officials at DOT and the USTR's office, provided for a two-year moratorium, but with the new provision that the USTR could "remove or modify" the restriction, in whole or in part, "if it is determined that such action would be in the national interest."[93] There was no explicit mention of reciprocity. For DOT and the USTR's office the compromise allowed Danforth to show to American carriers some tangible concern after MC-157 and the Section 301 and 305 inquiry had left them with nothing. The discretionary authority to determine the "national interest" in transborder trucking gave the USTR considerable latitude to decide what kind of bilateral outcome with Canada would justify lifting the moratorium. The State Department was displeased with a two-year moratorium under any conditions and never did finally approve the legislative language, although it did take part in dealing with Senator Danforth.

Public Diplomacy from the North

Although the three executive branch agencies all shared Canada's interest in quashing the Danforth amendment, the trucking dispute had escalated just when Ottawa was implementing an aggressive new diplomatic strategy for dealing with Washington. The strategy involved increased lobbying on legislation affecting Canadian interests and speaking directly to the American people over sensitive issues such as acid rain. The Department of External Affairs asked the federal Cabinet for an extra $650,000, and all but $150,000 of that would be spent to hire professional Washington lobbyists. The policy eventually implicated the Canadian government in the scandal over former Reagan White House official Michael Deaver, whom the Canadian Embassy had retained before he was legally eligible to offer his service for hire.

Following the new strategy, Ambassador Allan Gotlieb went directly to Senator Danforth to have the moratorium dropped. That move greatly displeased Gotlieb's counterparts in the State Department and the USTR's office, who regarded his single-handed effort as spurning the help of sympathetic allies. More broadly, they regarded Gotlieb's intervention as a departure from the discreet diplomacy that the State Department regarded as the proper form for dealings with Canada. American diplomats believed that such interventions would needlessly politicize sectoral issues such as trucking, attract public attention, and make it more difficult for legislators such as Danforth to retreat from positions such as the moratorium. They stood aside as the ambassador sought to change Danforth's mind. When it was clear that Gotlieb had failed, the State Department and the USTR returned to negotiate a less damaging version of the moratorium.[94]

Doubts about Domains

Achieving that compromise did not mean that all executive branch doubts about Canadian regulatory behaviour had been laid to rest. One question, over Canada's continued reference to its average rate of approving 90 percent of American applications, involved the basic matter of territory. In the view of a senior DOT official, such a summary statistic does not disclose the size and value of the authorities being granted and denied. Under the public convenience and necessity standard, and under the procedure of accommodating objections from already certificated carriers, a grant of authority would frequently involve minute actual changes. The 90 percent of authorities granted may therefore be marginal and incremental,

while the 10 percent denied may concern major traffic centres. Information provided by the Canadian government made the question impossible
to answer. The Canadian government's presentation at the Ottawa meeting did not include data about the territories contained in provincial
grants of authority to American carriers, and, since then, the Canadian
government had resolutely based its position on the summary percentage
figure. The issue, the official asserted, was not just discrimination but market access.[95] Reciprocity still underlay the issue.

Conflict in Earnest

The Department of External Affairs took the unprecedented step of asserting control over all communication between provincial regulators and federal transport officials and the American government. Because of the
previously non-contentious nature of transborder trucking and the wide
array of administrative and technical matters that arise, communication
between American and Canadian officials was always direct and informal,
and many of the officials knew their counterparts personally. When it
became clear that the bus bill would pass the US Senate, however, the
Department of External Affairs gave the directive to federal and provincial
transport officials that all communication on the issue must be channelled
through External Affairs and that no statements were to be made unless an
External Affairs official were present. That move was a telling index of the
seriousness with which the federal government had come to regard the
trucking issue. Informal communication was to be routed through official
diplomacy.

As the bus bill neared Senate passage, Canadian officials began displaying
the desired solidarity. The first note in the chorus that was soon to greet the
legislation came from Ontario premier William Davis, whose province is
home to almost half of Canada's trucking industry and the country's most
powerful trucking association. Addressing the Great Lakes Water Resources
Conference at Mackinac Island, Michigan, Davis gave some time in his
short presentation to trucking. He declared as offensive to "customary
Canadian-American practices" the Danforth amendment's "implication
that Canadians must prove their innocence in this area." The amendment
was a "sanction against Canadian commerce" and an example of congressional protectionism. It would be "most unfortunate," he concluded, if
such measures were to become "an element in our general relations."[96]

When the Senate passed the Bus Regulatory Reform Act with Danforth's
revised amendment on 30 June 1982, Canadian reaction was severe. In a
diplomatic note the Department of External Affairs expressed "profound
regret" over the action, which it characterized as "unnecessary, unwarranted and potentially harmful to international commerce." The Senate
deliberations, it charged, were based on allegations that had already been

disproved. Playing its strong diplomatic suit, the note charged that the bill "further discriminates against Canadian interests." Exploiting the executive branch's unhappiness with Danforth, the note added that those departments had agreed with Canada that a moratorium was unwarranted. The note took the unprecedented step of requesting a presidential veto of the bill.[97]

The Ontario minister of Transportation and Communications, addressing the annual conference of the American Association of Motor Vehicle Administrators, meeting fortuitously in Ottawa, accused American carriers of taking out their anger at deregulation on Canadian carriers. That was unfortunate, since interest in deregulation was increasing in Canada and more harmonious norms would be a likely outcome. However, he warned, deregulation in Canada would be made much simpler by "excluding Americans from any benefits." More broadly, he admonished the transport administrators, "You ... will be specific losers. All your cooperative efforts to facilitate truck movement through reciprocity, prorata agreements, uniform safety procedures and so on will be frustrated." In a concluding remark that was "just shy of an ultimatum," the minister stated that "any discrimination by the U.S. government against Canadian truckers is bound to create a backlash in this country. It may even lead to more direct forms of retaliation against Americans operating in Canada."[98]

Forms of retaliation were outlined by Toronto transport lawyer Joel Rose in a speech to the Transportation Law Institute's conference in Keystone, Colorado. He reported that the CTA, the provincial trucking associations, and the Canadian Conference of Motor Transport Administrators were working together to find ways of reprisal and that a meeting of the federal and provincial ministers of transport had been organized for 23 September to consider what actions to take. Rose outlined several possibilities: a Canadian inquiry similar to MC-157, a mirror two-year moratorium on American applications, and a show-cause review of the Canadian operating authorities held by American carriers to determine their compliance with obligations to the Canadian public.[99] Commenting on these developments, the *New York Times* regarded the trucking dispute as part of a broader pattern of tension between the two countries over issues ranging from expropriation of American oil holdings in Canada, to disputes over advertising on border television stations, to acid rain. Together these problems had created the most stressful time in bilateral relations in many years and made managing the Canada/United States relationship much more difficult.[100] A brief item in *Newsweek* suggested the possibility of a massive trucking tie-up at the border as carriers, deprived of single-line privileges, reverted to interline cargo transfers.

The Canadian government intensified its threats. On 17 August 1982 the Manitoba Highways and Transportation minister, Samuel Uskiw, cancelled a hearing on Yellow Freight's application to buy a portion of the Manitoba operating rights of another American carrier, GMW, Inc. In a similar move, the Quebec government scheduled a review of the applications of two large American carriers, St. Johnsbury Trucking Company and Consolidated Freightways. Writing to External Affairs Minister Mark McGuigan on 24 August 1982, Uskiw invoked reciprocity, citing a statutory prohibition in Manitoba law that prevents the province from granting authorities to jurisdictions that do not grant similar privileges to Manitoba carriers. The law would compel Manitoba to retaliate against all American applications. Fearing that such a "series of lock step" moves would harm vital trade relations between the two countries, Uskiw urged External Affairs to apply strong pressure to get the moratorium lifted. Failing that, the alternatives were either constricted transportation and higher transport costs or compromised Canadian sovereignty.[101] Commenting on the Manitoba delay, Yellow Freight senior vice-president Steve Murphy also invoked reciprocity: "I'm not wild about the moratorium, but maybe it's time to deregulate in Canada."[102]

As a preview of the kind of actions that could be taken, the Ontario Highway Transport Board denied the application of the Ohio-based bulk carrier Coastal Tank Lines, Inc., for two-way authority through the Niagara and St. Lawrence River gateways into Ontario. Already holding authority to transit cargoes into Ontario, Coastal filed this application in order to eliminate empty backhauls on return trips to the United States. The application followed the public convenience and necessity requirement of showing benefits now single line bi-directional service – and was supported by thirteen Canadian shippers. Disregarding that support, the Ontario board held that there was no evidence of sufficient traffic for balanced operations. A Quebec-based bulk carrier, Provost Cartage Inc., had been granted bi-directional authority into Ontario a year previously, even though it had very limited involvement in the province and much weaker grounds for showing traffic potential. In addition, Coastal had followed proper Ontario procedures in its application and had not brought up reciprocity. Those facts suggested more than normal regulatory protection. "Many persons might interpret this decision," stated Coastal's vice-president, "as the first indication of a backlash against the two-year moratorium on operating rights for Canadian carriers."[103]

The Danforth Compromise: A New *Pan American* Standard

The Canadian government had hoped that the House and Senate Conference Committee would delete the moratorium from the bus bill, but the final form did include it. As the bill was being readied for presidential approval, the ICC sent copies of the still unreleased MC-157 investigative record to the USTR's office and to DOT. Their use of the findings showed when President Reagan signed the Bus Regulatory Reform Act, 1982, into law on 20 September. As he did so, he partially lifted the moratorium for Canada, noting significant differences in access between the two countries but also noting the absence of discrimination. True to the compromise negotiated with Senator Danforth, the president declared that the partial removal was in the national interest and instructed USTR William Brock to reach an agreement with Canada in the next sixty days that would "ensure fair and equitable treatment of Canadian and United States trucking interests on both sides of the border."

Replacing the moratorium were three principles that the ICC was expected to apply on an interim basis. The one bearing directly on Canadian entry instructed the ICC to encourage "economical and efficient transportation" and "sound economic conditions in transportation including sound economic conditions among carriers." The president added that the ICC's determinations should be consistent with the directives of the USTR. The purpose of the three principles, Brock explained in a letter to ICC chairman Taylor, was to ensure that the commission consider the "competitive disadvantage facing U.S. motor carriers created by the differences in regulatory systems and investment policies between Canada and the U.S." Such consideration was to include the "effect upon existing carriers of granting new authority." He added that all pending Canadian applications should be re-opened and that opportunity should be given to the parties involved to present new evidence.[104]

In the view of the Canadian-American Motor Carriers Association (CAMCA), a small organization of American and Canadian truckers with transborder operations, these measures were similar to the defunct *Pan American* standard, under which the ICC could weigh adverse effects of entry on already certificated carriers. CAMCA also believed that these new rules were a "political compromise designed to avoid an explicit prohibition against issuance of all Commission operating authority to Canadian applicants" and to give the ICC discretion.[105] Adopting the new guidelines, the ICC introduced a temporary procedure to identify the nationality of applicants. Previously, the ICC did not require applicants to provide that information.

The president's action, said ICC chairman Taylor, "in effect takes Ex Parte MC-157 off the shelf." MC-157 had been on the shelf for five months because of the uncompleted status of the bus bill and the ICC commissioners' desire to stay clear of the bargaining between the executive branch and Senator Danforth. First the ICC had promised its report by mid-July. When that time arrived Chairman Taylor, citing "extraordinary circumstances," extended the report deadline to 18 August and announced that the ICC would not grant the pending Canadian applications until it was completed.[106] In August the ICC extended the deadline again, once more citing extraordinary circumstances as the reason. These evasive actions, complained a lawyer representing several Canadian carriers, had deprived the executive branch and Congress of sworn evidence at a time when that information had vital bearing on a policy question.[107] Nor was it clear, now that the moratorium was partially lifted but the MC-157 report was still unreleased, exactly what criteria the ICC would use in considering Canadian applications. Chairman Taylor said that MC-157's determination of non-discrimination by Canada would serve as the basis.[108] How that would be done while adhering to the USTR's directive to consider the welfare of American carriers was not explained.

The new ICC measures, the Canadian federal and provincial ministers of transport declared jointly, were intolerable. Meeting in Halifax on the issue, the ministers declared that the Canadian Council of Motor Transport Administrators (CCMTA) had been instructed to formulate retaliatory measures. These included developing "detailed information on the current involvements of American carriers in transborder operations in order to better identify and protect Canadian interests."[109] That information, said the CCMTA chairperson, would make it possible to shut down American carrier operations in Canada until the ICC removed all restrictions on Canadian carrier applications. Leaving the door open to negotiation, the chairperson added that such measures would be deferred pending ICC disposition of the delayed Canadian applications, now totalling 140, and action by President Reagan to lift the moratorium completely.[110]

ATA and CTA: Not a Big Ten-Four

With their public positions exactly juxtaposed, relations were poor between the ATA and the CTA. An editorial in *Transport Topics* expressed the ATA's view that the moratorium was "badly needed" and hoped that "equitable reciprocity" with Canada could be achieved. ATA general counsel Nelson Cooney saw the moratorium as a second-best solution made necessary by the ICC's consistent refusal to consider reciprocity. For the ATA, knowledge that the ICC had found no Canadian discrimination meant that the moratorium would at best be a temporary measure. Resolution of the reciprocity issue, however, would hinge on the USTR's being able to convince an entrenched and indignant Canadian government to make its regulatory rules compatible with American ones. "We don't think," Cooney said reflectively, "the moratorium was the best way to handle the situation."[111] CTA director Ken Maclaren emphatically agreed. The moratorium was "an act of war" to which Canada would have to retaliate by refusing to consider American applications.[112] That fraternal rupture, in the view of several American and Canadian transport officials, would take some effort to repair.

The ATA faced internal disunity as well. Some of its member firms had cross-memberships in the Canadian-American Motor Carriers Association, reflecting their trans-boundary interests. CAMCA organized a campaign to lobby members of Congress, the USTR's office, and the ICC to have the moratorium lifted. UPS, St. Johnsbury Trucking, and ten other American carriers operating in Canada participated in that effort, publicly diverging from the ATA's position. Roadway Express, another American firm with Canadian operations, did not join the lobbying coalition but wrote letters to executive branch officials requesting the moratorium's removal.

ICC: Finding an Exit

On 8 October 1982 the ICC released the MC-157 report. It found FIRA to be "discriminatory on its face" and capable of impeding investment by American carriers. Nevertheless, the ICC found no conclusive evidence of "any substantial chilling effect." With regard to Canadian entry norms, the ICC held that there was "general agreement by all the parties to this proceeding that the Provinces do not intentionally discriminate against American motor carriers in favor of their Canadian counterparts." Although acknowledging that the Canadian government had provided little actual statistical information on its grants of operating authority, the ICC concluded that the material Canada did provide supported the "near unanimous testimony" about the "fundamental fairness" of the provinces' regulatory practices. Referring specifically to Yellow Freight's denial in Ontario in 1978, the ICC held that the decision was in keeping with the provincial board's policy of withholding broad grants of general commodities authority. On the larger question of harm to American carriers from loss of their interline business, the ICC accepted the position of the Canadian government and the CTA that American carriers dominate transborder traffic and concluded that there was no substantial evidence of injury.[113] There was, therefore, no basis to fear that granting the set of pending Canadian applications would change the existing balance of transborder carriage and no basis for further detaining the Canadian applications.

The ICC's report circumscribed future action against Canadian carriers. In Canadian applications, reciprocity would now be considered only in the very narrow context of anti-competitive effects *within* the United States. That limitation ruled out any special treatment of Canadian applicants and any further inquiry into Canadian regulatory practices. In a statement addressed directly to the ATA, the commission rejected use of the *Pan American* standard on Canadian carriers. Treating Canadian applicants on the same basis as it did American ones, the ICC would presume competition to be in the public interest. That presumption had made protests almost impossible to sustain against domestic applicants and had opened the gates of deregulation. Now it would also be very difficult to show grounds for denying a Canadian carrier's entry.

That was soon demonstrated. Less than a month after issuing the MC-157 report, the ICC granted the pending application of Transx Ltd. Operating authority was issued over the ATA's objection that the ICC, in hearing American carrier protests, had considered only potential damage and had overlooked obvious harm to their international operations. In addition, the ATA had argued that the effects of Canadian entry should be considered not on a carrier-by-carrier basis with each application, but on a cumulative basis. Unswayed, on 16 November 1982 the ICC granted the application of Kingsway Transports Ltd. on the basis of the MC-157 findings and in the absence of evidence of harm to domestic competition. In limiting the grounds for denying Canadian applications as thoroughly as it did, the ICC showed its eagerness to be rid of extraterritorial trouble.

MC-157's conclusions may indeed have been generous and cursory. That was the conclusion University of British Columbia transport economist Garland Chow presented in a paper to the annual meeting of the American Economics Association in December 1982. Instead of making a careful evaluation, Chow asserted, the ICC was merely "passing judgment" on harm to American carriers. "On this judgment the ICC has much discretion, and indeed many of its conclusions can be questioned." Chow took issue with the position, put forward by the Canadian government and the CTA and accepted by the ICC, that American carriers dominate transborder trucking. Regarding the longer average lengths of haul in the American portions of transborder trips – the basis of the Canadian government's and the CTA's claim of American dominance – Chow compared the revenues actually earned in the two portions. He found that "both U.S. and Canadian domiciled carriers share equally in traffic participation (e.g., shipments and tonnage) but unequally with respect to the length of haul. Thus the American carriers do not dominate in the sense of having a larger market share of customer patronage."

Chow also took issue with the Canadian government's position that there was a significant American carrier presence in Canada. The approval rates of American carrier applications used to support that position, he asserted, overlook the territorial limits in those operating authorities. "The fact that Yellow Freight applied for new operating authority (it interlined over 90 percent of its Ontario freight in 1981) and was denied is evidence that these restrictions are binding."[114]

On the question of prospective harm to American carriers, Chow found from the Canadian carriers already certificated in the United States a "substantial potential for substitution of single line service for joint line service," affecting up to 60 percent of the existing transborder traffic. He also found that eliminating interline exchanges at the border would give Canadian carriers cost savings that they could exploit as lower rates. Finally, Chow predicted that Canadian carrier expansion into the United States would involve replacing terminal facilities at the border with facilities further inland. Although the depth of such expansion into the American market would be limited by the amount of transborder traffic available to support efficient vehicle utilization and competitive rates, Chow believed that Canadian carriers would find it attractive to expand into traffic centres at a moderate remove from the border, such as Chicago and Cleveland. In sum, Chow concluded, the ICC may have underestimated the competitive effects of Canadian entry. It should be noted that this assessment was made before the TL sector had emerged as a cheap, wide-ranging, and fast alternative to terminal-centred LTL carriage. TL's mobility makes it an ideal transborder mode, and it has been the most active and successful Canadian sector operating in that market. The ICC, in taking the sanguine position that it did, conceded much of the Canadian government's case and made the USTR's task of negotiating a "fair and equitable" agreement difficult and unpromising.

Negotiating from Strength

The conflict had given Canada a powerful negotiating position, and its stance, according to a USTR official, was "very tough." The USTR's goal was to get recognition from Canada that differences in regulatory systems could have a harmful impact on trucking trade between the two countries. The Canadian negotiators, proclaiming sovereignty, flatly refused to consider any changes to existing rules. The United States had created the problem by deregulating and should now live with the consequences. Reciprocity and balance, the Canadians insisted, were not components of the "fair and equitable" treatment being sought in the negotiations; rather, fairness and equity apply to the uniform enforcement of each nation's laws, and Canada's non-discriminatory treatment of American applicants had already been acknowledged.

Fully aware of its strong position, the Canadian side had as its goal producing a document that would enable the USTR to show that the situation as it existed was fair and equitable and have the moratorium lifted. For the longer term the Canadians desired to put into place some means of preventing future charges of non-compliance against Canada and the possibility of another moratorium. In this they were in agreement with the American negotiators, who also wished to secure a means of dealing with future complaints. The political climate for reaching a settlement was improved by a meeting between American secretary of state George Shultz and Canadian secretary of state for External Affairs Allan MacEachen. Both recently appointed, they agreed in Ottawa on 25 October 1982 that several trade irritants between the two countries, including trucking, had become overly politicized, and pledged to seek resolution of them.

The USTR's office handled the negotiations for the American side in consultation with DOT. The State Department was not a major participant. The Canadian side, as on previous encounters, was more numerous and senior. The Office of the Minister of International Trade was the principal negotiator. Advising the minister was a committee chaired by Transport Minister Jean-Luc Pépin, which consulted directly with the provincial ministers of transport and with the CCMTA. International trade officials from the Department of External Affairs were involved because of the broader trade implications of the negotiation. The two delegations met at the Department of External Affairs on 28 October 1982 to work out the basis of an agreement.

What emerged was a statement of five principles. The first committed both sides to efficient and competitive transportation between the two countries and to non-discriminatory regulatory treatment. The second was the crucial one. It pledged the two governments to provide "full, fair and equitable opportunities among truckers from both countries to compete for the carriage of international traffic." At the same time, it acknowledged "differences in the policies and economies of the two countries which may affect the competitive opportunities available to motor carriers," limiting the grounds for future challenges of transborder imbalances in traffic shares between American and Canadian carriers. The third principle asserted that both governments "welcome mutually beneficial investment" in motor carriage and favour "economically efficient competition." Although FIRA had not been much involved in trucking acquisitions, it retained arguable grounds to continue its mandate of vetting new foreign investment and to deny trucking applications that it judged to provide no significant economic benefit to Canada. The fourth principle pledged both sides to promote trade by "the most efficient and economical transportation possible, including single-line services," and to "endeavor to give significant weight to the needs and desires of shippers and consumers." For the United States the implication was that single-line services into its market from Canada were consistent with trade and deregulation. For Canadian provincial boards the implication was that efficient transportation was a desirable but – with the qualifying word "endeavor" – non-binding alternative to protecting domestic carriers. Finally, the two sides agreed to establish a "consultative mechanism" between the two countries to resolve problems affecting transborder trucking. Both sides retained the ability to take unilateral measures if problems submitted to the consultative mechanism were not resolved to their mutual satisfaction.

These principles were stated formally in an exchange of letters between USTR William Brock and Canadian ambassador Allan Gotlieb that, together, constituted an official understanding. In his letter of 17 November 1982, Brock stated that an affirmative reply from Gotlieb would end the moratorium on Canadian carriers. In his response to Brock, Gotlieb stated Canada's acceptance of the principles and added that Manitoba, which had suspended American applications, would resume processing them.[115] On 29 November 1982 President Reagan announced the end of the moratorium and complimented Brock on his successful efforts in securing "fair and equitable treatment for both Canadian and United States trucking interests on both sides of the border." He directed Brock to notify Congress that he had determined concluding the moratorium to be in the national interest and that he had instructed the ICC to begin an expeditious processing of all pending Canadian applications. The criteria for assessing those applications, he indicated, were contained in the Motor Carrier Act, 1980. Canadian applicants would thus enjoy the same free entry into the American market as did their American counterparts. The gates at the border were opened once again.

Business as Usual

Canadian reciprocity was not forthcoming. Just after the moratorium was lifted, officials at the Canadian embassy in Washington told the Toronto *Globe and Mail* that Canada had made no concessions in agreeing to the five principles. In Toronto the Chairman of the Ontario Highway Transport Board said that "we have no plans to change the way we operate."[116] Officials in External Affairs and the Ministry of Transport stressed the same thing to CTA executive director Ken Maclaren. In a letter to the CTA's international committee and its provincial managers, Maclaren reported having been emphatically told that there was "no intention to treat the agreement as a policy directive to provincial boards to grant U.S. applications for single-line authority" and that nothing from the "existing regulatory regime" had been conceded. Assessing these statements, Maclaren added, "I have no reason to suspect that any of them are trying to cover their tracks."[117]

Two applications in Ontario, from Roadway Express and Yellow Freight, were soon to test the situation. Roadway's was the more complex and interesting case. In 1981 Roadway had purchased a small Ontario carrier, Harkema Express, which had ceased operations after a Teamster strike. Because this was a foreign purchase, it had to be approved by FIRA. The purchase provoked great controversy in Ontario, where carriers charged that the purchase was simply a way of getting possession of Harkema's operating rights and opening single-line service to the border, thereby circumventing the normal entry barriers. FIRA approved the purchase in fall 1982 – just as the Trucking War was being resolved. The timing, in the view of the Ontario Trucking Association (OTA), was no coincidence. "We have seen our federal government bend over backwards to appease these American interests," declared OTA executive vice-president Stephen Flott.[118] This charge was strongly denied by Ontario Assistant Deputy Minister of Transportation and Communications Mark Larratt-Smith.[119] OTA protested before the Ontario Highway Transport Board (OHTB) that operating with Harkema's authorities amounted to "trafficking in licenses." The other points of objection were the more usual ones of new competition and traffic diversion. Large American firms like Roadway, Flott argued, could exploit their connections in the United States and divert traffic from Canadian carriers into single-line service, harming the business of Ontario truckers and forcing many to close down.[120] CTA executive director Ken Maclaren speculated that "if we do nothing, economic forces presently at play involving U.S. deregulation and a North American depression could force a dramatic overhaul in the structure of the trucking industry ... which very well may include significantly greater foreign penetration."[121] The OHTB ruled against Roadway on the grounds that its purpose was to use only the authorities that would cover single-line service to the United States and not to restore Harkema's full operations. Since the key point at issue was transborder traffic diversion and relative advantages and disadvantages on each side, and since a lack of data made it impossible for the OHTB to rule on that basis, Ontario Minister of Transportation and Communication James Snow ordered an inquiry into the balance of trade in transborder trucking services.[122] The report was later to figure in the politics of Ontario deregulation.

Yellow Freight's Ontario application, filed in February 1983, was for single-line service between Ontario and points in the American midwest. To avoid antagonizing Ontario carriers who already had single-line service into the northeastern and middle Atlantic states, Yellow conspicuously omitted those sixteen states in its application. It argued lower rates for shippers, faster service, and less frequency of cargo loss and damage. In rejecting the application, the OHTB ruled that Yellow already offered joint-line service and that if it wished to offer lower rates it should negotiate them with its Canadian partner.

Those developments did not please the USTR and DOT. A USTR official said that the Roadway denial, in particular, was galling because the firm had been a model applicant: politically discreet and concerned to fulfil all the requirements. The official characterized the Ontario board's grounds for denial as an "excuse" and objected directly to both the Canadian and Ontario governments. The displeasure was sufficient for the Ontario assistant deputy minister Mark Larratt-Smith to visit DOT in order to explain the board's decision. Roadway, however, did not complain to the American government, and no further action was taken. When Ontario subsequently denied Yellow Freight's application, there was speculation in the Canadian trade press that USTR Brock would protest to the Canadian government and that Senator Danforth, perhaps threatening another moratorium, might back a Yellow Freight appeal to the Ontario Cabinet, which has full discretion to override board decisions.[123]

The issue, however, passed without protest; instead, there developed in both DOT and the USTR's office a willingness to live with the regulatory differences between the two countries. A senior DOT official, who had been involved in the transborder issue from the beginning, reported that he was not at all inclined to conduct an analysis of Canadian penetration into the United States. Nor would the Reagan administration authorize the money necessary for such a study. His view of the situation, he related, was that "if things appear okay on the surface, let things lie unless a carrier comes forward and makes a specific complaint."[124] An ATA official indicated that he would "love to do a study" of the impact of Canadian entry but that there was no budget for such an undertaking. If the willingness to allocate research funds is any index, then the ATA's leadership, which had directed two years of opposition, had accepted the reality of the trucking imbalance and decided to accommodate it.

There were other motor carrier issues between the two countries in the years following 1982, but none had the conflict potential of the Trucking War. Canada objected to the Heavy Vehicle Use Tax, applied under the Surface Transportation Assistance Act, 1982, to American carriers and to Canadian carriers operating in the United States. The tax would be levied on each truck at a flat annual rate of about $400. The Canadian government and the CTA argued that the tax was discriminatory and sought a pro-rated figure based on annual mileage driven in the United States. The United States exempted Canadian carriers from the tax altogether in 1985.

Explaining Success

John Turner, former prime minister and leader of the Liberal Party in the 1988 election, expressed a common view of Canada's relationship with the United States: "In bilateral negotiations, the U.S. possesses substantially greater bargaining power than Canada." That advantage is used to get the better part. On trade issues, Turner declared, "the U.S. will not agree that a symmetrical exchange of national treatment for goods, services, and enterprises provides reciprocity and will, therefore, request additional concessions." Weakening Canada's position is its role as the side making demands, the absence of allies who are present in multilateral forums such as the World Trade Organization, and the ten-times greater size of the American market.[125]

Canada's inherent disadvantage in dealings with the United States has long been a rhetorical theme in Canadian politics and a staple of Canadian foreign policy analysis.[126] This view shares some of its basic assumptions with dependency theories of international political economy.[127] The political relationship between the two countries derives from Canada's position as a "geographically large zone within the U.S. economy rather than a distinct national entity."[128] The workings of that large economic unit require harmony and subordination from Canada: "industrial and resource production ... dance to rhythms written south of the border."[129] The political relationship is one of "informal American control of the Canadian state."[130]

Less categorical formulations see Canadian independence more qualitatively. Those regarding sovereignty as a matter of degree recognize the Canadian government's ability to act in its own interests, but they also recognize the opportunities in Canada's pluralistic politics for the American government and American corporations to lobby Ottawa for favourable policies.[131] Additional actors are the provincial governments, which often have complementary interests with the United States in matters involving resources and investment and have their own opportunities to pressure the federal government, weakening its ability to pursue coherent national economic policies.[132] Assisting the process are ideological allies within the Canadian government, who share American outlooks on economic issues and identify Canada's national interests with American ones.[133] The Department of External Affairs, according to a major study of Ottawa's relationship with the Reagan administration, had the reputation of "being supine vis-à-vis the Americans."[134] Finally there is the force of self-interest in Canadian business, which leads its members to pressure the Canadian government to "remove or at least modify ... policies causing the playing field not to be level." While such pressure can be expected to accompany the competitive differences arising from high levels of trade, Canadians are more "dependent on the U.S. economy and U.S. policies related to that economy than they are on [their own]" and are under greater pressure to comply.[135]

The course and outcome of the Trucking War do not fit these representations. The United States was in the position of making demands, not Canada. And far from being willing to consider harmonizing its policies with American deregulation, the Canadian government, coordinated by the Department of External Affairs, defined the issue as a basic matter of sovereignty and consistently refused to yield. It was quick to exploit tactical opportunities, did not hesitate to allow the dispute to escalate publicly, and was preparing retaliation. Nor was the CTA an advocate of harmonization. It benefited from asymmetry between the two countries and ended up in open conflict with its counterpart, the ATA. On the American side, the ICC wanted no part of the dispute and minimized its involvement, despite pressure from Congress and the executive branch. The executive branch's unwillingness to pursue a trucking agreement with Canada reflected broader views about reciprocity: "Specific reciprocity does not sit comfortably with the basic beliefs of most American policy makers. The United States has been and continues to be the strongest supporter of diffuse reciprocity, especially with regard to international trade."[136] Mindful of the trade policy and jurisdictional issues involved, wishing to prevent the trucking issue from becoming intractably politicized, and fully aware that the bargaining advantages were Canada's, the executive branch achieved a settlement that mollified Congress and left Canada's regulatory practices untouched.

These outcomes accord much more closely with views of Canada – US relations that emphasize a relative balance of advantages, despite the two countries' asymmetry in size and economic power. Close interdependence is the prime condition of the relationship, assuring bilateral impact across a range of issues.[137] Asymmetry, instead of being a disadvantage for Canada, differentially raises the salience of issues on its side and prompts the marshalling of resources for coherent and resolved action. Canada's parliamentary system is well suited for providing direction and control.[138] A strong belief in that capability was held by Allan Gotlieb, under-secretary of state for External Affairs, whose views on the department's role in foreign policy became influential in the late 1970s and early 1980s, and complemented the nationalist orientation of the Trudeau government. Gotlieb also believed that domestic economic policy is inherently part of foreign policy and requires a single strategy and centralized management.[139]

In 1981, Gotlieb and Jeremy Kinsman, chairman of the department's Policy Planning Secretariat, published an article advocating that Canada resurrect the Third Option, a policy originally enunciated in 1972. The Third Option advocated "a comprehensive and long-term strategy to develop and strengthen the Canadian economy and other aspects of its national life." The strategy's purpose would be to reduce Canada's exposure to economic disruptions from the United States and build a stronger Canadian society.[140] The Third Option was prompted in 1971 by President Richard Nixon's imposition of import surcharges and financial controls, which brought home to Canada the fact that its economic security depended on a political relationship of quiet diplomacy and special consideration, leaving it vulnerable to actions such as Nixon's.[141] More broadly, the Third Option addressed popular concerns that had built through the late 1960s over the degree of American ownership and influence in Canada. The Third Option's primary policy effects, true to its purpose, were domestic.[142] FIRA can be seen as the Third Option's clearest expression, although it actually resulted from an earlier initiative. Otherwise the policy's practical impact was modest. Its most important foreign policy application was an unsuccessful effort to secure a special "contractual link" with the European Community.[143] Never embraced by much of the Canadian business community, and enjoying lukewarm support in other parts of the government, the Third Option became dormant by the mid-1970s.

In arguing in 1981 to revive the Third Option, Gotlieb and Kinsman emphasized that its focus was domestic industrial policy that and its objective was increased sovereignty and control. "The nature of the Canadian economy and society," they wrote, "has required government involvement to channel aspects of long-range development in beneficial ways. Similarly, it is axiomatic that the benefits of development have to be worked at by Canada. They will not fall out of a free trade, free investment, free-for-all continental economy. This is not an option for Canadian development."[144]

National economic policy was inherently related to foreign policy, and the unifying concern was sovereignty. Referring to relations with the United States, Gotlieb wrote of sovereignty "not in the legal sense, but in the discretion over the security of national interests which, inevitably, are not identical for both sides." To be successful in its effort, Canada needed to "adopt a strategic approach," and the architect and manager of that strategy would be External Affairs.[145] Acting on these views, the Trudeau government undertook a significant ministerial reorganization in 1982 by grafting the trade section of the former Ministry of Industry, Trade and Commerce onto External Affairs.[146] The department's mandate was to perform "a comprehensive linking role between the concerns of the government outside Canada and within Canada."[147] These political and administrative currents were in full circulation when transborder trucking arose as an issue. Implied reciprocity and sovereign control of regulation fitted exactly with the view that domestic economy and foreign policy were intertwined. External Affairs' ability to give diplomatic effect to these views was shown in its allocation of senior-level attention, its success in coordinating the Canadian participants, and its involvement at the very outset of the dispute.

Another factor balancing bargaining advantages between the two countries is the Canadian parliamentary system's ability to manage the politicization of issues by channelling interest group pressure and focusing publicity.[148] Issues in the United States, in contrast, become politicized in Congress, diffusing purpose and opening the way to conflicts with the executive branch.[149] Such divergence occurred when DOT, State Department, and the USTR opposed the Danforth amendment, enabling Canada to use that opposition to bolster its own case. Despite an earlier show of disunity over FIRA, Canada was able to mount a united front of federal, provincial, and interest group resistance to the moratorium and give it public play.

Interdependence also provides Canada the means for consequential retaliation.[150] Since there were American carriers also seeking authorities in

Canada, a moratorium could be placed on their applications. Raising the stakes, Canada could begin suspending the authorities of American carriers already in force. Restraining the United States, on the other hand, was an awareness of a broader range of concerns, the disruptive possibilities of conflict over trucking, and a general reluctance to push any given dispute to "an extreme conclusion."[151] There was no appetite in the executive branch for pressuring Canada into negotiating reciprocity, even though some officials in the USTR's office could see using the moratorium to extract concessions. Nor were there efforts to link Canadian concessions to issues requiring favourable treatment by the United States; instead, the interest was to find a settlement and get out.

Strength and Action

One index of the latitude to act is independence from organized pressures.[152] By that measure, ICC demonstrated latitude. Although it eventually yielded to congressional pressure to conduct an investigation and to apply a moratorium, it firmly resisted carrier protests of its decisions, refused executive branch and ATA appeals to consider reciprocity, and generally minimized its involvement. One could dismiss that behaviour as bureaucratic self-protection, but one could also see it as a conscientious effort to keep to a legal mandate. That performance followed upon an equally firm pursuit of deregulation, first through in-house reform and then through an aggressive interpretation of the Motor Carrier Act. The same was not true elsewhere. Initial divisions in the executive branch and between the executive branch and Congress reflected a conflict between attending to the complaints of American carriers and dealing with a unified and determined Canadian government. This conflict made it impossible to assemble a united front. Given the structure of the dispute, Canada's tactical advantages, and its refusal to make concessions, it is difficult to see how greater unity would have altered the outcome. There were too many reasons to keep the matter from escalating further.

Action was easier on the Canadian side because there were no domestic divisions. The provinces, apart from unexpected differences with the federal government over FIRA, backed its position and were wary of direct dealings with the ICC. The CTA was a strong supporter. Governmental priorities of the time favoured resistance. The one interest that might have had divergent preferences was Canadian shippers. As was noted at the beginning of the chapter, regulatory reformers could argue that mirror deregulation would benefit both sides through cheaper and more efficient transport. The CITL, the major organization of Canadian shippers, might be expected to appreciate that benefit, but no evidence was found of its involvement in the Trucking War. One reason, as will be seen in the next chapter, was that the CITL was initially wary of deregulation and did not support it until later.

The CITL feared that deregulation, and episodes such as the Trucking War, would sow disruption and uncertainty in trucking markets. This political consonance notwithstanding, External Affairs' resolute management of the dispute reflected a notable organizational capacity to orchestrate coherent action and to seize opportunities.

Conclusion

We have seen what happens when unilateral action disrupts a symmetrical arrangement. When the ICC treated Canadian carriers on the same terms as it did American ones, it enabled them to capture the traffic they once shared with their American interline partners. American carriers soon complained that no equivalent opportunities were open to them in Canada. The grievance was over a trade in services imbalance, but the origin of the problem was in the two countries' domestic regulatory rules. That fact conflated reciprocity, a trade issue, with discrimination, a regulatory issue. Standing firm on sovereignty, Canada refused to consider the trade solution of reciprocity and insisted that the problem was regulatory. Denying discrimination, Canada shifted expectations for adjustment to the American side and, when the ICC implemented a regulatory solution, claimed injury.

A regulatory remedy was imposed on an unwilling ICC by the congressional moratorium. Although the moratorium was implemented, the ICC otherwise managed to limit the scope of its involvement and exit before the conflict was over. DOT and the USTR were clear that the underlying issue was reciprocity, but they also recognized Canada's unwillingness to consider it. These facts, along with the structural obstacles to a bilateral services agreement, resulted in regulatory remedies being preferred to diplomatic ones. With reciprocity off the table, and with the applied regulatory remedy the point of intense Canadian complaint, diplomatic settlement left the American side to offer unilateral hospitality. Canada successfully maintained sovereign control of its border and kept its norms intact, preserving its regulatory order. With regulation successfully defended, Canada's diplomatic objective of protecting its sovereign practices had been achieved.

American deregulation posed an opened market alongside a still-regulated one. As Canadian carriers expanded transborder services and established themselves in the United States, lower rates and better service produced an increasing disparity, bringing deregulation home economically and raising again the question of harmonization. This time the latitude for foreign expansion was in Canada's decentralized jurisdiction, and reciprocity was an inter-provincial conflict. Deregulation and sovereignty were again issues, but this time they were raised by watchful provinces.

5

The State Withdraws: Reform, Trade, and Federalism in Canada

Canada defended its regulation in the Trucking War but deregulated five years later. This sequence raises an interesting question: If diplomatic pressure was not the impetus, then what was? The answer is an amalgam of the domestic and the international. On the domestic side, interest in regulatory reform had been activated by the crisis of stagflation in the mid-1970s, and subsequent studies of trucking found much inefficiency and waste. In 1980 the Economic Council of Canada, directed by the Trudeau government to examine regulation and to recommend remedies, endorsed the industry's complete deregulation. Political action came later from the Liberal government's minister of transport, Lloyd Axworthy, who put pressure on the Canadian Transport Commission to lower airfares and on provincial governments to reform trucking. His successor, the Conservative government's Donald Mazankowski, continued the initiative on a more comprehensive basis, which resulted in legislation in 1987 that affected air, rail, maritime, and motor carriers. Rail and trucking reform was backed by shippers anticipating lower rates and was opposed by carriers anticipating competition.

Some of these elements were similar to those that occurred in the American experience, with economic malaise directing interest towards regulation, elected politicians prompting action, and prospective results motivating supporters and opponents. Canada, however, had already acted on regulatory reform. The National Transportation Act (NTA), 1967, which partly deregulated Canadian rail rates, preceded American rail deregulation by thirteen years. Although motor carrier rates were in provincial hands, the NTA gave some play to market forces, encouraging railways and motor carriers to find their proper niches.[1] The NTA itself had followed the work of the MacPherson Royal Commission on Transportation, which took up the complex and troubled question of railway rates and regional development. Regulatory reform was not new political business in Canada.

On the international side, Canada's deregulation of trucking, coming after deregulation in the United States, was subject to cross-border comparisons.

The effect of such comparisons can be considerable. Political economists Jeffrey Frieden and Ronald Rogowski hypothesize that international price differences motivate domestic reform, with the strongest pressures coming from sectors that bear higher costs than do international competitors. Although these sectors may be shielded by various protections and subsidies, the differences still show in "shadow" prices, which reflect the true disparity and tell domestic producers how non-competitive they actually are. As trade expands, cost disadvantages generate compelling domestic political pressure for reform. The potential gains attract political support. "The greater the dead-weight loss from a prevailing arrangement, the likelier it becomes that some political entrepreneur will succeed in changing it."[2] Such entrepreneurship materialized in the person of Lloyd Axworthy, although his initial beneficiaries were not producers but airline passengers, who had been comparing deregulated American airfares since 1978. Governments may have their own interests in reform, and lifting restrictions may lead to what they consider to be desirable ends.[3] As trade has expanded over the last quarter-century, and as governments have sought to assist domestic firms in world markets, an important area of endeavour has been domestic infrastructures. Telecommunications and transportation are particularly important because of the competitive need for fast and inexpensive linkages.[4]

Both elements were present in trucking deregulation. American motor carrier rates presented striking cost comparisons to Canadian shippers, who made that the basis of their case. The government's position was informed by efficiency. At a time when Canada's international competitiveness had become a concern for both Liberal and Conservative governments, efficient transport could be supported as a desirable end.

Cross-border comparisons also raise the question of policy emulation. Occasions to consider other states' policies arise internally from dissatisfaction and externally from interdependence. Dissatisfaction prompts an interest in different policies, and interdependence conveys their practical effects. Both focus attention. The practical effects of policy may require adjustment and compensation, while results elsewhere may show what can be achieved. Similarity between states is an important consideration. The best candidates for emulation are programs and policies that are not unique in their components or requirements, that do not depend on unusual or singular institutions, and that require similar mandates and competence. Whether it is practical to adopt such policies or programs depends on the degree of correspondence between institutional forms, rules, and experience. Institutional similarity among advanced industrial states provides a wide range of candidates, and high levels of correspondence favour adoption.[5] With regard to trucking regulation, as was seen in Chapter 2, the similarity between Canada and the United States was high.

The main difference was in federal organization. Also favouring adoption is a clear cause-and-effect relationship between policy and outcome. The stronger that relationship, the fewer the risks of surprising and unwanted consequences.

Both supporters and opponents of trucking deregulation in Canada referred to the American experience as a highly relevant precedent. Adduced as positive evidence were lower rates and improved service; adduced as negative evidence were disruption, layoffs, and concern about highway safety. At the same time, the set of trucking regulatory studies commissioned by the federal government used as their comparative reference not the United States, but Alberta – a province that had never applied entry controls on intraprovincial carriers. The play between domestic and international influences will be seen throughout this chapter and will be evaluated in the conclusion.

Attention is a key political resource, for it determines which problems and solutions are acted upon.[6] In the view of institutional analysis, attention is not steady, particularly at senior ranks, but shifts irregularly among sectors in response to varying cues, demands, and political incentives. The result is a discontinuous conjuncture of problems, attention, and solutions. Problems may have long been identified but not attended to, and appropriate solutions may sit awaiting adoption. Change occurs when a problem and solution are brought together. With trucking, the problem and the solution had been identified by 1980, but change had to await the attention of a senior politician. Lloyd Axworthy, having become the Trudeau government's minister of transport in 1983, put public pressure on the Canadian Transport Commission to cut airline fares. His interest in trucking had been preceded by some of the provinces, which were conducting regulatory reviews. When Axworthy turned his attention to that industry, he persuaded the provinces to take up the key issue of entry standards, thus beginning the process of deregulation in earnest.

During the time that trucking deregulation was awaiting senior sponsorship, the Trudeau government, alarmed by the 1981 recession's heavy damage to Canada's industrial sector, had launched two initiatives focused on competitiveness and trade: a Department of External Affairs consultative study and, much more elaborate, the Macdonald Royal Commission. As liberalizing reforms involving Canada's prime trading partner, deregulation and free trade would seem to be obviously connected. And the fact that they were on the policy agenda at the same time supports that impression. However, the government's assessments of trade prospects did not emphasize trucking – the prime transborder mode of transport. The External Affairs review, which did much to concentrate political energy on trade, contained merely one sentence – referring to all transport modes – about regulatory reform. The Macdonald Commission's report, which recommended

Canada-US free trade on the basis of a comprehensive review of Canada's economic sectors and public policy, barely mentioned trucking deregulation, noting only that the Economic Council of Canada supported it. In the Commons Standing Committee on Transport's hearings on regulatory reform legislation, free trade was treated as a separate issue, even though the transborder implications of deregulation were much discussed. How does one account for this apparent disjuncture? One explanation is federal: these were federal initiatives and trucking regulation was a provincial responsibility. Government reform legislation was a set of standards for the provinces to adopt; it was not directly instrumental. Another explanation is institutional: deregulation and free trade entered the political agenda as responses to different problems. Whether or not free trade begot deregulation is less obvious than one might expect.

Change can be most easily implemented in the face of opposition when authority is centred in a single agency with clear jurisdiction. Latitude diminishes when power is scattered among a number of agencies and across levels of government and when "a wide range of politicians and bureaucrats can claim some jurisdiction [and] no institutions exist to link their activities."[7] With trucking deregulation, there was no federal agency. The authority given to the Canadian Transport Commission in 1967 by the NTA had been left in the hands of the provinces. Parliament could legislate a set of new standards, but it was up to the provinces to adopt them. And provincial enthusiasm was mixed. Only Alberta shared the federal government's dedication to open roads (implementation simply meant widening Albertan hospitality). Other provinces, attentive to their motor carriers' fear of competition, delayed. Ontario stalled the longest, and Manitoba was the most openly defiant. Just as it did in the Trucking War five years earlier, reciprocity became an issue when provinces that had dropped their controls complained about the unfair advantages enjoyed by still-protected carriers from Ontario. This time the conflict was played out within a domestic jurisdiction. Although harmonization of entry standards was achieved among the provinces by 1989, remnants of regulation remain in Manitoba, Saskatchewan, and British Columbia.

Decentralized Jurisdiction, International Traffic
Ottawa's reluctance to become involved in interprovincial trucking regulation, as was seen in Chapter 2, led it to delegate that authority to the individual provinces, with the Motor Vehicle Transport Act, 1954, sustaining ten separate regulatory jurisdictions and ten sets of rules. Constitutionally, the Canadian provinces' jurisdiction over property and civil rights enabled them to establish differing regulatory arrangements and to restrict interprovincial trade in both goods and services.[8] Those regulatory boundaries discouraged the growth of a national trucking industry. With no federal

agency to regulate interprovincial trucking, and with the standard of public convenience and necessity in place, carriers faced multiple applications
and tiring, expensive proceedings. That impediment hindered the growth
of nationwide trucking.[9] Regulatory policy in the United States, though it
had excluded new entrants, did enable carriers to assemble interstate operations and to expand through buyouts and mergers, allowing dense and
omni-directional traffic flows to develop, particularly after deregulation
had removed restrictions. That density, together with the expanse of the
national market, made the American motor carrier industry more thoroughly domestic than Canada's and limited the importance of international traffic.

In Canada the American border is a focus of trucking, and when deregulation was implemented in 1989 Ontario and Quebec accounted for 85 percent of the transborder traffic.[10] In the years following the Trucking War,
approximately half of Canada's exports to the United States were loaded in
Ontario, and some 65 percent of Ontario's exports travelled by truck.[11] By
1990, the portion of Ontario's exports going to the United States had grown
to over 90 percent, and trucks continued to carry two-thirds of it.[12] For
many Canadian carriers, the transborder market was more important than
were those in their neighbouring provinces.

An index of the carriers' role in transborder trucking was the election in
1984 of a Trimac Ltd. executive to head the ATA's National Tank Truck Carriers Conference; this recognized the position of the twenty large Canadian
bulk carriers operating in the United States, the volumes of trade in liquid
petroleum and chemical commodities, and the stature of Calgary-based Trimac as the third-largest bulk carrier in North America (it is now the
largest).[13] The Trimac executive's being elected to head a major body of the
ATA also showed the association's willingness, soon after the Trucking War,
to accept Canadian carriers into its leadership. That same international
exposure provided a realistic basis for Canadian carriers' concerns about
American competition. Deregulation, they feared, would see large and efficient American carriers stream in to occupy key centres and traffic lanes.
International concerns were very much part of the provincial reviews
because the provinces controlled carrier entry on their respective segments
of the border.

The rest of Chapter 5 will examine these issues in more detail. With the
federal and provincial governments all involved in deregulation, the sum of
legislative and administrative events is quite large. Instead of reviewing
them entirely, I will focus briefly and selectively on the federal government
and Ontario as well as on the subsequent manoeuvring among the
provinces. The size of Ontario's carrier industry and its pivotal position in
international traffic made it the reference point for the other provinces as

they calculated the timing and degree of their actions.[14] Ontario's deregulation was also the most protracted, visible, and politically contentious. Deregulation in the Atlantic provinces, in contrast, received little attention, even in the trade press. Altogether, given the domestic and international dimensions of carrier entry, the legacy of transport reform, the decentralized jurisdiction, and the simultaneous political attention to deregulation and trade, the transition in Canada was far more complex than it was in the United States. In Canadian trucking deregulation, advocates of a mutual consciousness between International Relations and Public Policy have a strong case.

Plural Initiatives

Regulatory reform originated at the provincial level, while deregulation originated at the federal level. The provincial governments undertook reviews of their motor carrier regulation on limited and pragmatic grounds. The remedies envisaged were not drastic, and none of the provincial reviews opted for free entry. Federal interest in trucking had begun with the first ministers conference of 1978, which produced a prime ministerial directive to the Economic Council of Canada to conduct a comprehensive review. These developments set the stage for Axworthy's involvement, although that came following an interlude of economic nationalism that was not hospitable to open-market reforms. When the federal government's attitude subsequently changed, its concern with transport costs and efficiency clashed with the carriers' wishes to keep their protections, thus making the provincial governments prime sites of conflict.

Federal interest in transport regulation was rooted in the complexities and controversies of railway rates. Because of the impact of freight rates on production costs and, more contentious still, on regional inequality, railway regulation and subsidies had always involved more than simple efficiency.[15] At the same time, rates and subsidies alone were inadequate to promote national industrial development and to reduce regional disparities.[16] In 1951, the Turgeon Royal Commission, assigned to deal with provincial complaints about rail rate increases, recommended a number of changes to relax rate control, and these were incorporated into the Railway Act, 1955. Subsequent rate increases raised more complaints, and in 1958 the federal government partially reversed the increases and compensated the railways with subsidies. The resulting conflict between reasonable rates and adequate rail service led, in 1959, to the creation of the MacPherson Royal Commission. Its recommendations were to end rail rate regulation entirely, to abandon restrictions on private rates between rail carriers and shippers, and to centralize responsibility for the railways within a single agency. These recommendations were at the core of the National Transportation Act, 1967.[17]

The CTA, which had long regarded both the railways and Ottawa as enemies, welcomed more competition in the rail market.[18] Eliminating subsidies and setting rail rates according to true costs would place the two modes of transport on a more equally competitive footing. For their part, the railways did not get the right to set confidential rates with individual shippers, but they liked the prospect of operating on a longer regulatory leash. The NTA, in its partial reform of rail rates, marked a more general move towards free-market thinking: "Non-interventionist ideas and policies slowly worked their way throughout the policy system, culminating in the post-1975 move toward transportation deregulation."[19] That date might more precisely be set at 1978, when regulatory inefficiency was identified as an important issue, as we will see presently.

Canadian economists, like their American counterparts, had analyzed trucking regulation. A working bibliography prepared for the Ontario government's Public Commercial Vehicles Act Review Committee in 1981 listed several dozen Canadian sources. Until the late 1970s, however, most Canadian research had focused on procedural rather than substantive questions.[20] That began to change when the Trudeau government, responding to the same problems of inflation and energy costs that were troubling the Ford administration in the United States, introduced national wage and price controls in 1975 and created the Anti-Inflation Board (AIB) to monitor them. Although that move represented a massive increase in federal controls, it made deregulation a political issue when the AIB, true to the spirit of its mandate, became concerned about costs and efficiency. At the AIB's prompting, a year later the federal government announced a "fundamental examination of the major structural components of our economy and our society."[21] That line of thought led to regulation, and in 1977 the AIB released a report, *The Impact of Regulation: The Case of Trucking*.

Prime Minister Trudeau convened a first ministers conference on 13 February 1978 to discuss burdens on the Canadian economy and ways of addressing them. A major burden, the conference agreed, was government. A review of regulation at all government levels was authorized, and Trudeau instructed the Economic Council of Canada to undertake this task and to prepare a set of recommendations. His letter to the council specifically connected regulation and efficiency. "Increasing government regulation," he wrote to the Council's chairwoman, Sylvia Ostry, "might be having adverse effects on the efficiency of Canadian firms and industries and on the allocation of resources and the distribution of income."[22]

The same initiative established the federal Interdepartmental Committee on Competition and Regulation in Transportation, composed of the Department of Consumer and Corporate Affairs, the Canadian Transport Commission, and Transport Canada. Cabinet, as part of a "medium-term economic strategy," directed the committee to undertake research to "analyze the role of competition in transportation, leading, where appropriate, to recommendations regarding the content and application of regulation."[23] The committee's research agenda covered trucking's structure, conduct, and performance. The results were prolific. By 1982 the committee had produced a series of twenty analyses of all aspects of the Canadian trucking industry, focusing on the questions of competition and efficiency and on provincial regulatory practices.[24]

Regulatory and market differences among the provinces made comparison and evaluation complex tasks. Instead of looking to foreign regions, however, the committee had the advantage of an unregulated jurisdiction at home – Alberta. The three studies that conducted the most extensive econometric analysis used Alberta as their point of comparison with the other provinces, particularly Ontario.[25] The contrasts were striking. The summary report based on the three studies found that Ontario's heavily regulated common carriers had costs and revenues that were fully twice those of Alberta's.[26] Another impressive comparison involved the incidence of private carriage. As was seen in Chapter 2, private carriage is the transport of goods in the shipper's own vehicles. Under regulation, which forbade private carriers hauling goods for compensation, operations tended to run up empty miles, making it an expensive alternative to using for-hire firms. Capital outlay on trucks represented further costs. Because, in the 1970s, private carriage had grown to account for half of the intercity freight in Canada, the study assumed that shippers would choose it only if for-hire rates were quite unattractive. That proved to be true: the incidence of private carriage was highest in the most-regulated provinces and lowest in Alberta. One example was Imperial Oil Ltd.'s uses of private and for-hire carriage for its bulk product distribution. Seventy-five percent of Imperial's carriage in Ontario was private, compared to 25 percent of its carriage in Alberta.

Taking into account other factors that might affect the difference between Alberta and the other provinces, the report concluded that rates in heavily regulated provinces were causing Canadian shippers to abandon for-hire trucking. "This observation alone," noted the author in reference to national economic efficiency, "is likely to have implications for the delivered prices of many goods-producing sectors in the Canadian economy, for intermodal competition in transport, and for the overall efficiency of trucking, the dominant mode of freight transportation in Canada." The policy recommendation was clear: "In the absence of regulatory reform designed to lower the for-hire rate/private cost gap ... policy makers should consider the removal of cost-increasing regulation on private carriage."[27] That change would allow private carriers to haul goods for compensation.

Policy emulation, as was seen at the beginning of this chapter, involves looking abroad for models and experience. The focus of the Interdepartmental Committee's research was domestic. Of the twenty studies of trucking regulation prepared, only one – a literature review – had an international focus.[28] The three studies that carried out the major economic analysis all focused on comparisons between Alberta and other provinces. When these studies did cite foreign data and results, it was to test their own conclusions. The summary report acknowledged the example of American deregulation but was careful to point out that "Canadian experience with regulation (and deregulation) ... is rooted in a different historical, social and economic context, which tends to complicate considerably the analysis of performance of regulated industries."[29] After carefully reviewing factors that may affect results among jurisdictions, the report stated: "While substantial differences may exist, the fact remains that the essential economics are the same." Unregulated carriers, the study concluded, "appear to be cost-conscious, efficient, capable of paying reasonable wages, and appear to have no problems in attracting capital."[30] The supporting empirical case was domestic.

The importance of domestic research and experience was also emphasized in a comparative study of American and Canadian regulation that was conducted for the Institute for Research on Public Policy. While acknowledging the American case, the author cautioned against the "natural temptation" to borrow from it: "In reality, the experiences, while similar in many respects, are significantly different in other critical ways ... Studies undertaken in the last five years in Canada have enabled us to delineate some of these differences and hopefully avoid the pitfalls of universalist solutions."[31]

That judicious approach did indeed characterize the Interdepartmental Committee's work, and it is possible to infer an underlying political strategy. For those wishing to promote regulatory reform, it was not wise to make American experience the point of reference. This was particularly so in the early 1980s, as we will see shortly.

"This is a most difficult time for Canadian Governments," began the Economic Council of Canada's interim report, reflecting its terms of reference and the sense of economic malaise that underlay its mandate.[32] Released in 1979, the interim report was a survey of Canadian regulatory values, objectives, and procedures, and the final report, released in 1981, examined particular areas of regulation, covering trucking, along with railways, airlines, and taxis. A broad-gauged review such as this would offer an occasion for policy analysts to seek foreign experience and models; but, instead of looking abroad, the council kept its scrutiny internal. The section on trucking, drawing directly on the Interdepartmental Committee's studies, focused entirely on the domestic industry. To support the committee's conclusions about workable competition, the council made brief references to foreign deregulated jurisdictions – Australia and the United Kingdom – and to American research findings on economies of scale. The council's final report, still keeping carefully to its domestic terms of reference, recommended the complete deregulation of trucking.[33]

Economic Nationalism, Stagnated Reform

Despite Trudeau's initiative and these impressive responses, transport reform did not become a prominent issue.[34] In 1979, in fact, Trudeau reversed his position about the burdens of government and proposed more economic intervention: NEP and the active use of FIRA. Both were designed to increase Canadian control of the economy. In the view of Stephen Clarkson, the change originated during the Liberals' brief time in opposition and was the electoral expedient of a tired party looking for ideas.[35] When Trudeau returned to power, the impact and publicity of these programs wrapped his government in the robes of economic nationalism.

Because of reform's low priority on the new agenda, a special committee established in the House of Commons to act upon the Economic Council of Canada's recommendations had little to do. W.T. Stanbury, an academic participant in the council's review, was not optimistic that the Liberal government would ever become an active reformer because pragmatic political considerations favoured the interests of Ontario and Quebec – Canada's industrial heartland and the electoral base of Liberal governments. Those interests specified continuing economic nationalism and protectionism. In addition, in Canada deregulation was identified with the excesses of Reaganism and Thatcherism, therefore making it difficult for a Liberal government to espouse.[36] That was particularly so in light of Canada's tradition of regarding regulation as an instrument for achieving progressive economic, political, and social purposes.[37]

Even though the Trudeau government was sympathetically inclined towards domestic industries, the truckers believed that their natural allies were the provincial governments. Historically, that view grew out of the CTA's long opposition to federal support for the railways. Tactically, provincial governments are promising partners when groups can identify their concerns with provincial ones and when the issue involves federal-provincial cooperation.[38] Identifying with the provinces over matters affecting jobs and regional welfare supports the political posture of defence against the federal government. The trucking associations followed exactly that strategy, as we will see. The provincial governments were generally not enthusiastic about reform, and protecting local trucking businesses was a feasible political rationale.

The Provincial Level: Pragmatic Dissatisfactions, Limited Change

Compared to the federal regulatory reviews, the provincial ones were more immediate and practical. In 1976 the government of Ontario, responding to growing discontent among motor carriers and shippers over the complexity of regulation under the province's much-amended Public Commercial Vehicles Act, appointed the Select Committee on Highway Transportation of Goods to examine all issues relating to motor carriage and regulation in the province. Reporting to the provincial legislature a year later, the committee recommended a formal review of the Public Commercial Vehicles Act.[39] The provincial government, however, waited until 1981 to convene the Ontario Public Commercial Vehicles (PCV) Act Review Committee, and it waited until 1989 to pass new legislation. The review itself took two years and included representatives from motor carriers, the Teamsters, and shippers. Reflecting the divided interests of these parties, the committee's report stopped short of recommending an end to entry controls.

The interests defending regulation were powerful enough to derail the PCV Review Committee's consensual approach to reform. Although the Ontario government originally intended to proceed by rational consensus building, the committee was unable to agree on the key issue of entry, and its proceedings foretold a long and disjointed process in the broader provincial arena. The difficult passage to deregulation in Ontario provides a good example of conflicting economic interests. It also shows how international considerations may pervade public policy in trade-based jurisdictions, even in seemingly prosaic areas like trucking regulation.

The PCV Review Committee conducted hearings and deliberations for the next two years, and in June 1983 it submitted its recommendations as part of its report, *Responsible Trucking: New Directions*, which recommended changing the PCV Act.[40] The government's intention to conduct a serious evaluation and to reach a workable consensus showed in the composition of the PCV Review Committee. It was headed by an assistant deputy minister from the Ministry of Transportation and Communications, and it included representatives from regulated carriers, owner-operators, private carriers, the Teamsters, manufacturers, and shippers. Transport Minister James Snow's address to the just-constituted committee reflects a Canadian political preference for handling contentious issues through consultation and negotiation. Snow had sought to "ensure the widest possible range of interests around the table," and though he expected that the members would consult closely with their respective constituencies, "it is critical," he emphasized, "that you regard yourselves primarily as representatives of the road transport industry as a whole, upon whom the government is relying for expert advice." Recognizing the probability of conflict, he appealed to their sense of public duty to settle differences and warned that failure to reach a common set of recommendations would leave the members and their associations "no choice but to live with a set of government-imposed solutions."[41]

During its two years of deliberations, the committee focused on getting a working list of problems and preferred outcomes. In general, all sides agreed on the need to achieve greater flexibility in trucking. There was agreement on legitimizing and expanding contract carriage, which in Ontario had an ambiguous regulatory status, and on giving independent owner-operators greater latitude in working for certificated carriers. A difference emerged with regard to removing restrictions on private carriers and allowing them to haul cargoes for hire and to lease their drivers and vehicles to other shippers and carriers. Shippers favoured the flexibility they would gain, but regulated carriers opposed this new source of competition. More basic was the question of entry controls. In principle, both shippers and carriers favoured abolishing the test of public convenience and necessity. Carriers, however, wanted to keep entry and rate controls in some form. They favoured a market test, in which an application could be challenged on the grounds that it would deny certificated carriers a fair opportunity to compete for traffic. That measure, the carriers believed, would keep out large firms that might attract disproportionate amounts of business.

Compromise appeared to have been achieved. The final report recommended replacing the test of public convenience and necessity with a simple fitness test and only using the market test in the exceptional circumstances of a large carrier's application. In not advocating the divestiture of all entry controls, however, the committee reflected the conflicting interests of the organizations represented. Furthermore, the report only obliquely dealt with the central issue of American carrier entry. As deregulation began to take more practical forms, consensus dissolved.

The Canadian Manufacturers Association (CMA), which favoured carrier competition and free entry for American firms, was unhappy with the market test, as were American carriers interested in expanding into Ontario. Both suspected that the market test was simply a way to relax entry controls while keeping large American firms out. The provision that only exceptional and disruptive cases would activate the test supported that suspicion. The PCV committee acknowledged that the market test was intended to protect against an undesirable concentration of carriers, including the "threat of domination of Ontario markets by giant competitors from the U.S."[42]

Taking up American entry directly brought out clearer divisions. These appeared in submissions to the OHTB when it prepared a study of transborder trucking following the controversy (discussed in Chapter 4) surrounding Roadway Express's effort to purchase an Ontario carrier and the denial of regulatory approval. The OHTB heard sixty-two submissions from Canadian carriers, the OTA, the CITL, the CMA, and the ATA.[43]

As might be expected, the OTA strongly opposed American entry. The problem, insisted Stephen Flott, the OTA's executive vice-president, was that there was not *enough* regulation. "There is no political will in Ontario today," he stated, "to support the Public Commercial Vehicles Act as it is now written."[44] Lax enforcement meant that the province was semi-regulated. Pirate trucking was taking business from honest firms, and informal discounting, driven by the 1981 recession, was making posted rates vestigial. That left Ontario carriers, according to Flott, with the "worst of both possible worlds" of regulation and deregulation.[45] Carriers in Manitoba raised a similar complaint. Pirate truckers, the Manitoba Trucking Association charged, were skimming off 20 percent of the traffic.[46]

The OTA's solution was tougher regulation, and one idea was to change the law to allow carriers to bring charges against violators of the PCV Act, something only inspectors and law enforcement officials could do. The OTA's position recognized that market forces – both legal and illegal – were deregulating trucking. Because of informal discounting, some truckers came to believe that the eventual transition to an open market would be less drastic in Canada than it was in the United States because Canadian carriers were being more gradually introduced to rate competition. In the face of those market pressures, government action would have to be more vigorous if regulation were to be preserved. In requesting this, the OTA was moving against the trend of practice and outlook. A more general pressure was also at work. As the centre of domestic and transborder trucking, Ontario was receiving the country's highest levels of application, thus making entry policy an unavoidable issue.[47]

Less expected was the opposition of the CITL, an organization of shippers. Its American counterpart, the National Industrial Transportation League, had been a strong supporter of deregulation, as was seen in Chapter 3. The CITL's concern was that deregulation in Canada would foster the growth of giant carriers and that Canadian National and Canadian Pacific would boost their trucking subsidiaries into dominant market positions.[48] The CITL was also concerned that the end of rate filing would make it difficult for smaller shippers to have orderly price information. The CMA, on the other hand, strongly supported complete deregulation and free entry for American carriers. The two organizations' constituencies may explain their different positions. The CITL represented 500 smaller firms in a number of different industries. These firms doubted their bargaining position in the absence of posted rates, particularly against giant carriers in a concentrated deregulated industry. The CMA, in contrast, represented large firms who had greater confidence in their negotiating power.[49]

The OTA and the CITL argued that American carriers in Ontario would have unequal advantages, and they pointed to differences in the two markets, repeating an argument made during the Trucking War: while American carriers could expand into Ontario with small and incremental additions to their networks, Ontario carriers would have to make proportionately much larger investments in order to offer a comparable assortment of American traffic centres to Canadian shippers. One carrier estimated the price of setting up an American network to be $500 million.[50] Comparing operating costs, Canadian carriers pointed to tax and fuel price advantages enjoyed by American carriers in the United States, making it possible for them to offer deeper discounts than Canadian carriers. Several Ontario carriers testified that if an open international border were inaugurated, then cost differences would prompt them to relocate their businesses to the United States. The OTA also mirrored American complaints about interline traffic diversion – the catalyst of the Trucking War: American carriers holding Ontario authorities could capture transborder traffic and bypass their Canadian partners. By 1982, however, that argument had to contend with the fact that a number of the OTA's larger members were already operating in the United States.

The CMA strongly denied that Ontario carriers were at risk. Replying to the OTA's objections to American entry, the CMA found it "paradoxical that the Canadian industry maintains it cannot survive if large U.S. carriers are allowed into Ontario while at the same time its members are aggressively expanding into the U.S. We see no reason why direct-line transborder transportation should be reserved exclusively for Canadian-based carriers."[51] Predatory pricing, the CMA asserted, can be controlled through existing competition law. "It is not the number of firms in the marketplace that determines the intensity of competition," the CMA asserted. "What is important is the availability of potential substitutes and the relative ease to enter the industry."[52] The CMA'S support for free entry for American carriers was explicit: Canadian shippers would be able to sell their products more widely and enjoy more efficient transportation. With the prospect of international trade becoming more competitive in the 1980s, that was an important consideration.[53]

The ATA denied that American carriers have "secret competitive weapons or strategies" and forecast that they would fail in a deregulated Ontario if their prices and services were inferior. Siding with the CMA, the ATA held that there would be long-term damage to Canadian manufacturers if regulation forced them to use expensive and inefficient carriers. Addressing respective advantages in transborder traffic, the ATA maintained that Ontario carriers had long enjoyed disproportionately generous shares of profit from interline operations with American carriers. The ICC had magnified those advantages by giving Canadian carriers one-way entry and by awarding Canadian carriers authority for purely domestic American traffic – in contrast to Ontario's barring American carriers from intraprovincial service.[54]

Sympathy and Firebombs

The OHTB report made no recommendations but showed sympathy for the Ontario carriers: "It appears that the concern expressed [by Ontario carriers] is not for protection from competition but for recognition of the fact that differences do exist and such differences are not of the making of the trucking fraternity in either jurisdiction but do affect one much more than the other." Drawing the regulatory implication, the report added: "To apply equal opportunity for markets to those who are not equal leads to further inequality or, as one submission concluded, 'Hopefully the minnows will not be forced to swim with the sharks.'"[55] Critics noted, however, that in repeating the Ontario carriers' testimony on transborder trucking with no base of reliable data, the exercise was a political sop to their complaints about American competition.[56] That made the OHTB's report similar to the ICC's MC-157 investigation, but, unlike the ICC, the OHTB recognized harm from foreign carriers.

The Ontario government acted on the OHTB's views with a set of regulatory guidelines, announced in summer 1984. These were to be in force while the PCV Act Review Committee's recommendations were being worked into law. Transport Minister Snow acknowledged the need to allow American carriers into Ontario, but he promised that the new regulatory legislation would "protect the interests of Ontario carriers in the long term." In the meantime his government "recognized the concerns of this province's trucking companies regarding competition from large U.S. firms."[57] The number of trucks an American carrier could operate in Ontario, he promised, would be limited.[58]

The reviews in other provinces were more circumscribed. The governments were essentially satisfied with the regulations they had, and in none of the provincial reviews was there the reformist enthusiasm seen in the United States.[59] In British Columbia, the last province to undertake a review, the initiative came from the British Columbia Motor Transport Association itself, which wanted to see a set of streamlined regulations to reduce the bureaucratic burden on the province's carriers. The association had no desire to end entry and rate controls. Truckers in other provinces also wanted to reduce red tape. A survey of carrier firms in the four Atlantic provinces in 1981, for example, showed that 75 percent were dissatisfied with existing regulations. The Atlantic Provinces Transportation Commission, reflecting these dissatisfactions, submitted a set of reform proposals to the provincial governments. This included granting contract carrier licences automatically and granting unopposed common carrier authorities without a hearing. The commission stopped short, however, of recommending an end to the test of public convenience and necessity.[60] Nova Scotia subsequently established a new licence category to grant entry on a fitness-only basis to Nova Scotia firms, but it did not extend that privilege to out-of-province carriers.

Manitoba minister of highways and transportation John Plohman outspokenly opposed change. He told the 1984 convention of the Manitoba Trucking Association that "it is simply not realistic to talk about deregulation" and that the province's trucking industry would always be regulated.[61] In Quebec carriers wanted more enforcement of route and commodity restrictions in order to curb an epidemic of pirate trucking. Violations were pervasive and easily outstripped the province's meagre resources, thus creating an atmosphere of lawlessness.[62] Truckers entering Quebec on Highway 401, for example, would form convoys and drive by the border weigh scale en masse, defying authorities to stop them. On two occasions, the border station was firebombed. The probabilities of arrest and prosecution for regulatory violations were small enough to lead transport specialists to view Quebec's system as unenforceable.[63] Removing controls, however, was even less appealing. Deregulation's prospect, left in provincial hands, was slow headway at best.

Political Ascension under Axworthy

Lloyd Axworthy, who became Liberal transport minister in 1983, had become keenly interested in airline deregulation. Much as Senator Edward Kennedy had done with his Senate committee hearings on airline regulation in 1978, Axworthy could benefit politically by holding out the promise of lower airfares to voters who were already enjoying American fares by driving to airports across the border.[64] There was speculation in the trucking and airline industries that Axworthy was using a popular cause to raise his political profile.[65] In 1983 he began putting public pressure on the Canadian Transport Commission to cut airfares, and in 1984 he broadened his pressure to remove all restrictions from air licences in favour of a reverse-onus standard.[66] Reverse onus, as was been earlier, shifts the burden of proof from applicants to opponents.

Inferring political entrepreneurship, journalists noted the proximity of this initiative with a Liberal leadership contest and an approaching federal election.[67] Pursuing airline deregulation through the CTC instead of through legislation, it was speculated, was a faster way of achieving competition, fare cuts, and political credit.[68] For his part, Axworthy maintained that "we were trying to change Transport into a consumer-oriented department."[69] Pursuing a reformist agenda against resistance in the ministry, he maintained, had made it necessary to bring in outside consultants on contract.

Officials in both the ministry and the CTC believed they had ideas to contribute. According to one account, "When Axworthy has gone public with his thoughts on specific issues – without ministry or Canadian Transport Commission staff aware of his thinking – or brought in outsiders to help him formulate policy, the bureaucrats feel left out of the process."[70] Thoughts of reform in those precincts were not new. The ministry had been a member of the interdepartmental committee that coordinated the regulatory studies of trucking. The CTC had conducted its own study of easing airline rate control in 1981, and the ministry had prepared recommendations on the matter in 1982.[71]

Responding to Axworthy's public statements, the CTC quietly began changing airline regulation. In early 1984 it held a hearing on airfares and, under its power to interpret public convenience and necessity, not only began relaxing rate controls but also entry controls.[72] The ICC, as was seen in Chapter 3, had done the same thing with trucking regulation in the late 1970s. Responding to political prompting from the White House and to the views of new pro-deregulation commissioners, the ICC reinterpreted public convenience and necessity broadly enough to remove most restrictions. In both cases emphasis was shifted from necessity, which favoured carriers, to convenience, which favoured customers. The CTC's approach was beneficial, in the view of some, because change would be introduced incrementally. By the end of the CTC hearings, Morris Kaufman, a Winnipeg lawyer Axworthy had appointed to advocate the public benefits of deregulation, was persuaded that a drastic transition "was not appropriate for Canada."[73]

In late 1983 Axworthy decided to step up the pace of the provincial motor carrier reviews, and in a December meeting with the provincial ministers of transport he got an agreement that provincial reforms would be conducted under a uniform set of priorities and that the Canadian Council of Motor Transport Administrators, an intergovernmental coordinating body, would draw up proposals for reform. In April 1984, the federal and provincial deputy ministers of transport met in Ottawa to consider the draft proposals. That same day there was a meeting with motor carrier industry representatives to hear their views. Meeting with the provincial transport ministers again in May 1984, Axworthy secured a set of explicit terms of reference for regulatory changes.[74] So radical that "even the most liberal of the provincial reviews weren't seriously considering them," the changes included replacing the public convenience and necessity entry standard with a simple fitness test, dropping all requirements to file rates, and extending the list of non-regulated commodities.[75] The CTA, which believed something much less sweeping had been prepared, was caught by surprise.[76] Axworthy also secured commitment from the provincial ministers that their governments would proceed immediately with regulatory reform. A working group of the CCMTA was charged with preparing a uniform set of recommendations by fall 1984.[77]

In obtaining these far-reaching concessions, Axworthy reminded the provinces of the unproclaimed part of the NTA, which provided for federal regulation of interprovincial trucking by the CTC. Axworthy's keen interest and the possibility that interprovincial regulation might be taken out of the provinces' hands may have facilitated agreement. Addressing the ministers,

Axworthy took up the theme of efficiency. One disadvantage was Canada's decentralized jurisdiction: "Next to the American approach, our patchwork system of regulation seems fraught with problems." It imposes regulations that "are often contrary, inequitable and inconsistent." Broadening the perspective, Axworthy asserted: "I believe we must shake off the shackles of protectionism if we want our economy to grow. Instead, we should embrace a new growth philosophy. Economic approaches like deregulation will lead to growth."[78] Conservative opposition critic Donald Mazankowski fully approved of Axworthy's efforts but argued that they should be part of a comprehensive policy. He began acting on those views when the Conservative government of Brian Mulroney took power in fall 1984. In the meantime, Canada-United States trade had entered the agenda. There, too, liberalization, growth, and efficiency were central themes.

Recession, Reconsideration, and Trade

Growth and efficiency had become painfully pertinent. If the first ministers had found the economic climate discouraging in 1978, then 1981's climate was positively alarming. The recession, which had begun in that year, was deep and widespread, and it was particularly cruel to the manufacturing and export sectors. There was growing fear that the government had no means of containing it. Trucking, a derived-demand industry that follows economic fluctuations immediately, was badly affected. On the west coast, slumping lumber exports cut motor carrier traffic by 35 percent. In Ontario and Quebec, stagnation in the automobile and manufacturing sectors drove many carriers to the margin. "I don't think I've ever seen it so bad," observed CTA president Ken Maclaren. "The industry is in real trouble."[79] Within the federal government, the cabinet Priorities and Planning Committee, alarmed by deepening recession and escalating conflict with the United States over NEP and FIRA, launched a broad policy re-evaluation in 1981 that focused on trade competitiveness and Canadian-American relations.

The trade part of the review came under the direction of the Department of External Affairs. Bolstered by consultations with the provincial governments and business, the department's task force concluded that achieving a secure trade relationship with the United States was the paramount concern. The review emphasized Canada's export dependence on the American market, the relatively high percentage of the economy associated with trade, and the serious effects of the recession on the manufacturing sector.[80] Early in the review, Canadian diplomats in Washington sounded out American trade officials on the idea of bilateral sectoral free trade and received a favourable response. Sectoral free trade was put forward in the External Affairs report to Cabinet and was adopted in August 1983 amidst active discussion and debate, although the department, aware of free trade's highly divisive history, advocated simultaneous pursuit of freer multilateral trade under GATT.[81] Although the sectoral free trade initiative faltered on the inability of the Canadian and American governments to agree on which sectors to include, the idea retained the support of key officials in External Affairs, who presented it to the new Tory government of Brian Mulroney in fall 1984.[82]

The External Affairs background study surveyed efficiency and trade prospects in Canada's domestic economic sectors. The study's brief section on transport focused on seaport improvement, and the carrier rates considered were maritime ones.[83] In the discussion paper transport appeared in a section on domestic policy and trade. Again the reference was to bulk commodity exports, and the focus was maritime: developing coal and grain terminals and improving major seaports. Reference to all other modes was contained in this sentence: "The gradual deregulation of the transportation industries would further assist in industry competitiveness and productivity."[84] This incidental treatment of transport regulation, in a comprehensive summary of domestic economic sectors and international competitiveness, was repeated in the Macdonald Commission's studies and report.

The Royal Commission on the Economic Union and Development Prospects for Canada was convened by the Trudeau government in November 1982 out of the same apprehension that had prompted the Department of External Affairs study. The commission's interest in identifying "what policies should be installed to handle changing world competitiveness" led it to examine Canada's domestic and external aspects in detail. According to Richard Simeon, the commission's Research Coordinator, the commissioners, too, were shaken by the severity of the recession and had come to the view that "Canada now existed in a highly threatening, increasingly competitive world environment."[85] Amidst such turbulence and instability, Canada's "small, open economy" could no longer support nationalist economic policies.[86] Canadians, the commission's report asserted, "must resist pressures to introduce more protection into our economy; we must, instead, slowly reduce and eventually remove our protective trade barriers as we proceed by way of bilateral and multilateral negotiations with our trade partners."[87] In addition to turbulence, vulnerability, and recession, the commissioners were "mesmerized by the realization that 80% of Canada's exports were going to the U.S."[88] Having defined Canada's economic problems as based in trade and competitiveness, the commissioners saw "no credible alternative" to free trade negotiations with the United States.[89]

Domestically the commission recommended "an end to those patterns of government involvement in the economy which may generate disincentives, retard flexibility, and work against the desired allocation of resources."[90] Such thoughts did not lead to efficient transport and deregulation. Although the seventy-two volumes of background studies covered industrial, finance, and competition policy elaborately, only one touched on trucking in a two-page mention of interprovincial barriers.[91] The volume on regulation and federalism examined airlines and telecommunications.[92] The final report's brief reference to trucking noted that "the deregulation of U.S. trucking also affects the Canadian trucking industry" as well as that the Economic Council of Canada supported deregulation. No specific recommendation was made: "A gradual movement towards partial deregulation of trucking is sensible, keeping in mind the differences in the nature of the Canadian market."[93]

Why did two major federal initiatives on public policy and trade, undertaken at a time of great economic uncertainty, give such cursory attention to domestic and international transport's prime mode? Much of the reason may be federal. Delegating trucking jurisdiction to the provinces created a lacuna in Ottawa. Air, maritime, and rail modes of transportation were Transport Canada's responsibility, but trucks were not. Reflecting that separation, a detailed commentary on Transport Canada's mandates, programs, spending, and key policy issues for 1982 made no mention of motor carriage.[94] Nor did it appear in a policy survey by Arthur Kroeger, the deputy minister of Transport.[95] Although a federal body, the Interdepartmental Committee on Competition in Transportation had coordinated the review of trucking policy because the first ministers conference had ordered an evaluation of both federal and provincial regulation. When the time came to draft common terms of reference for the provincial ministers of transport, the task went not to the Ministry of Transport, but to the CCMTA – a federal-provincial coordinating body. Because the working paper was the only tabulation of provincial reform proposals at the time, opposition transport critic Donald Mazankowski requested a copy during a session of the Commons Standing Committee on Transport. Nick Mulder, administrator of the Canadian Surface Transportation Administration of Transport Canada, responded that the paper was a federal-provincial document and would have to be requested from the committee chair – an Ontario assistant deputy minister.[96] That same division was to show up later in reform legislation. Railways, airlines, and maritime carriers were dealt with directly by modifying federal legislation. The federal legislation for trucking, the Motor Vehicle Transport Act, delegated regulation to the provinces. In modifying the act, the federal government would set out new standards that the provinces themselves would have to apply.

An institutional interpretation would stress that transport deregulation and free trade had been activated by two different problems – stagflation in the 1970s and trade worries in the 1980s. As we saw in Chapter 3, the concept of policy-oriented learning regards external disturbance as providing the necessary catalyst for change. With deregulation and free trade, one catalyst preceded the other. The fact that deregulation was on the policy agenda at the same time as free trade was owed, at least partly, to its delayed uptake by politicians. Once there, the separate nature of regulatory reform and trade agreements could be expected to keep the two processes distinct. As will be seen, because regulatory reform was a matter of changing domestic legislation, discussion in the Commons Standing Committee on Transport excluded the free trade question, although full play was given to the legislation's international aspects. Free trade, for its part, was proceeding through bilateral negotiations. Transport and trade became directly linked when trucking, along with other industries, wound up on the table in the free trade negotiations; but in the end deregulation was accomplished not by a trade agreement but by domestic legislation. The effect of the legislation was to establish a de facto regime of free trade in trucking services. These domestic and international dimensions will appear as we proceed.

Exploiting Discretion

Major change seemed to be in the offing. On Transport Minister Axworthy's initiative, the CCMTA had worked during the summer and fall of 1984 to develop new regulatory guidelines. In February 1985, under the Conservative government's auspices, the transport ministers from all the provinces signed a memorandum of understanding in which they agreed to implement a reverse-onus entry standard on 1 January 1987. The provincial boards would presume entry of a carrier to be in the public interest unless shown otherwise.[97] Because it shifted the definition of public interest, reverse onus was a significant change. In the United States the reverse-onus provision in the Motor Carrier Act, 1980, enabled the ICC to abandon public convenience and necessity altogether and to open the gates to the interstate market. In addition to this fundamental change, the transport ministers agreed to adopt a uniform fitness test by 1 January 1986, to standardize application criteria, and to encourage carriers to expand interprovincially. That, too, had radical possibilities. When the ICC went beyond the Motor Carrier Act's intentions, it did so by abandoning reverse onus for a simple fitness test.

Despite the pro-market rubric and the implication of fundamental change, the provinces still had regulatory jurisdiction. More important, the Memorandum of Understanding allowed them to retain wide discretion in interpreting the public interest: "In adopting [the proposed reverse-onus entry test]," the CCMTA's report acknowledged, "the provinces would not abrogate their right to regulate in a manner consistent with provincial policy objectives." Detriment to the public interest included:

- adverse impact on the stability of the trucking industry
- undue reduction of competition
- market dominance by one or several carriers.

More important, the report allowed "adverse effect on the respondent" as grounds for protest, retaining the protective spirit of public convenience and necessity. Even more latitude was granted by allowing the boards to consider a new carrier's impact on "economic or social development." Finally, recognizing Cabinet discretion, the report allowed applications to be denied for "any public policy considerations declared by the government."[98]

These measures represented a CCMTA compromise between shippers, who favoured an end to all controls, and truckers, many of whom favoured increased enforcement of existing regulation.[99] In agreeing to the CCMTA's provisions, the CTA acted out of the same sense of realism that, five years earlier, had led the ATA to abandon its all-out opposition to regulatory reform in Congress and to support the reverse onus provision of the Motor Carrier Act, 1980. Both organizations realized that regulatory reform was politically inevitable and supported a measure that abandoned public convenience and necessity but stopped short of free entry. The ministers of transport endorsed what they believed to be a politically supportable compromise. There remained, however, the cushions of provincial jurisdiction and regulatory discretion. While keeping their governments in line with federal intentions on inter-provincial trucking, the ministers left the latitude, for provinces wishing to use it, to retain tight controls.[100] For their part, the CTA and the OTA began mounting an opposition campaign. They were backed by the CLC, whose president, having viewed American Teamster layoffs and contract concessions since 1980, condemned deregulation as anti-union.[101]

Although Canadian carriers supported the efforts to forestall deregulation, their pragmatic business judgement led some of them to begin positioning themselves for an opened market.[102] In 1985 Overland Express merged with Dominion Consolidated Truck Lines, creating the largest motor carrier in Ontario. The deal produced a larger fleet, a more extensive network, and greater traffic density, thus enabling Overland to increase its coverage of Ontario and to gain broader access to the United States. In another acquisition, Reimer Express of Winnipeg took over Inter-City Truck Lines of Ontario, giving Reimer enlarged operations in Ontario and creating one of Canada's largest carriers. In a move explicitly based on the experience of American and Australian carriers that had survived deregulation, Canadian Motorways of Winnipeg purchased Direct Transportation System of Toronto, giving Motorways access to six provinces and forty-nine states through terminals and agents in ninety-one traffic centres. According to the president of Motorways' parent company, Federal Industries: "In the U.S. and Australia, large, well-financed trucking companies have been the clear winners under a new regulatory environment. We are convinced this pattern will hold true in Canada."[103]

Tory Government and Market Discipline

The Progressive Conservative government of Brian Mulroney, elected in fall 1984, had firm convictions about markets and competition, and the new minister of transport, Donald Mazankowski, was a strong supporter of regulatory reform. As the Conservative economic development critic in 1982, he told a *Financial Post*-sponsored transportation conference: "It is clearly time for a regulatory housecleaning. Many regulations and indeed some agencies have outlived their usefulness and should be scrapped or at least scaled down."[104] Addressing a CTA conference several months before the election, Mazankowski added a stiff dose of market discipline: "Competition and the market system," he asserted, "is the reality of the '80s. The most important challenge is the necessity of being more competitive and aggressive – more market-oriented in exploiting our domestic and international opportunities." Looking afield, Mazankowski saw deregulation's effects in the United States along with a "growing impetus for free trade, the reduction of tariffs under GATT, new intermodal competition as a result of railway deregulation, and the increasing trend toward an integrated North American economy."[105] The outlook was plain: "Canadians will not further support the continuing interventionist, deficit ridden, highly regulated, crown corporation proliferated economy of the '70s, and so, like it or not, every industrial sector will be faced with that reality sooner or later."[106]

In 1985 the government released its transport White Paper *Freedom to Move*. The White Paper set out the government's basic premise, which was that market forces, not regulatory agencies, would be the "guiding hand behind company decisions on routes, fares and service."[107] The benefit would be lower-cost and more competitive transportation. Its surface freight transport provisions covered both railways and motor carriers. For the railways the White Paper proposed opening rail fares to price competition and allowing the railways to establish confidential rates with shippers. For captive shippers without a negotiated rate with their rail carrier, the paper proposed access to the nearest interchange point at rates that were under regulatory authority. These measures reflected Mazankowski's view that the NTA, 1967, had given the railways too much advantage over shippers. The railways' reaction was mixed. They had pressed for confidential rates in order to compete with American rail carriers, who had been granted that privilege under deregulation in 1980. The railways opposed the captive shipper provision, arguing that many of the important interchange points are at the American border and that Canadian rail traffic would be diverted through the United States.

Freedom to Move's provision for motor carriage was to endorse the 1985 Memorandum of Understanding. Responding to truckers' fears about American competition, the White Paper recommended negotiating a bilateral agreement in order to ensure an equitable balance, and it rejected regulatory solutions. This approach avoided both introducing new controls into a process designed to remove them and adding a federal layer to an interprovincial undertaking. It also reflected a perception that the issues of the Trucking War had not disappeared. The Brock-Gotlieb memorandum that ended that conflict was the basis of the White Paper's bilateral approach. The memorandum recognized that the two countries' regulatory practices could differ, and it established the Joint United States-Canada Consultative Committee to deal with serious imbalances. The memorandum also endorsed the principle of non-discriminatory treatment. On non-discrimination, the White Paper expressed concern that any regulatory controls on American entry might attract retaliation from the United States. On the Consultative Committee, the White Paper stated that the ideal measure would extend the committee into a long-term bilateral mechanism.[108] Truckers regarded the lack of regulatory measures to deal with American entry as "ominous."[109]

In the government's view, the Consultative Committee was working adequately. Appearing before the Commons Standing Committee on Transport in 1984, Nick Mulder, administrator of the Canadian Surface Transportation Administration of Transport Canada, reported that the Consultative Committee had been looking into complaints. One complaint was Ontario's denial of operating authorities to Roadway Express and Yellow Freight in early 1983, which was discussed in Chapter 4. Having investigated that issue and the broader transborder situation, Mulder reported that the Consultative Committee found that "the problems are not as acute as is sometimes alleged in the newspapers or in the Congress of the U.S."[110]

A broader question was whether the government was committed to protection or harmonization. In the same testimony Mulder noted that he had conferred with the Consultative Committee, along with the provincial governments and the representatives of the trucking industry, on ways of "harmonizing the decision-making process." Policy emulation can be read into this statement, if one takes harmonizing to mean adopting another state's forms and procedures. Mulder's meaning was more limited, although the implication was expansive. He personally favoured the integration of the two carrier industries, he told the Commons Committee, but only balanced integration. In the absence of regulation, ways of creating imbalances would be present on both sides. The purpose of getting the Consultative

Committee's views was to "sort out these things and make sure that their regulatory authorities on safety and fitness tests are consistent with some of the other regulatory decisions that we make."[111] The implication was that the ministry had a transborder perspective on competition. Integration was inevitable, Mulder asserted, "because we have the biggest trading partners on both sides."[112]

On 26 June 1986, Bill C-19, An Act Respecting Motor Vehicle Transportation by Extra-Provincial Undertakings, was introduced in the House of Commons. Its purpose was to amend the Motor Vehicle Transport Act to incorporate the Memorandum of Understanding. Appearing before the Commons Standing Committee on Transport, John Crosbie (who became transport minister when Mazankowski was appointed deputy prime Minister) spoke of efficiency and economic growth. [113] The committee conducted simultaneous hearings on C-19 (the trucking legislation) and on C-18 (the railways, maritime, and airline legislation). Appearing before the committee was a parade of shippers and carriers.

Although the CTA's main concern was competition from other motor carriers, it saw two intermodal implications. The first was that the railways, free to offer discounts, could injure truckers by capturing backhaul traffic to central Canada from the east and west. The second concern was confidential rail rates. The CTA accepted them as necessary in transborder traffic but advocated keeping them posted in Canada. In light of these concerns, one could argue that railway deregulation, along with illegal discounting in trucking, would force motor carrier deregulation through price competition regardless of the truckers' preferences and any legislative reform. If there were no reform, then route controls and public convenience and necessity would still be in effect, thus preventing a fully open market (unless regulators reinterpreted their entry standard). Informal discounting would be the agent of change.

De facto rate deregulation of trucking would be an appreciable prospect if railway and truck transport were relatively undifferentiated products. By the mid-1980s, however, commodity and service characteristics had established distinct transport sectors. The railways' natural niche had become the long-distance movement of bulk commodities. Those commodities' low unit-values and large-volume shipments make rail the most efficient mode of transport. Trucks, in contrast, are relatively small cargo containers suited to high unit-value goods. The railways' disadvantage with high unit-value goods was that they could not offer the same rapid service or exact deliveries and could not move small volumes as conveniently as could trucks.

Many high unit-value goods must travel quickly. When these goods consist of components moving between production points or finished goods moving to meet retail demand, speed and punctuality can be decisive. We will see why this is so in Chapter 6, where I discuss just-in-time and flow-through logistics. One reason these schemes were adopted in the 1980s and 1990s was the level of trucking service that had become available. Trucking's advantages were not new. As we saw in Chapter 2, trucks began diverting express and small-consignment traffic from the railways in the 1930s, and the resulting injury to the latter was one of the principal reasons that the Canadian and American governments imposed regulation. In the 1980s the trend began to equalize in favour of the railways, when they began offering expedited container and trailer service (although, even now, their on-time performance and ability to custom-tailor transportation lags behind that of trucks).

The views of shippers are an important consideration. If they regard the two modes of transport as non- or semi-substitutable, then the competitive prospects would be less than the would be if they saw them as highly substitutable. An index of their views appeared in the Commons Committee hearings. The railways, arguing against the captive shipper provision, maintained that they have no captive shippers. The CITL responded that 75 percent of their members are captive to one of the two railways. The difference was transport substitutability. The railways claimed that the widespread availability of truck service rendered the captive shipper provision of the legislation unnecessary. The CITL saw things differently. Although its members may be close to highways, "for many captive shippers, the type of goods – particularly bulk resource commodities – are unsuited to truck transportation."[114] Because lower rail rates would shape shippers' overall price expectations, they would be part of more general pressures to reduce truck rates but not directly negotiable ones. Those would come from other truckers themselves. It was on that prospect that the CTA, the Teamsters, and the provincial associations focused their prime attention.

In making their case to the Commons Transport Committee, they cited American experience. The Canadian Teamsters emphasized layoffs, deteriorated working conditions, and cash-strapped carriers cutting corners on safety. As the two industries were highly similar, they argued, the same consequences would appear in Canada.[115] The Ontario Trucking Association seconded these views and adduced the experience of California.[116] That state had deregulated intrastate trucking in 1980, but by 1986 its public utilities commission had become so concerned about rate cutting and truck safety that it re-introduced partial rate regulation. By establishing a zone of rate flexibility, the commission hoped to allow rate negotiations while maintaining a price floor adequate to sustain safe operations. Transport committee member Les Benjamin (NDP, Regina West) cited California's experience, and deregulation's effects on American trucking in general, as highly relevant.[117] The California example was used in debate in the House of Commons by an Opposition speaker, who saw a "very timely lesson for Canada" and grounds to reject the bill.[118]

Not all of the trucking industry's transborder comparisons were negative. Speaking to the *Financial Post* transport conference in 1982, the president of bulk commodity hauler Trimac Ltd. noted that its subsidiary, based in Louisville, Kentucky, had increased its capacity by 50 percent under the first two years of American deregulation.[119]

Price comparisons figured in the shippers' case, and there was some dramatic evidence. A 1984 Ontario Ministry of Transportation and Communications study, for example, showed that carrier rates from Toronto to Atlanta (1,617 kilometres) could exceed the rates from Buffalo to Atlanta (1,451 kilometres) by more than 65 percent.[120] Overall, transborder truck rates were 30 percent to 60 percent higher than American domestic rates for comparable distances, and, reportedly, the transborder market had the highest profit margins.[121] Aggregate effects in the United States were equally striking. In the 1970s American transportation costs had averaged 8.1 percent of GDP, and by 1989 they were 6.3 percent. Total logistics costs in the United States in the 1970s were 13.7 percent of GDP, and by 1987 they were 11.1 percent. Private trucks, with their new freedom to haul cargoes for hire, had reduced empty miles by two-thirds.[122] The direction of these trends was apparent by the early 1980s.[123]

At the business level, Canadian shippers were hearing of carriers offering American shippers 20 percent and 30 percent discounts as openers in price negotiations, and American carriers serving Canada were beginning to offer those prices in transborder service.[124] A 1983 advertisement from St. Johnsbury Trucking, a Massachusetts-based regional LTL carrier, promised discounts of up to 30 percent between the U.S. Northeast and Quebec and Ontario. Addressing the Commons Transport Committee, the CMA's National Transportation Committee chair stated: "Our contacts with U.S. manufacturers indicate that they have benefited enormously from deregulation. Canadian shippers, on the other hand, are at a disadvantage."[125] With the bulk of Canada's exports competing in the American market, and with transportation accounting, on average, for between 20 percent and 35 percent of the total costs of production – the biggest cost factors in manufacturing after wages and materials – the American shippers' gains from deregulation represented net advantages in contending for market share.[126]

Strongly in favour of the legislation, the CMA and the CITL could "see the day when transportation [would] be less the discrete industry sector it is today and more an organic component of a North American product-and-service network." Also strongly favouring deregulation was the Coalition of Concerned Shippers, a lobbying group of fourteen industry associations. Like the CMA and the CITL, their interest was cheaper shipping costs and lower prices for their goods, and they advocated their point strongly before the Commons Transport Committee.[127] Arguing that production should drive transport and not vice versa, shippers looked forward to a blurring of boundaries between the two sectors.[128] That, indeed, has been one result of deregulation, as Chapter 6 will show.

In its report to Parliament, the committee agreed with the White Paper that American carriers could have a significant impact on a deregulated Canadian industry, and it advocated the White Paper's recommendation that the government negotiate an agreement to ensure a "fair and equitable balance of trade in transborder trucking services."[129] Between regulatory reform and free trade the committee's proceedings maintained a clear distinction, and on one occasion the chair, Patrick Nowlan (PC, Annapolis Valley-Hants), ruled out of order questions and comments from NDP transport critic Les Benjamin concerning the implications of free trade. That, Nowlan insisted, was beyond the focus of the committee.[130] For its part the government believed that transborder traffic would adjust itself through competition. How that actually occurred will be seen in Chapter 6.

Transborder competition was addressed in testimony from the Department of Consumer and Corporate Affairs' acting director of the Regulated Sector Branch. Citing a study conducted for the department by University of British Columbia transport economist Garland Chow, the official reported that 80 percent of transborder traffic is short-haul service. He acknowledged that large American carriers had an advantage in long-haul service, but maintained that transborder trucking "is in a particular market niche where the Americans have no competitive advantage." Another finding was that Canadian shippers and receivers controlled over 60 percent of transborder traffic. "In other words, it was the Canadians who were deciding what carriers they would choose and not the American shippers."[131]

The draft trucking legislation, however, departed significantly from the Memorandum of Understanding, which had agreed to a reverse-onus standard but had contained no further easing of entry controls. Bill C-19, however, made reverse onus a transitional measure to be supplanted by a fitness test on 1 January 1991. At that date, entry standards in Canada would be virtually the same as those in the United States. Recognizing the provinces' latitude not to enact the new regulatory measures, the standing committee recommended as a fallback that the federal government reclaim its power to regulate interprovincial trucking and write a simple fitness test into the new NTA. If that were done, then Canadian interprovincial regulation would parallel American interstate regulation in both jurisdiction and entry standards.

The draft legislation dropped an important qualification. The Memorandum of Understanding had specified that, under reverse onus, an application could be opposed on the grounds that granting the operating authority would be potentially detrimental to the public interest. The new legislation deleted the word "potentially," thus considerably narrowing the grounds for protest. The legislation specified no special criteria for dealing with applications from American carriers and left it to the provincial boards' discretion to determine which to grant and which to deny. Clearly referring to the Trucking War, however, the new act did give the federal minister of transport the power to resolve cases of unfair or restrictive treatment of Canadian carriers by foreign jurisdictions through consultation and, failing that, through empowering provincial boards to suspend the authorities of foreign carriers. On the kinds of foreign entry issues most likely to arise in normal applications, however, the new act gave Canadian carriers no specific protections. That matter was very much a concern at the provincial level.

Liberal Victory, Failed Consensus

In Ontario the Conservative provincial government appeared to be moving quietly towards reform. After watching three years of deliberations about the PCV Act and hearing the same arguments against deregulation, the government was ready to legislate. At its fall 1984 convention the OTA passed a unanimous resolution calling on the government to postpone introducing its new trucking legislation, slated for 14 December 1984. If it did not, the resolution declared, "the OTA will have no recourse but to oppose the bill, when it had genuinely wanted to support a reregulatory trucking bill."[132] The bill was not radical. Its core provision was a market test, representing an effort to reconcile the two sides.

The OTA's hopes for even more limited changes appeared in its talking of "reregulation" rather than "deregulation." After all the deliberations in the PCV Act review, the OTA still wanted to preserve, not eliminate, controls. That provided further evidence that the review's effort at conciliatory policy making had not worked. If anything, the two sides were further apart. That showed clearly a year after the PCV report was issued, when the Ontario government convened a working group of carriers and manufacturers in order to reconcile their differences and to advise the government on drafting the new legislation. On the basic issues there was sharp division: the market test, abandoning rate filing and allowing secret carrier contracts with shippers, and the amount of discretion the OHTB should have to deny applications. The OTA, calculating that consultation would probably never resolve those questions, argued that the government should wait on introducing the legislation until there was agreement. The CMA argued that the government should simply proceed with its intentions.[133]

The Conservative government's legislation died with the provincial election in 1985. The new Ontario Liberal government, ruling with the support of the NDP, was conciliatory and cautious about deregulation and outspokenly hostile to free trade and unprotected competition with American firms. If deregulation could be blocked in Ontario, the OTA believed, then deregulation might be thwarted across the country, since other provinces would be reluctant to lower their barriers until they were lowered in Canadian trucking's heartland.[134] The new government assured the OTA that it would not unquestioningly follow the previous government's initiatives but would make its own determinations and draft its own policies. It was in no hurry.

The Feds Move

The draft Motor Vehicle Transport Act met with dismay. John Plohman, Manitoba minister of highways and transportation, accused Mazankowski of breaching the Memorandum of Understanding by setting a time limit on the reverse-onus test and, worse, by specifying a fitness test to replace it. That, he objected, had never been agreed to.[135] The memorandum had merely stated that a fitness-only test would be studied, and it made no mention of terminating reverse onus. Moreover, he charged, the federal government had acted against the spirit of the memorandum by changing the grounds for protesting an application from "potentially detrimental" to the public interest to "detrimental," making it "even more likely that reverse onus will be tantamount to immediate, complete deregulation." To the same effect, charged Plohman, the bill broadened the public interest criterion by specifying the "economic or social development *of Canada*," implying that narrower, province-based interpretations of the public interest in denying an application would be against the spirit of the legislation.[136]

The CTA was equally strident. Mazankowski, the CTA charged, had promised regulatory reforms when he got the provincial ministers to agree to the Memorandum of Understanding, but, instead, the actual legislation amounted to "almost total deregulation." Canadian carriers "had been sold down the river." The CTA also believed that the terms of protest had been "loaded almost 100% in favor of the applicant, leaving the opponent with little or any hope of convincing a transport board that granting authority to the applicant would be prejudicial to a substantial number of shippers, carriers and/or the public interest."[137]

While some governments were more dissatisfied with the new legislation than were others, all opposed the loss of regulatory discretion contained in the act's restrictive wording of the public interest criteria. The provincial governments all expressed concern that limiting the grounds for protesting applications would make it too easy for American carriers to obtain authorities. In making no mention of special regulatory treatment of American applicants, the new law would open the market to competition that Canadian carriers, alleged to have higher taxes and operating costs, would be unable to match.[138] There was no indication in the legislation that the federal government would change those disadvantages. The only solution, in the view of the Manitoba minister of highways and transportation, was for Ottawa to seek a bilateral agreement with the United States for an "even balance of trade in trucking services."

Unbinding the Public Interest

All the provincial governments were under intense lobbying pressure from Canadian motor carriers and provincial trucking associations to get the draft bill modified. The Manitoba and Quebec highway ministers, together with the CTA and the provincial associations, prevailed on John Crosbie to eliminate a section of the draft bill that specified a uniform and nationwide definition of public interest that the provincial boards would have to apply in administering the reverse-onus test. The crucial determination of when an application is not in the public interest was now left to the boards' discretion. The only public interest language remaining in the act was "likely to be detrimental."[139] The provinces were also successful in having the date for the transition from reverse onus to fitness-only pushed forward to 1993.

Provincial officials were quick to cheer this victory. Donald Norquay, chair of the Manitoba Motor Transport Board, stated that each of the provincial boards, in ruling on applications under the new legislation, would now have latitude to decide "what truly is in the public interest." Not all interested parties were pleased. Shippers were very unhappy, claiming that the government had gone back on its undertakings to them and had not consulted the Commons Standing Committee on Transport, where they were well represented. Particularly displeased was the CITL. As we saw earlier, the CITL had initially opposed deregulation and free entry for American carriers but became strongly pro-deregulation after polling its members in 1984.[140]

The new provincial latitude horrified the CTA. It had lobbied hard to get the provinces more leeway to respond to the needs of local truckers, but it found the new legislation "anathema." The CTA claimed that it had sought uniform entry rules for years but that it now feared that the provinces' discretion under the new act would lead to an interpretive patchwork across the country. That would leave Canadian carriers with the worst of both deregulation and federalism: increased competition and Balkanized regulation.[141] Disparities were already appearing. Manitoba, Alberta, New Brunswick, and Nova Scotia were ready in early 1985 with revised entry standards but delayed implementing them because they did not want to extend unilateral advantages to the holdout provinces of British Columbia, Saskatchewan, Ontario, and Quebec.[142] The Motor Vehicle Transport Act (MVTA), 1987, became law on 19 August, after relatively brief debate in Parliament.

Plural Progress

Provincial implementation was disconnected. New Brunswick passed legislation adopting reverse onus in 1985 but did not proclaim it into law. Saskatchewan, notwithstanding its minister of highways and transportation's statement that "deregulation of the highway transportation industry has no place in Canada," adopted reverse onus administratively in April 1986 – over a year in advance of the federal legislation. Moving in a different direction, Manitoba took advantage of regulatory latitude and soon after the MVTA's passage in 1987 adopted a "shared onus" entry standard. Under shared onus, an applicant, in order to counter evidence by protesting carriers that granting operating authority would produce layoffs and distress, would need to show offsetting public benefits.[143] Since the carriers whose entry might cause such disruption would most likely be large, efficient, and American, the administrative intention was protective.

Alberta, in contrast, strongly opposed the MVTA's reverse-onus provision because the provincial government wanted to move immediately to a simple fitness test and complete deregulation. The provincial board reluctantly agreed to hold hearings on protested applications, thereby complying with the conditions of reverse onus, but it made clear its preference for free entry. Looking to the other provinces, however, the board was apprehensive about adopting a policy of hospitality in Alberta while restrictions remained in place elsewhere. That was the same dilemma facing the ICC when Canadian carriers began applying in 1980, and Alberta adopted the ATA's preferred solution of reciprocal treatment. In British Columbia matters were far less advanced. By summer 1987, on the eve of passage of the federal MVTA, the provincial government had still not decided what issues to include in its regulatory review and was cautiously conferring with the British Columbia Motor Transport Association. Nova Scotia had still taken no action.

Ontario's moves were the crucial ones, and the Liberal government's attitude was leisurely. Putting political distance between his government and its Conservative predecessor in Ontario and the national Conservative government in Ottawa, in 1985 and 1986 the Ontario transport minister consulted with shippers and carriers in the United States on their experiences with deregulation and called for more studies in Canada. The Ontario government was still committed to a market test, which would contradict the federal legislation's reverse-onus provisions. During 1986 and 1987 the minister gradually came to support a reverse-onus entry standard, but he pressured the federal government to proceed slowly with deregulation. As the MVTA neared passage in the federal Parliament, Ontario joined with Manitoba, British Columbia, and Quebec in urgently seeking delay. The OTA caused more delay by launching a provincial court case to determine whether it is the minister of transportation and communications or the

Ontario Highway Transport Board that has the final authority to award international and interprovincial operating authorities under the MVTA.

With Ontario occupying the pivotal position in Canadian motor carrier regulation, these postponements meant that the federal government faced the choice of taking up its jurisdiction over trucking by invoking the dormant part of the NTA or of using negotiation and persuasion. It chose the latter. With the provinces firmly attached to their regulatory powers, the federal government – as it did when it faced the same question following the *Winner* decision in 1954 – feared that its regulatory authority would lead to a protracted power struggle with the provinces and to chaos in road transport. Its preference, unless deregulation stalled completely, was persuasion. Two concurrent developments leavened these considerations: free trade negotiations and concerns over motor carrier entry policy within the forty-nine continental American states.

Trade and Trucks

Canadian truckers opposed free trade because an agreement including trucking services would eliminate any protective latitude remaining under reverse onus. The trade principle of right of establishment would remove barriers to American carriers setting up business in Canada, and the principle of national treatment would bar any special regulatory provisions. The ATA favoured inclusion of trucking services in the agreement. One reason for this was equity: over 1,000 Canadian carriers had received ICC operating authorities since 1980. Although the ATA knew that the Canadian federal government was pursuing deregulation, it believed that a trade in trucking services provision would make it possible to challenge any remaining restrictive practices under trade law.[144]

Transportation is an important trade-in-services area. The 1985 Shamrock Summit between Prime Minister Mulroney and President Reagan produced a work plan for transportation. The plan focused on such matters as packaging, hazardous materials, and transborder movement of railway cars. In the broader context of free trade negotiations, however, both American and Canadian trade experts expected that the United States, in the name of equity and reciprocity, would seek an end to Canadian regulatory barriers on trucking.[145] The United States had abandoned that objective in the Trucking War because Canada had insisted that the issue was regulatory and would not be pressured into changing the way it managed its transportation. It is entirely appropriate, however, to seek reciprocity and open access in free trade negotiations.

Free entry into the American market had produced a very favourable balance for Canadian carriers. According to Statistics Canada, fully 94 percent of the carriers involved in international trucking were Canadian-owned, and Ontario-based carriers alone earned 60 percent of the $1.1 billion revenues generated.[146] A subsequent study by Trimac Consulting Services found a similar earnings percentage and showed that Ontario carriers accounted for as much as 80 percent of the truck trips across the Canadian-American border.[147] More systematic studies were conducted in 1991, and their results will be seen in Chapter 6.

The draft free trade agreement included transportation services. Anticipating Canadian deregulation, the draft agreement stipulated that both American and Canadian carriers must benefit equally from regulatory liberalization in either country. The provision would be redundant under the MVTA's reverse-onus provision, which discouraged provinces from excluding applicants. Its use would be in discretionary rulings against American applicants, making it an anti-discrimination measure. If the boards did abide by the spirit of the MVTA in international carriage, then the situation could be assumed to be in accordance with free trade in services – a de facto free trade regime based in regulation.

A feature of Canadian federalism allowed still one way for protective discretion to remain in place. The Canadian Constitution lacks a supremacy clause that would require the provinces to comply with a trade agreement negotiated by the federal government. Furthermore, Canadian constitutional law does not hold that international agreements, such as the one covering bilateral trade with the United States, are part of Canadian municipal law. There is also the fact that international conventions, which signatory governments are obliged to implement in their domestic laws, require provincial implementation on matters that come under provincial jurisdiction. With the provinces having jurisdiction over trucking, there was no built-in legal provision for enforcing their compliance with a free trade agreement.[149] Areas under provincial jurisdiction would thus require the provinces to pass implementing legislation and that, in turn, would depend on the federal government's ability to persuade them to do so.[149] Free entry of American motor carriers under a services agreement would not be automatic.[150]

These points suddenly became moot. At the very end of the free trade negotiations, pressures from American maritime interests, who feared that Canadian vessels would haul goods between ports in the United States, led to transportation being dropped from the final version of the free trade agreement. That disappointed the Canadian side, which had hoped to gain access to the American transportation market, although, in exchange, Canada was able to exempt its cultural industries, whose future was a point of fierce resistance among free trade opponents.[151] That outcome left transborder trucking where it had always been – in the sphere of regulation.

Trucking was included in the North American Free Trade Agreement, but its main provision was to open the Mexican trucking market. Canada concluded a separate trucking agreement with Mexico in 1994, but the United

States, under presidential order, has continued to restrict entry of Mexican trucks until safety practices are brought into harmony. The result has caused interline congestion at the Mexican border, and by 1999 both Mexican and American carriers had become impatient with the delays and complication.

Federalism Reversed

The federal structure of regulation in both countries allowed non-reciprocal treatment of carriers *within* the provinces and states because both retained jurisdiction over trucking within their borders. Here the United States was in the more restrictive position, and the incentives of the Canadian and American trucking associations were reversed. Before 1980 the United States had uniform standards for both inter- and intrastate trucking. Most state governments had supported the Motor Carrier Act, 1935, and those that did not use public convenience and necessity to control entry began doing so, producing a symmetrical set of practices at both levels of government. New Jersey was the only state never to enforce entry controls. The two levels of regulation produced two levels of jurisdiction. ICC operating authorities entitled carriers to carry goods interstate, but permission to haul between points within individual states had to be obtained from the state regulatory commissions. After the Motor Carrier Act, 1980, possessing broad new ICC authorities still meant being barred from intrastate markets. Some states were more generous than others, but forty-three had entry controls at the time of the free trade negotiations.

Only the states of Alaska, Arizona, Florida, Indiana, Vermont, and Wisconsin had deregulated their intrastate carriers by then, and California, having done so in 1980, reintroduced rate regulation in 1986. Maryland, Ohio, and Texas subsequently reformed trucking regulation. Maryland moved to complete deregulation. In Ohio the changes were limited to contract carriers, and in Texas they were limited to liberalizing the scope of statewide grants of operating authority. As we saw in Chapter 3, there was desultory interest in the Reagan and Bush administrations in completing deregulation at the state level, and in 1995 that was achieved under the Clinton administration. At the time of the free trade negotiations in 1987, however, state controls were an issue.

The ATA, having accepted deregulation in interstate motor carriage, opposed any advance into state jurisdictions and would not give unqualified support to the draft free trade agreement. Canadian carriers, in contrast, welcomed state-level deregulation. For them, moving into intrastate service was a means of balancing cargo patterns and equipment utilization and gaining traffic density. Large states such as California, as was demonstrated by the growth of profitable regional carriers, were attractive markets in their own right. With only the states of North Dakota, Washington, and Oklahoma showing any interest in deregulating their carriers, however, the prospect for widespread intrastate access was not promising. Implementing reverse onus in Canada, however, would leave provincial markets open to Americans without securing equal access to American states. For Canadian carriers this was reciprocity reversed.

The ATA was also uneasy. Knowing the serious possibility of intraprovincial deregulation in Canada, and knowing the Reagan administration's interest in rolling back state jurisdiction, the ATA feared that American trade negotiators might strike a bargain with Canada: American access to Canadian provinces would be exchanged for Canadian access to American states. Trade negotiations were thus a means of eliminating remaining state regulation and, at the same time, achieving a balanced arrangement with Canada. The ATA warned the Senate Finance Committee of this possibility in a presentation on 17 August 1987. When transportation was dropped from the final draft of the Free Trade Agreement, trucking was taken out of the reach of trade rules, and the issue of access to American states was left unchanged.

Reciprocity and Resistance

With the federal Conservatives proceeding after the 1988 election towards implementation of the Free Trade Agreement, with the Motor Vehicle Transport Act passed the previous year, and with provincial governments working their way towards legislation, intrastate entry became the OTA's last-stand issue for delaying deregulation. The Ontario Liberal government, after years of hearings, consultations, and being lobbied, hoped to finally have the Truck Transportation Act in place by summer 1988. The legislation contained a reverse-onus test as its entry standard, with public interest as the grounds for protest of new applications. The OTA conceded that its members had come to accept reverse onus for other Canadian applicants, but it insisted that the act contain a reciprocity clause for American applicants. Such a clause would grant entry under reverse onus to American carriers domiciled in states granting easy entry to Ontario carriers but would retain public convenience and necessity for carriers from restrictive states. The ATA, having advocated reciprocity in the Trucking War, found the OTA's position reasonable.[152]

The OTA, however, hoped that demanding reciprocity would delay and complicate the Ontario government's legislation. Following the feverish electoral politics over free trade, Canadian public opinion was kept aroused by ongoing debate and by the agreement's pending approval in Parliament. Since one of the strongest arguments against free trade was that American business and government would take advantage of Canada, any depictions of Canadian firms suffering unequal treatment would attract attention and provide a favourable political context. As the provincial government's Resources Development Committee was holding hearings on the Truck Transportation Act during the summer of 1988, the OTA, using the issue of reciprocity, directed one of the most massive lobbying campaigns in its history. This campaign was directed towards the leaders and members of the three provincial parties, the news media, and even on mayors and municipal governments. Stressing the Ontario Liberal government's continuing opposition to the Free Trade Agreement, and holding that the province's trucking legislation would usher in free trade in trucking services, the OTA charged that the government was abandoning its principles.

Although Ontario's Office of the Attorney General advised that a reciprocity clause would be unconstitutional, the OTA's gambit again succeeded in stalling progress on the bill, which the minister had hoped to have in force by the end of summer 1988. There was a subsequent delay over the wording of public interest. Instead of agreeing with the MVTA that the public interest test should demonstrate that an application would "likely to be detrimental to the public interest," the minister specified that it should demonstrate that an application would be "significantly detrimental to the public interest." The OTA challenged this as going beyond the intent of the MVTA.

Entry hearings were still the order of business at the highway board, and the OTA was opposing nearly all applications for interprovincial authority. That added administrative congestion to legislative delay. Having decided to proceed, the minister was becoming increasingly frustrated, and, as the delays extended into 1988, he decided to make blanket use of his discretionary power. His office began issuing public commercial vehicle licences on its own in order to circumvent a hobbled highway board. Feeling the spirit of deregulation, the minister's office, by October 1988, had awarded 512 new PCV licenses and had rejected only ten. The OTA believed that between one-fifth and one-third of those had gone to American carriers. Questioning the boundary between elected government and regulatory boards, the OTA filed suit in the Supreme Court of Ontario challenging the minister's right, under the MVTA, to issue operating authorities.

The OTA was upheld. On 21 October 1988 the court ruled in a two-to-one decision that only the OHTB has the right to issue licences. That decision prevented the minister from administering new authorities and returned responsibility to a clogged OHTB. The decision, the OTA hoped, would overturn the licences issued by the minister and set back deregulation. In retaliation, officials in the minister's office said that the ruling brought into question *all* interprovincial licences issued since 1954 because all authorities bore an Ontario transportation minister's signature. If that were true, then carriers holding those authorities would have to park their trucks.

That possibility did not stop deregulation, but it temporarily confounded the OTA.[153]

Non-Reciprocity, Neighbourly Wrath

Ontario's delays raised reciprocity with other provinces. The Quebec government, after several years of hesitation, enacted its legislation in early 1988, bringing the province into compliance with the MVTA. This dismayed the Quebec Trucking Association (QTA). Its members would now have to accommodate new competitors from Ontario, who still enjoyed a protected home market. Ontario also drew displeasure because its PCV review, being the most elaborate of the provincial efforts, was responsible for advancing reform – an ironic accusation in light of Ontario's five years of foot-dragging. "With Ontario in the forefront," stated a senior member of the QTA, "the provinces agreed to deregulate the trucking industry and convinced us to go along with it. So our government deregulated our transport industry, but the others (with the exception of Alberta and Saskatchewan) haven't done so. This leaves us with the impression that we've been stabbed in the back, especially by Ontario."[154]

The QTA's members urged the Quebec transport minister to delay proclaiming Quebec's new law until Ontario adopted the same entry practices. The Quebec transport minister responded to the situation by taking up the US Congress's solution in the Trucking War six years earlier – a moratorium on issuing Quebec authorities to Ontario carriers until Quebec carriers could enter Ontario on the same terms. The minister also promised the QTA to ask federal transport minister Benoit Bouchard to convene a federal tribunal to take over the regulation of interprovincial trucking and to enforce a uniform set of national rules. The governments of Alberta and Saskatchewan also complained to the federal minister about their carriers' restricted access to Ontario.

Two organizations at opposite sides of deregulation had become concerned enough to seek federal remedy. The CITL saw the irregular expanse of provincial regulation as harmful to shippers. It took up provincial conformity with the MVTA at its 1988 annual convention in Calgary and voted to request the federal government to monitor the provinces' administration of entry applications for compliance with federal policy.[155] On the opposite side was the CTA, which was alarmed that uncoordinated reform was dangerously fragmenting the Canadian market. At an executive meeting in Ottawa in June 1988, the CTA passed a resolution requesting the federal government to establish uniform procedures to ensure consistent provincial implementation. Left on their own, said one CTA member, the provinces "will take protectionist attitudes and may discriminate against some applications." Matters had combined badly for the CTA. Protection at the international boundary was failing, and protection within it was uneven. As American competition was impending, Canadian carriers could not be sure of expanding within their own country.

None of these appeals produced results. The federal government held that the current situation was preferable to the conflict and confusion that would result from reclaiming its regulatory powers from the provinces. The situation dragged on. A year later, in July 1989, the Quebec transport minister objected bitterly to the OTA that Quebec carriers were still having difficulty obtaining Ontario authorities, even though the province's new Truck Transportation Act had been in place since that January.

If Ontario was loitering its way towards deregulation, then Manitoba was openly defiant. A chief objection was the MVTA's broad wording concerning public interest. It had been possible to make determinations of public convenience and necessity, said Manitoba Motor Transport Board director of policy Adam Hrabinski, when one could assume that unrestrained competition was not in the public interest. "It is an entirely different matter," he said, "for a transport board to weigh public economic and social development goals against the promotion of international commerce as set out in the Memorandum of Understanding. The Political judgements should be made by parliament, legislatures and cabinets, not in provincial transport board hearing rooms."[156]

At issue was the proper radius of regulatory authority and the prospect that controversial decisions could reach beyond unhappy carriers. Trade in services was also a consideration. Manitoba was a net exporter of trucking services, both to other parts of Canada and to the United States, and it was home to several of Canada's largest carriers. Its trucking regulation had also been Canada's most strict and comprehensive.

Although regulators may have been uncomfortable with interpreting the MVTA's new social and economic goals, reverse onus gave them leeway to protect local carriers. "We can do what we want," stated Donald Norquay, chair of the Manitoba Motor Transport Board in 1988, "deregulate or strictly regulate, depending on our views as to what likelihood and severity of adverse effect will be 'likely detrimental to the public interest.'"[157] In taking that position, Manitoba joined Ontario in being one of the last holdout provinces. In another echo from the Trucking War, in 1989 Norquay charged that other provinces, retaliating against his board's strict procedures, were discriminating against Manitoba carriers applying for authorities in their jurisdictions.

The situation in other provinces was less discordant but still contentious. In British Columbia, in 1988 the Motor Carrier Commission did begin granting interprovincial authorities under the terms of the MVTA, but the minister of transport remained adamantly against deregulating intraprovincial transport. Nova Scotia's deregulatory legislation died in 1988 when the provincial legislature adjourned for the summer. Even Saskatchewan, which in practice had become one of the generous jurisdictions, still required evidence of shipper support from carrier applicants – a holdover from the days of public convenience and necessity.

Fatigue and Open Roads

Ontario's Truck Transportation Act was passed on 15 January 1989, and the OTA conceded political defeat. By early 1990 all major American carriers who had sought Ontario authorities now possessed them and began appearing quickly on Ontario's highways. Lowering the barriers in the hub of transborder traffic was the final act of regulatory withdrawal. Across the country, regulatory practices remained different in their particulars, although the overall effect was to open provincial motor carrier markets. Reporting to Parliament in 1992 on the implementation of the Motor Vehicle Transport Act, 1987, Transport Canada found:

- British Columbia was granting most applications but favoured retaining reverse-onus proceedings until 1995 to protect niche markets.
- Alberta favoured unrestricted entry.
- Saskatchewan was continuing to deny applications that would potentially harm intraprovincial carrier operations.
- Manitoba, having earlier used its interpretations of the public interest to restrict entry, by 1992 was discouraging only large LTL applications.
- Ontario and Quebec had moved to a fitness-only standard.
- New Brunswick and Nova Scotia had reluctantly accepted reverse-onus, but New Brunswick still retained "vestiges of heavily regulated licensing."

Altogether, the report concluded that Canada was ready to move from the reverse-onus phase of implementation to a fitness-only standard.[158]

Since then, market-based symmetry has allowed free movement in both directions, making carriers and shippers directly interactive in both domestic and transborder commerce. Carriers from both sides have continued getting Canadian and American operating authorities, reflecting the rising volume of trade and the appeal of expanded and unified operations. The operational side of this transformation will be discussed in Chapter 6.

Conclusion

In any trade-based jurisdiction, it is always important to look at the relative influence of domestic and international factors on major policy changes. As we have just seen, domestically, a set of federally conducted studies showed a strong case for efficiency; internationally, price comparisons showed higher transport costs. What effect should be ascribed to each?

Traditionally, such questions are answered by applying the test for policy harmonization. Harmonization is a coordinated effort between governments to eliminate differences in particular policy areas in the interest of facilitating important transactions. In Colin Bennett's view, harmonization is most easily achieved when states work within an international regime (i.e., a formal or informal arrangement among states to pool expertise, design policy, and coordinate implementation within specified policy areas). Intergovernmental organizations, which may be part of such regimes, can serve as sites where expertise is pooled, common objectives established, and collective actions coordinated. Because regimes arise from recognized areas of interdependence, seek mutual action, and have visible results, their work provides the clearest examples of harmonization.[159]

The United States and Canada deregulated through domestic legislation, with no bilateral coordination. Canada, in fact, specifically rejected coordination in the Trucking War. Without bilateral activity, harmonization becomes more difficult to prove. Adopting similar policies is evidence neither of imitation nor of irresistible transnational forces. Policies that closely resemble each other may have important domestic sources and motivations. "The lesson for policy analysts," in Bennett's words, "is to try to reject the influence of domestic factors before concluding that one of the transnational forces must be responsible."[160]

We saw a set of domestic antecedents. Postwar controversy over rail rates led to their partial deregulation in the NTA, 1967. Economic concerns brought reform to the political agenda of the 1970s. Regulatory waste was the focus of the First Ministers Conference in 1978. The same concern framed the Economic Council of Canada's and the Interdepartmental Committee's research and recommendations. The basis of the key studies was domestic comparisons. Economic efficiency framed Axworthy's reform advocacy as well as that of the Mulroney government. On more limited and pragmatic grounds, the provinces were conducting regulatory reviews on their own. An important part of the politics of deregulation was inducing the provinces to adopt the federal government's more comprehensive standards.

The international influence was trade. Although domestic recession prompted the Department of External Affairs review and the Macdonald Royal Commission, both defined international competitiveness as the central concern. The two exercises ranged widely over economic and industrial policy, but neither joined competitiveness to road transport costs and regulation. Shippers did make that connection. Their case was framed under the rubrics of economic efficiency and international competitiveness, but their practical point was lower transport costs in the United States. In the same businesslike spirit, the federal government's interest in international trucking showed in its support of the expansion of Canadian carriers into the American market, which the inclusion of transport services in the Canada-US Free Trade Agreement would have facilitated.

A case could be made that either the domestic or international factors would have been enough to prompt change. On the domestic side, the First Ministers Conference and subsequent empirical research had identified regulation as a burden on the economy. Axworthy sponsored trucking deregulation in the name of efficiency and growth, and his successor, Mazankowski, was also keen to act. Even though neither of the two federal trade studies gave more than cursory attention to road transport, they did put economic and industrial competitiveness front and centre. Lower transport costs could easily fit within this framework. The continuous element, however, was market efficiency, not trade. Initially opposed to free trade, the Mulroney government continued and expanded market-based transport reform. In the Mulroney government's hands, free-market initiative might have sustained deregulation.

A complicating consideration is that Canada's decentralized trucking jurisdiction makes it difficult to discern a coherent advocacy coalition. As was seen in Chapter 3, the advocacy coalition concept suited the American case because it had a more limited set of participants: economists, the White House, and the ICC. In Canada, because trucking was delegated to the provinces, there was no centre of coalescence; consequently, advocacy was dispersed and reform complicated. At the same time, Ottawa did have the unproclaimed part of the NTA in reserve as well as a coherent reform agenda. By taking up its jurisdiction over interprovincial trucking, Ottawa could deregulate by writing a liberal entry standard into the NTA.

On the international side, lower carrier rates in the United States made Canadian shippers a dissatisfied constituency. Their point of reference was not the inefficiencies shown in domestic research, but the lower costs of their counterparts in the United States. What if there had been no domestic initiative and no supporting research? Shippers could simply point to disadvantages in their prime export market. The importance of that market for Canada's economy would make a strong case in their favour, and the climate of apprehension over international competitiveness would provide an attentive context. The two largest trading partners, as the Transport Canada official noted to the House of Commons committee, are on both sides of the border. Recognizing that position, the government was negotiating free trade.

Together, these are potent sets of factors, and one way of reconciling them is to consider their sequence. Given the strength of domestic reform's antecedents and momentum, the shippers' price comparisons were introduced into a longer process, assisting but not determining the outcome. This interpretation is reasonable. In the debate over deregulation in Congress, as we saw in Chapter 3, American shippers also argued cheaper prices – domestic ones, in that instance. Their influence was not politically decisive because the case for reform was already well advanced. In Canada, the international price comparisons are potent enough to make deregulation something more than domestic reform. At the same time, the antecedents and momentum are too strong to warrant characterizing the process as international harmonization.

Canada's ability to act on trucking reform, as we saw, was constrained by federalism. The federal government had no significant impediments to drafting and enacting the content of reform when it modified the MVTA, but it had delegated regulation to the provinces in 1954 and could not directly implement the legislation. We saw the result: an array of preferences ranging from openness in Alberta to continued restriction in Manitoba. Ontario's protracted experience shows the difficulties governments face when two important constituencies end up on opposite sides of an issue. In comparison, the ICC's administrative changes and its implementation of the Motor Carrier Act shows the latitude available when a single agency has jurisdiction and political backing. In considering this comparison there are two points to remember. First, the CTC achieved the first stages of airline deregulation by administrative rule making – much as the ICC had done with trucks. One reason for its ability to act was that it had a clear federal jurisdiction and another was that it was prompted by a powerful minister. Second, adopting a fitness-only test not only opened interprovincial trucking markets, but also intraprovincial ones, thus producing reform at both levels of government. In the United States fifteen years elapsed before a uniform set of liberalized intrastate rules was enacted. One reason for this, as we saw, was lukewarm interest in the executive branch; but the comparison is worth noting.

What about international latitude to act? Again, interpretive emphasis can be placed either domestically or internationally. If the emphasis is placed domestically, then efficiency would be a net gain regardless of any trading ties. Trade amplifies the gain, with lower delivery prices expanding the number of exportable goods. The fact that a major trading partner has previously adopted the same reform simply means that one's improved efficiency and trading costs will match accompanying gains abroad and yield mutual benefits. If the emphasis is placed internationally, then external price comparisons denote constraint and adaptation. Both the federal government's trade policy review and the Macdonald Royal Commission were occupied with economic globalization and interdependence. Both decided that protectionism and import substitution were no longer possible in a world where the trends were in the opposite direction. Significantly cheaper American trucking rates gave such thoughts a practical regulatory focus. With competition and interdependence fully in view, the question of keeping existing domestic policies would be impossible to defer for long.

Domestically and internationally, the strongest constraint on the latitude to act was federalism. Deregulation posed Ottawa's long-standing interest in transport reform against the provinces' equally long-standing unwillingness to surrender their trucking jurisdiction and their local protections. As a matter of domestic reform, the provinces were at best lukewarm about the complete removal of entry controls; as a matter of international competition, the entry of American carriers was the focus of apprehension. For both, provincial jurisdiction and regulatory discretion were important safeguards. The federal government's incentives, both domestic and international, were much less constrained.

If these considerations connect plausibly with the events we have seen, they show a blend of international and domestic causes. In the same vein, an analysis of the foreign and domestic sources of reform in Canada's agriculture policy states that "it is difficult to separate the effects of these international developments from domestic pressures for neo-liberal policies."[161] A companion study of Canadian telecommunications policy finds that American experience provided important "ideas, models and allies," but it concludes that "domestic actors used the American experience, and international agreements, to their own ends."[162] It is reasonable to conclude that such blended causality – warranted empirically but unsatisfying taxonomically – is present in trucking reform. An offsetting satisfaction is the complementarity we have seen between public policy and international relations.

6
After Deregulation

When the United States and Canada deregulated trucking, they removed rules that had governed the industry's sectoral organization. Common carriers had enjoyed protected domains and rates while truckload and contract carriers were kept at the margins. Deregulation allowed all sectors to contest traffic as they chose, and the motor carrier industry quickly reorganized. Common carriage's expensive terminal networks, which regulation had supported on behalf of widespread service to the public, quickly became liabilities. TL and contract carriage, which had always been potentially flexible and efficient, expanded and thrived. Favouring their advantages was the rapid growth of integrated logistics schemes in industry. These schemes depend on the custom-tailored transportation that TL and contract carriers can readily provide.

Deregulation in the United States involved a largely domestic transition, but there were two important international aspects to deregulation in Canada. The first was the arrival of American carriers competing for transborder traffic. Although Canadian carriers had received the same access to the American transborder market in 1980, the Canadian carrier industry's smaller size magnified the impact when American carriers subsequently headed north. These carriers were used to competition, having survived nine years of turmoil and attrition in their home market, and the largest ones dwarfed their Canadian counterparts.

The second international aspect to deregulation in Canada was free trade. Canadian deregulation coincided with the implementation of the Canada-United States Free Trade agreement and it continued under the North American Free Trade Agreement. The effects were very positive. Between 1989 and 1997 transborder revenues increased by 145 percent and tonnage by 107 percent. By the mid-1990s both countries had recovered from the recession, and the American economy was booming. Transborder traffic soared, with revenues increasing by 30 percent between 1995 and 1997 and tonnage by 41 percent. The American economy's appetite for imports made revenues and tonnage highest on southbound traffic.[1] As these results began appearing earlier in the decade, Canadian carriers began expanding transborder operations, and by 1997, 72 percent of the largest carriers were operating in the United States. Representing 42 percent of carrier revenues, transborder service had become a "lucrative niche."[2]

Revenues and tonnage also reflect a regional diversification of trade. Transborder trucking had always been concentrated in Ontario and the American northeast and upper midwest. On the American side, traffic from Canada has moved into the west and south; on the Canadian side, Quebec, the Prairie provinces, and British Columbia have enjoyed the same increases. Some of these gains reflect growth in regional corridors, with traffic between British Columbia and the western states rising by over 200 percent.

Diversification also shows in the composition of trade. A striking index is the 863 percent increase in southbound general freight between 1989 and 1997.[3] General freight is the category for all manufactured goods that fall outside basic industrial classifications such as motor vehicles and paper products. Because general freight includes such a broad assortment of manufactures, it shows a spectrum of export growth. By 1997 general freight had moved into second place, behind motor vehicles and parts, in Ontario's southbound traffic. Overall, manufactured products moved up the top-ten commodities list. With motor carriers continuing to transport two-thirds of Canadian-American commerce, figures such as these provide a logistical view of the trade relationship.

The outlook was far less bright in 1990, as Canadian carriers struggled with deregulation. We will look first at the immediate effects of an opened market and American competition. Next we will see how trucking's sectors have fared, noting the rapid rise of TL and the impact of integrated logistics. Finally, we will look at the industry's development under free trade, as reflected in regional destinations, commodity levels, and operating patterns. Together these changes amount to a transformation.

Opened Borders and Competition

On American Memorial Day weekend 1990, Canadian truckers blockaded the bridges over the Niagara, Detroit, and St. Clair Rivers. A smaller stoppage had begun the previous week in Quebec, spreading quickly to Ontario and then to border-crossing points between Vancouver and Washington State. The results were almost immediate. General Motors shut down its Oshawa plant as parts from the United States stopped arriving, and other automotive plants in Ontario soon did the same. Disrupted supply from Canada was soon felt in the United States. The truckers repeated their blockade the following April, and in May 1991 they converged on Highway 401 in Toronto to jam traffic and marshalled their trucks on Parliament Hill in Ottawa. The April blockade was not as well-attended as was the first one, but the traffic slowdown in Toronto caused huge congestion and was front-page news. Deregulation and American competition were the issues.

Most of the blockaders were owner-operators. Canadian carrier firms themselves did not support the blockades, and the OTA kept its distance. Also disavowing support, the CTA sent a letter to federal transport minister Doug Lewis declaring its appreciation of the "financial and economic pressures facing both trucking companies and independent operators" from American competition.[4]

Canadian carriers had been operating in transborder markets since 1980, but their advantage was single-line service, not rates. When Canada deregulated, American carriers were able to offer their own single-line services – and at rates honed by almost a decade of survival in a deregulated market. Competition picked up quickly. In 1989, the first year of deregulation, one-third of the shippers across Canada and two-thirds of the shippers in Ontario reported more carriers seeking their business. Many of those carriers were American. In Ontario, the number of American carriers with provincial authorities grew to 1,362 in 1990 and increased further to 2,066 in 1991. The number operating in Canada rose from 3,000 in 1989 to 5,323 in 1991.[5] Arkansas-based J.B. Hunt Transport, then the largest TL carrier, reported that its Canadian business had doubled between 1988 and 1990.[6] American carriers concentrated on high-volume traffic in the automotive and newsprint industries and offered attractive discounts, producing overall rate differentials with Canadian carriers of 10 percent to 20 percent.[7] Muskoka Transport, an Ontario TL carrier, reported in 1989 that a Hunt representative had visited one of its shippers and offered a price of US$1,800 per truckload to haul to a customer in Georgia. That rate undercut Muskoka's by $250. In late 1989 Ford Motor Company of Canada shifted $50 million of its yearly trucking account to American-based carriers.[8]

As American carriers began entering the Canadian market, conditions in the economy combined badly. The Canadian dollar appreciated from a low-seventy-cent (US) range in the mid-1980s to a mid-eighty-cent range in 1991, adding over 7 percent to Canadian costs. A serious recession began in both countries in 1990. The American carrier industry was badly affected, and in 1991 bankruptcies reached their highest level since deregulation eleven years earlier. On the Canadian side the recession added one more dimension of difficulty.

Operating ratios depict the situation. As we saw in Chapter 2, an operating ratio is the percentage of revenue claimed by operating costs. An operating ratio of 93 is considered prosperous, 95 is healthy, and 97 is viable.[9] At 100 costs equal revenue. By 1988 the American carriers still in business had achieved an operating ratio of 95. It fell again to 97 in 1991, and the three largest LTL carriers had ratios in the high 90s. Canadian carriers' operating ratios declined from 96 in 1988, the year before deregulation, to 100 in 1991.[10] In 1992 their operating ratio improved only to 99.8.[11] Adding to costs were debt burdens. According to the National Transportation Agency, Canadian carriers were bearing "at least twice" the debt of American carriers.[12]

Bankruptcies among Ontario's and British Columbia's carriers doubled in 1991, and across the country they increased from 381 in 1989 to 763.[13] Only five of the 381 bankruptcies in 1989 involved firms with liabilities of over $1 million, but in 1991 sixty-five of the 763 bankruptcies involved large carriers, and 85 percent of those carriers were in Quebec, Ontario, and British Columbia – the provinces with the heaviest transborder traffic. There was one positive comparison. The bankruptcy rate for Canadian carriers was no higher than it was for other business sectors, while the post-deregulation bankruptcy of American carriers was double that of other businesses.[14] Even so, thirty-seven of the firms appearing on the 1988 list of top 100 Canadian carriers were gone by 1993, having closed or merged with other carriers.[15]

The blockaders acknowledged that deregulation was here to stay, and many were at pains to point out that they had no complaints against the American carriers themselves; rather, they blamed Canadian government policies, from higher fuel prices to longer tax depreciation periods, for a relative disadvantage. Also singled out were higher Canadian interest rates, which made it more expensive to replace inefficient equipment, and the high exchange rate of the Canadian dollar. The federal transport minister visited the blockades at the Ambassador Bridge. Soon afterwards he formed the Task Force on Trucking Issues and commissioned eight studies of competitiveness in transborder trucking.[16] The Ontario government commissioned a study of its own.[17]

Costs and Competitiveness

The findings produced a mixed picture. First, American international carriers were also found to be suffering. Of 100 American international trucking firms surveyed, 35 percent reported losing money in 1989, and the ones located in the northeast had the lowest return on equity. Overall, American international carriers had a lower return on equity than did American domestic carriers.[18] One implication of these results was that rates in the two countries were competitive and comparable. Furthermore, no study found that Canadian carriers were suffering because of "institutional barriers" in the United States impeding backhauls to Canada. The major factor was comparative costs.[19]

There, too, the picture was mixed. American-based carriers had a tax advantage in that they had more generous depreciation allowances on their equipment and, in some cases, lower state taxes, but Canadian carriers enjoyed lower corporate and payroll taxes and paid no excise tax on new equipment. By sector, LTL carriers tended to fare better under the Canadian tax regime, as did small TL carriers, although to a much less degree. Large TL carriers were better off under the American tax regime.[20] Ontario carriers enjoyed a "marginal" advantage in all significant federal and state/provincial taxes, with the greater advantages being in comparison to high-tax states like Michigan and the smaller advantages being in comparison to lower-tax states like Arkansas. For Canadian policy, the implication was that corporate tax remedies would not provide much help.[21]

American carriers were found to have a 6 percent overall advantage in operating costs. Larger Canadian carriers suffered a 3 percent disadvantage and smaller ones a much more serious 9 percent disadvantage. By region and firm size, the firms comparing the least favourably were small Quebec carriers, whose costs were 114 percent of American ones. Altogether the least competitive provinces were Ontario, Quebec, and Manitoba – a discouraging finding, given the fact that three-quarters of Canada's trucking industry is located there. Saskatchewan and the Atlantic provinces compared the most favourably.[22] Canadian equipment costs, representing truckers' most important capital category, were 106 percent of American ones.[23]

At the same time, Canadian driver costs were found to be 10 percent below American ones, due largely to the medical benefit expenses borne by US carriers. Additional American disadvantages were higher social security and workers compensation charges.[24] Canadian unionized wage rates were relatively high, with those in Ontario 20 percent higher than the non-union rates of large American TL carriers.[25] On the other hand, the Canadian driver force is less unionized than the American one, and the TL sector (seen shortly) is an excellent place for using non-union owner-operators.

Cheaper American diesel fuel prices were acknowledged but assumed to equalize. Truckers buying diesel in the cheapest locales still must pay taxes according to the miles they drive in each jurisdiction.[26] Keeping accurate records of fuel purchases and mileage by state and province is one part of drivers' paperwork. Agreements between states and provinces enable them to divide the fuel taxes they collect according to the mileage figures carriers report.

Currency exchange rates did inflate overall Canadian costs. In July 1991, two months after the second border blockade, the eighty-seven-cent Canadian dollar produced a 7.5 percent operating cost disadvantage for Canadian carriers.[27] The cost difference would reduce to 3 percent with the Canadian dollar trading at eighty cents (US). A seventy-five-cent Canadian dollar would produce a 1 percent cost advantage.[28] The KPMG study ranked the high value of the Canadian dollar only behind deregulation itself as the industry's greatest difficulty.[29]

In the poorest condition were owner-operators, who had the worst of both worlds, with earnings 15 percent to 25 percent lower than those of American owner-operaters and with costs 7 percent higher. To those problems were added their dependence on Canadian carriers, who were themselves coping with recession, cost disadvantages, and competition from American carriers. One heavy employer of owner-operators, Frederick Transport of Dundas, Ontario, saw one-third of its owner-operators go broke in the first year of deregulation.[30] The problem was significant. Of the approximately 18,200 Canadian jobs in transborder trucking, owner-operators accounted for about 4,200. They were also more heavily used in Canada, with one sample showing a two-to-one difference over American carriers.[31] The owner-operators blockading the bridges had good reason to feel beset.

The federal reports offered little remedy. The Canadian carriers' most serious disadvantages, they concluded, were structural ones beyond the reach of simple and direct measures. Helping Canadian carriers adjust and restructure was the best the government could do. The task force did recommend removing a four-cents-per-litre federal diesel fuel excise tax, speeding up tax depreciation on existing trucks, and reinstituting a 7 percent investment tax credit on new trucks. But much less was actually adopted. For the tax years 1991 and 1992, Canadian motor carriers, as well as railways and airlines, could claim a 3-cents-per-litre rebate on their fuel purchases, but the intention was easing short-term cash flow. The tax depreciation rate for trucks was accelerated but remained half that requested by the CTA and was lower than the American rate. Since depreciation reduces taxable income, the CTA noted, the change would only help those carriers actually making money.[32] Underpinning these measures was the government's belief that costs – not taxes – were the issue.

The Ontario report expressed concern about the large gap between unionized Ontario wages and those of non-union American TL firms. One suggestion entailed expanding into the United States, using non-union American drivers, and transferring the earnings back to Canada to offset the higher costs.[33] A less positive suggestion entailed "reviewing arrangements with unionized drivers." Less positive still, the report recommended that the provincial government find the "means by which unproductive and surplus capacity could be removed permanently from the industry" in the interests of saving and consolidating the most viable operations.[34] The Ontario Liberal government, which commissioned the report, subsequently lost an election, and its New Democratic successor was occupied with other reforms and controversies. Trucking policy simply gave play to competition. The transborder market was a principal focus.

The carriers standing to benefit most from transborder expansion were Canadian. The federal study found illegal cabotage to be rare on both sides of the border, which meant that neither side was taking unfair advantage.[35] The study also found American carriers not interested in expanding into Canadian domestic service. They regarded international traffic as an extension of their primary business in the United States. That view was confirmed by simulation results in the Ontario study, which showed no gains for American carriers from access to domestic Canadian traffic. On the other hand, Canadian carriers were shown to gain improved productivity and financial performance with access to American domestic traffic.[36] "It seems desirable," the report concluded, "to undertake additional analyses to determine whether a relaxation of cabotage rules on both sides of the border would give Ontario-based transborder carriers a competitive advantage without posing a serious problem for Ontario based domestic carriers."

Contrary to the blockaders' fears of cut-throat competition, a subsequent study found that rates did not fall greatly after deregulation. Surveying a set of samples from intraprovincial trucking in Ontario, the study found that commodity characteristics – not competition – appeared to be the strongest factor affecting rate levels. If the same were true more generally, and particularly in transborder markets, then deregulation's effects had been overstated by both its opponents and its supporters.[37] In the meantime, sectoral reorganization was recasting the trucking industry.

TL Carriers: Deregulation's Winners

Following deregulation in the United States, TL carriers emerged rapidly from firms in the irregular-route common carrier sector. When they were regulated, those firms served the general public but did not travel fixed routes.[38] Freed of their common-carrier obligations and their restriction to particular regions, they could serve individual shippers and operate nationwide. In Canada, TL was defined more by industry structure than by regulation. As was true in the United States, general freight was the domain of large LTL carriers, and Canadian carriers handled both LTL and TL consignments.[39] Small Canadian TL general freight carriers operated differently from American irregular-route carriers in that they used freight brokers to arrange hauls and to consolidate small shipments into full-trailer loads. These operations were possible because Canadian freight brokers were less regulated and more numerous than were American freight brokers.[40] Utilizing small and sometimes illegal carriers (uncertificated or without appropriate operating authorities), freight brokers could charge attractively low TL rates.[41] Even so, small TL carriers operated at the margins of the large LTL carriers in Canada. Attracted by the mode's advantages, new TL carrier firms organized in both countries. From these various origins, they challenged the large, incumbent LTLs in the basic categories of costs and service.[42]

TL carriers haul full-trailer volumes directly from shipper to receiver with no intermediate handling in terminals. With no investment in terminal networks, the main capital cost of entry is the trucks themselves. Free to go wherever they are required, TL carriers have a naturally high mobility. By serving individual shippers door to door, they lend themselves to specialized and individual applications, and can be adapted readily to particular logistics. Together with low capital cost entry barriers, these conditions bring TL "very close to meeting the classical economic definition of pure competition."[43]

Terminal-free operations also give TL carriers a significant operating cost advantage over LTL carriers. Line-haul costs in TL represent more than 90 percent of operating costs, while line-haul costs are 34.6 percent of LTL operating costs, with the largest portions of the remainder representing pickup and delivery, terminal, and platform costs.[44] TL's simpler cost structure favours small and medium carriers. In fact, TL operating ratios increase with market share, reflecting diseconomies of scale. The threshold is $100 million in annual revenue.[45] With more trucks in motion, larger operations require computerization and elaborate dispatching systems to ensure new loads at the points of delivery – TL's main operating constraint.[46] Computers keep a continuously updated inventory, allowing dispatchers to match loads with the nearest available vehicles. A survey of TL carriers found load-size economies (an absence of empty miles) among the firms using computerized routing, reflecting high equipment utilization.[47]

Another TL advantage is labour costs. TL carriers are non-union, and the major LTL carriers, with few exceptions, are union. The cost difference is striking. Those of MS Carriers, one of the largest TL firms, are 38 percent of revenues, while those of Yellow Freight System, one of the three largest LTLs, are 67 percent of revenues.[48] For Canadian carriers the gap is narrower: the TL sector has labour costs of 29.4 percent of revenues compared to 43.4 percent for LTL.[49] Non-union carriers also have flexible work rules, allowing adaptive scheduling and operations.[50]

TL's mobility enables close coordination with shippers. That advantage is especially useful in supply-chain management, which involves the scheduling of production and distribution according to the volumes required at each point in the process. To keep those volumes to a minimum and to keep supplies arriving when they are needed, scheduling must be exact. These requirements favour TL carriers, which can provide direct point-to-point service and tailor vehicle movements to the shippers' schedules. Overnite Transportation, the seventh-largest LTL, opened a special TL division in 1994 to link Ford and Chrysler automotive plants in Ontario and the American midwest with plants in Mexico. The goods shuttle by rail container from a facility near Chicago to Mexico City. Overnite provides the truck transportation between the rail facility and the Canadian and American plants. As an index of the intensity of dedicated logistics operations, the division's trucks average twenty hours a day on the road.[51] Integrating itself even further into a supply chain, the Mackie Group in Ontario expanded from trucking into manufacturing by operating an automotive subassembly plant for the General Motors plant in Oshawa. The finished components are loaded into Mackie's trucks to arrive in exactly the same sequence as the cars moving along the assembly line. The firm's computers are linked directly to those at the GM plant, and the volume is 2,000 truckloads per week.[52]

A successful supply chain depends on rapid communication and dependable responses at all stages. On-line data interchange between shippers and carriers and satellite-linked dispatcher-driver communications make it possible to coordinate truck movements closely.[53] In more general TL service, satellite tracking adds value by enabling a shipper to know within a kilometre the location of an expected consignment and makes computerized dispatching instantaneous. Carriers without satellite technology stay in touch with their drivers by telephone. Challenger Motor Freight, based in Cambridge, Ontario, was one of the first Canadian carriers to adopt satellite technology to track its 700 tractors and 1,800 trailers throughout Canada, the United States, and Mexico. Smaller carriers have also been adopting this technology. As an index of the size of operations that can benefit, Winnipeg-based Gershman Transport, whose fleet is 116 tractors and 264 trailers, coordinates all its operations with computer and satellite.[54]

TL has been an ideal mode for Canadians expanding into the transborder market. Easy mobility puts the entire United States within reach and eliminates the need to invest in an American terminal network. Canadian carriers have been expanding into the United States since the early 1980s, and many are LTL firms that have opened TL divisions.[55] Examples are Cabano TL, a division of Cabano-Kingsway, and Jet Transport, owned by Manitoulin Transport. Canadian Pacific's former American TL carrier, Highland Transport, is now owned by Westminster Holdings of Toronto. Operating a TL carrier as part of a larger transportation business combines the advantages of both large and small firms. The parent firm provides volume discounts on equipment purchases along with marketing and administrative resources and reputation.[56] Simpler operations and the ability to use owner-operators provide the cost advantages of a small firm.

Long-Haul LTL Carriers: Merged and Vanished

Common carriers in both countries became known as LTL carriers after deregulation. They did not fare well. In the United States, only five of the fifty largest LTLs have survived since deregulation in 1980.[57] In Canada, all of Canada's nationwide LTL carriers had closed by 1997. Federal Industries, one of Canada's principal carrier groups, merged twenty-one duplicate terminals and sold off surplus equipment after deregulation, but these measures were not enough. In 1992 Federal sold one of its major carriers, Kingsway Transports, to Quebec-based Cabano Ltd. Federal's other major LTL, Motorways, lost 40 percent of its freight volume in the three years following deregulation, and its revenues fell from $300 million to $50 million.[58] Federal closed Motorways in 1993 and exited trucking altogether the following year. Earlier in 1993 Reimer Express Enterprises, another of Canada's major carrier groups, had closed Ontario-based Inter-City Truck Lines. Canadian Pacific got out of trucking with the sale of its LTL carrier CP Express and Transport to employees in 1994 after four years of losses totalling over $170 million.[59] After a major refinancing and reorganization in 1996, the carrier went out of business the following year. Large American transportation companies also exited long-haul LTL. In 1996 Roadway Systems and Consolidated Freightways spun off their American and Canadian LTL operations in order to concentrate on their other transportation businesses – primarily regional LTL, TL and package carriers, airfreight, and logistics-provider operations.[60]

In both countries, deregulation had exacerbated LTL's comparative disadvantages. LTL carriers constitute the only sector using large terminal networks; all others operate directly from shipper to receiver or use smaller regional networks. As we saw in Chapter 2, terminals impose some additional 25 percent in operating costs. After deregulation the largest LTLs sought to raise efficiency by organizing their operations into hub-and-spoke systems, with large terminals feeding local and regional traffic into trunk routes.[61] Hub-and-spoke preserves regional service and promotes full loadings on the trunk hauls, but passage through each hub generally delays a consignment by a day.[62] With straight-line transits available from the other sectors, LTL's terminal networks became costly impediments. They do, however, allow small shipments to be handled, small traffic centres to be served, and pickup and delivery service to be provided. These service advantages probably account for the long-haul LTL that survives.

LTL's impediments were fully present in Canada. "Once you get very big, with terminals throughout Canada," according to one LTL manager, "you have to maintain high fixed overheads."[63] That is particularly the case when traffic densities are not high enough to support terminal costs. In the words of the vice-president of TNT Overland, "Canada is different from the U.S. The Windsor-Quebec City corridor is the closest thing we have to the critical mass or market density" needed to sustain a large terminal system. "Covering the rest of Canada gets to be very expensive."[64] Commenting on the closing of Motorways and the decision of its parent firm, Federal Industries, to get out of trucking, Federal's CEO John Pelton made a more general assessment: "I don't see any future for national LTL trucking."[65]

Complicating the outlook for long-haul LTL in Canada is a shifting directional trend in traffic. "The reality is there is less and less freight going east and west across the country," observed Pelton.[66] Domestic shipments actually declined until 1994.[67] Revenue on movements from Ontario to Manitoba, Saskatchewan, and Alberta were reduced from $1 billion in 1990 to $889 million in 1995.[68] The time period suggests that the recession was a factor, since the traffic was domestic. There is no breakdown between LTL and TL carriers for 1995, but in 1990 LTL carriers claimed only 39 percent of those revenues.

Following transborder traffic growth as a Canadian long-haul LTL carrier would have required very large outlays in American terminals – just when the surviving American LTLs were paring back their own networks and bypassing them with straight-through service. The dispersion of traffic centres in the United States favours carriers that are not bound to fixed routes and terminals or that operate in carefully selected corridors.[69] Being free of terminal networks, as we saw, favours TL carriers. Operating in moderately sized markets favours regional LTL carriers, as we will see next.

Regional LTLs: Smaller Is Better

Both Canada and the United States have regional LTL carriers. Their operations are terminal-centred, but the economics are more favourable. Under deregulation regional LTLs have proved efficient and profitable. Covering shorter distances makes it possible to operate on a direct-load basis and eliminates hub-and-spoke networks.[70] In busy traffic lanes, simpler networks and no intermediate handling encourage economies of density.[71] At the same time, using terminals enables regional LTLs to offer pickup and delivery and handle small consignments, providing a service advantage over TL and contract carriers, which handle only full-load consignments and are often unsuitable for small shippers.[72] There is ample regional traffic to haul: fully 64 percent of Canadian truck tonnage in 1992 moved between 25 and 299 kilometres.[73] Con-Way, the most profitable American regional LTL, handles almost two-thirds of its freight on a one-day basis at distances up to 1,200 kilometres.[74]

Intraprovincial trucking, which contains much of the demand for such service, continues to be a major market. Of Canada's domestic freight, measured by tonnage, over 83 percent is picked up and delivered in the same region. Trucking within Ontario accounts for fully one-third of Canada's intraregional total.[75] Because regional LTLs have such promise, and because there are growth possibilities in their markets, they can be attractive parts of larger operations. One regional LTL operated by a large parent firm is Lakehead Freightways, owned by Ontario-based Manitoulin Transport Group.[76]

Regional LTL carriers can move into direct competition in longer-distance service by forming connective alliances among themselves. In 1993, 45 percent of Canadian carriers reported being involved in partnerships or alliances with other carriers.[77] With the growth of international traffic, Canadian and American regional LTLs began forming transborder alliances, as we will see later.

Contract Carriers: Simple and Efficient

Both contract and TL carriers offer full-trailer transport for individual shippers, the difference between them being that TL carriers circulate their equipment among a number of shippers while contract carriers devote their vehicles to particular clients. Even that distinction is blurring as TL (and many LTL) carriers seek to establish long-term relationships with major shippers and tailor their services to highly specific requirements. Contract carriage has grown in the two countries since deregulation, and its primary advantage is service characteristics. Dedicating vehicles to particular shippers makes contract carriers ideally suited to complex and continuous logistics arrangements. Contract carriers can assign trucks and drivers to be used completely according to the shipper's direction. A survey by the Council of Logistics Management shows how attractive such service can be. Of eight long-term trends identified in carrier-shipper relations, the most significant was a shift away from LTL to contract carriage.[78]

Contract carriage's low capital costs and simple operating structures make it attractive both as a single enterprise and as part of a larger trucking business. As an index of the continuing feasibility of small-scale operations, only a few American contract firms, such as Miami-based Ryder Dedicated Logistics and Pennsylvania-based Penske Logistics, are very large. The Canadian equivalent of contract carrier operations is often performed by firms offering other kinds of trucking services. Canadian carrier groups with special contract divisions are Mississauga-based TNT North America, Hartland, New Brunswick-based Day and Ross, and St. John New Brunswick-based Sunbury Transport. Five years after deregulation in the United States, almost all LTL carriers had acquired contract carrier authorities from the ICC, blending the two forms of business, as had LTL carriers in Canada.[79] Some contract operations can be extensive. Calgary-based Trimac Ltd., North America's largest bulk carrier, does 70 percent of its business on a contract basis.[80] One of its major clients is Imperial Oil Ltd.

Private Carriers: Holding the Line

In both service and price, deregulation affected the decision to use private trucking. TL and contract carriers can now offer the kind of highly specialized service previously available only through private carriage, and they can do so more cheaply.[81] Competition puts shippers in a position to negotiate favourable rates and services. Private carrier managers must please not only the firm's customers, but also the firm's own management, who are very aware of transport substitutability.

At the same time, deregulation has made private carriage more attractive in other ways. The capital costs of a fleet can be avoided by leasing the trucks. Full-service leasing, made possible under deregulation, helps avoid some of the operating costs by providing private carriers with both vehicles and drivers together with maintenance and benefits packages. These arrangements closely resemble contract carriage, for in both the shipper procures vehicles and drivers for dedicated use. Deregulation in the two countries also allows private carriers to haul cargoes for hire, thus improving equipment utilization and lowering costs.

Many private carrier operations, bearing high costs and inefficient utilization because of regulation, were quick to convert to TL and contract once those services became available. Much of the early growth of TL and contract carriers, in fact, came as shippers reduced or abandoned their private fleets. In Canada, the percentage of shippers using private fleets declined from 48 percent in 1988, the year before deregulation, to 33 percent in 1993. Of those shippers, however, 73 percent indicated that their fleets had not changed since the previous year.[82] In the United States as well, movement from private carriage had stabilized by the early 1990s.

The levelling off occurred for several reasons. First, the easily converted traffic had already been taken by for-hire carriers or was balanced by the private carriers' new ability to carry freight for hire. Second, TL carriers had reached the limits of their ability to offer more closely integrated and specialized service than remaining private fleets, which had been kept because they could meet high requirements. Moreover, private fleets do much better than TL carriers with regard to recruiting and retaining drivers because they offer better pay and working conditions.[83] Finally, private fleet managers are well aware of the availability of for-hire carriers and have been busy cutting costs. According to a survey by A.T. Kearney, a consulting firm, per-mile operating costs of private fleets have been steadily declining since 1983.[84]

The service advantages possible with private carriage often show indirectly. Sales can be significantly affected by the quality of transportation.[85] A firm's sales department, for example, may be able to negotiate a premium price on the basis of premium transportation. That bonus should be credited to the firm's private carrier operation. A closely managed private fleet may also do better than for-hire carriers in responding quickly to supply fluctuations. Savings from the smaller inventories that this makes possible should also be credited.[86]

Private carriage's future may again come into question as shippers adopt more comprehensive logistics schemes, casting cost and service comparisons into a broader perspective and revealing new opportunities for substitution. Sixty-two percent of the firms surveyed in one study had outsourced logistics and transportation. Within that group 56 percent had done so to concentrate on the firm's main business, 50 percent to reduce payroll, and 48 percent to cut capital costs.[87] The third-party firms taking over transportation negotiate with for-hire carriers or use their own fleets. By improving transport management, however, third-party firms may raise an existing private fleet's efficiency and service enough to warrant keeping it.

The New Logistics

"Just-in-time" inventory management, the core of integrated logistics schemes, uses transportation to lower production costs. Manufacturing and distribution are organized to eliminate idle stocks, storage capacity, and intermediate handling so that "the amount of inventory held at any point in the system is the minimum to operate."[88] The reductions are dramatic. In the words of a manager of administration and special projects for General Motors, "It was amazing before: If we had a major storm, we could run for a week with the materials on hand."[89] The savings come from taking capital out of supplies and materials and from reducing costs of storage and warehousing. Supplies arrive during "delivery windows" set exactly to production requirements and dock space. Delivery windows do not stay open long. One carrier, for example, which hauls Chevy Blazer bodies from a plant in Lorain, Ohio, 400 kilometres to Pontiac, Michigan, must meet a delivery window of fifteen minutes.[90] Product is shipped to its next stage as soon as it comes off the line.

Minimal inventory levels at each site eliminate buffers in the system and require rapid and dependable transportation. Instead of less frequent deliveries of large quantities, the requirement is continuous replenishment of small quantities.[91] Efforts by industries to reduce vertical integration bring more suppliers into their production networks and multiply the requirements for coordination and transport. The ultimate objective, in one carrier executive's words, is "virtual inventories" in which shippers substitute information and rapid movement for goods on hand.[92]

Of the automakers, Chrysler has been the most comprehensive in adopting just-in-time. To enable dealers to offer a broad selection of colours and accessories, Chrysler has put some of its assembly lines on a four-hour system. According to a Chrysler production specialist, "Chrysler broadcasts [to suppliers] the trim specifications four hours before the car hits that point in the assembly line. When the car arrives, seats of the proper color arrive in a module that is placed into the car. The sequenced parts come in, truck after truck, all day."[93] Logistics are complex and exact: "Getting the whole supply base to work together is the key."[94] Coordinating those networks is supply chain management. As producers reduce vertical integration and bring more suppliers into their networks, the requirements for coordination multiply. Transporters provide the connective linkages and are expected to be punctual. In a closely scheduled network, a late delivery is a major service failure.

One might expect to find such networks radiating from large firms to nearby suppliers and to be concentrated in densely industrial regions. A survey of manufacturers who had adopted closely scheduled logistics found that firm size, distance from suppliers, and the nature of their regional location had little or no bearing on their decision.[95] An example of a far-flung network is Ford Canada's St. Thomas assembly plant, which uses a global set of suppliers. Africa is the only continent not sending parts to St. Thomas, and the foreign content of the cars is high enough to qualify them as imports. Coordinating that extensive supply chain requires an elaborate computer system.[96]

One might also expect that scheduling vehicle movements according to supply requirements and not fleet efficiency would produce partial loads and inefficient utilization. That too, the manufacturers survey found, was not the case. Adopting just-in-time does not automatically produce higher transportation costs.[97] Altogether, the authors concluded, it is a widely applicable strategy. Motor carriers figure centrally because of their mobility and adaptability. In the words of one transport analyst, "a just-in-time production system cannot function without a strong and efficient trucking industry."[98] Accounting for 5 percent to 10 percent of the industry's growth between 1983 and 1993, just-in-time has been a boon for the firms able to adapt.[99] Helping firms in supply chains to plan and manage their logistics has been an expanding area of the trucking business.

Flow-through logistics apply the same strategy to distribution by eliminating intermediate storage and handling. Some arrangements are based on supplying particular levels on a continuous basis, with rapid adjustment for changes in demand. Procter and Gamble, for example, operates a continuous replenishment program with selected large customers such as Wal-Mart; under this program it assumes responsibility for keeping the store shelves full. Carriers are required to handle uninterrupted currents of traffic.[100] As with just-in-time, flow-through logistics depend on receiving accurate data from all points in the system in order to keep supplies from either running out or accumulating and in order to coordinate all processes continuously.[101] And, as with just-in-time, the scheme depends on extremely dependable and closely managed transportation.[102] As an example of a coordinated process, Oshawa Foods, a large Ontario grocery distributor, has computerized its inventory management, delivery scheduling, and truck routing in a single system in order to meet variable supply requirements, select efficient backhauls, and monitor the sales performance of individual stores.[103] Such logistics services may also be contracted to outside firms. J.B. Hunt Transport and Schneider National Carriers, the two largest TL firms, develop flow-through programs with major shippers.[104] TNT Logistics is a major third-party transport management firm in Canada, along with Ryder Dedicated Logistics.

These advantages are not limited to large shippers. Those who are too small to use dedicated transportation can pool their traffic and achieve the same speed and efficiency. Freight consolidators organize the shipments. A study conducted for the Warehouse Education Research Council in 1993 found shippers pooling 33 percent of their outbound shipments and expecting to increase that to 43 percent by the year 2000.[105] Such consignments are ideal cargoes for both TL and contract carriers.

Distribution and manufacturing can be combined in a centralized operation. From a single facility near Toronto, IBM Canada serves both its retail clientele and a set of manufacturing sites operating on just-in-time. In setting up the operation, IBM closed fourteen warehouses in the area. For IBM's carriers the requirement is flexible, continuous, and prompt transportation from a single point.[106] Other corporations that have rationalized their transportation into continuous streams between production points, suppliers, and sales outlets are Quaker Oats, Whirlpool, and 3M.[107]

A related trend is the "core carrier" concept, in which shippers deal with a reduced number of carriers in order to lower transaction costs, simplify shipping management, and involve carriers more closely in logistics operations and planning. In the words of one transport specialist, this represents "a shift away from a transactional, 'you call, we haul' basis to a contractual basis."[108] According to the executive director of the Atlantic Provinces Trucking Association, shippers "want to reduce the number of carriers they deal with, often to as few as two, and maintain a closer relationship with them."[109] Ford Canada, which once used twenty-two common carriers to distribute parts from its Oakville plant to its dealers in the Maritimes, has given that work to a single provider. Across a large corporation the reductions can be massive. General Motors, for example, once did business with 4,000 carriers and now uses 500. Fifty to sixty carriers handle its inbound TL shipments.[110] One survey of shippers found a widespread move to reduce the number of carriers used and to develop more elaborate, protracted, and extensive relationships with the ones remaining.[111] The core carrier concept favours carriers with the resources to take up major shares of traffic and is especially favourable for TL carriers.[112]

In more radical core carrier arrangements, a single carrier takes over the shipper's logistics, providing cargo and inventory management along with transportation. One version was seen earlier with the replacement of private carriage. In more comprehensive arrangements, third-party logistics providers manage a client firm's transport-related operations. The services range from selecting and dealing with carriers to assuming responsibility for transport planning and management. In 1993, Ricoh/Savin Canada, which had used thirty-five carriers, turned over its logistics to a single carrier, which handles transportation along with product inspection, packaging, installation, and demonstration.[113] With logistics expenditures claiming 25 percent to 45 percent of production costs in manufacturing, shippers concerned with cost-cutting may find outsourcing attractive.[114] According to one logistics specialist, "The most active customers are corporations that have gone through leveraged buyouts and are carrying enormous debt loads. They want to concentrate on their core businesses, cut costs and not have to bother with transportation planning. This is where the clever carrier enters the picture, building an inventory and traffic service tailored to the client ... in effect becoming an integral part of the client's business."[115]

In 1992, third-party payments accounted for 17 percent of intercity motor carrier revenues.[116] A Deloitte Touche survey of Canadian manufacturers in 1996 found 96 percent of them planning to outsource some part of their logistics in the next five years and 65 percent having already done so.[117]

Serving a large company may require considerable investment by the carrier. When the General Motors' Saturn Division chose contract carrier Ryder Dedicated Logistics to be its "lead logistics provider" in 1989, Ryder invested $40 million on information systems, new facilities, and equipment.[118] One way of avoiding much of the investment in equipment is to lease it. An official of Ryder Canada sees increasing partnerships between truck leasing firms, contract logistics providers, and carriers.[119] Leasing also adds extra degrees of flexibility and adaptability.

The levels of service available since deregulation have raised shippers' expectations accordingly. Instead of being willing to trade off price against service, shippers have come to demand both. A 1993 survey by the National Transportation Agency found shippers rating price, just-in-time capability, and overnight delivery as their highest priorities.[120] These expectations have added to carriers' post-deregulation adjustment. Regarding the demands of his shippers for excellent service and competitive rates, the vice-president of a large Ontario LTL carrier said, "They simply expect it."[121]

Free Trade, Rising Traffic, Diversification

Canadian-American trade doubled in the 1980s, and two-thirds of that increase, measured by value of goods, was motor freight.[122] Between 1976 and 1989 Canadian transborder trucking revenues, in constant dollars, more than tripled – from $524 million to $1.7 billion – and by 1997 transborder revenues were nearly ten times those of 1976. Truck crossings on the

Ambassador Bridge, the busiest gateway between the two countries, rose from 330,000 a year to over a million – a volume of almost two trucks per minute.[123] At the second-busiest gateway, the Peace Bridge between Buffalo and Fort Erie, commercial traffic increased almost 30 percent between 1990 and 1994 (a record gain) and rose another 15 percent in the first half of 1995.

Domestic traffic in Canada recovered after the recession but trailed the transborder increases. Carrier revenues from Quebec and Ontario to the western provinces, having dropped in the early 1990s, increased by 58 percent by 1997; but, in the same period, Quebec and Ontario transborder revenues increased by 153 percent. Tonnage between Quebec and Ontario and the western provinces grew by 60 percent, while their (Quebec's and Ontario's) transborder tonnage grew by 106 percent.[124] These changes reflected an overall shift of the domestic/international balance. The share of motor carrier revenues earned domestically fell from 74.6 percent in 1988 to 64.1 percent in 1995, while the share of transborder revenues increased from 24 percent to 36 percent. That increase was spread across all commodities and was reflected in both revenues and tons. In Statistics Canada's words, that result "supports the conclusion that a reorientation of trucking activity from east/west to north/south has occurred under the FTA and NAFTA."[125]

Applications for operating authority mirrored the increase in traffic. In 1989, the first year of deregulation in Canada, there were 10,000 applications for extra-provincial operating authorities. Of these, 23 percent were from American carriers. By 1994 American carriers held 7,831 operating authorities. The distribution by province was:[126]

Ontario	3,113
Quebec	1,349
Prairie provinces	2,051
British Columbia	820
Atlantic provinces	501

The National Transportation Agency, which conducted the survey, cautioned that the figures may be inflated because of the need to obtain authorities from each province, while a single authority gives interstate access to all of the United States.

Following five decades of tight controls, one might expect a temporary surge of applications, followed by a decline. Applications did drop to 6,000 by 1991, but they began increasing again in 1993 – just as transborder traffic was beginning to accelerate.[127] One might also expect that nine years of ICC hospitality to Canadian carriers would have filled the Canadian carriers' demand for interstate authorities; instead, the pattern was one of steady increase. The number of Canadian applicants tripled between 1986 and 1991 and rose by another 30 percent by 1994 to 1,200 per year.[128]

"Fleets could look on [free trade] as either a blessing or a curse," observed a CTA policy adviser. "The forward-looking ones took advantage of it."[129] A National Transportation Authority survey of Canadian carriers found them expanding their American operations and attributing their efforts to free trade.[130] By 1991, 45 percent of Canadian carriers were depending on transborder operations for more than 40 percent of their revenues.[131] By 1993 the number of Canadian carriers with American operations had tripled.[132] The dominant flow of traffic is southbound, accounting in 1997 for 57 percent of transborder revenues. Reflecting their ability to find backhauls in the United States, Canadian carriers earn 43 percent of their transborder revenues moving goods into Canada.[133]

Among Canadian carriers, TLs reaped the largest gains, with over one-third reporting volume increases ranging from 10 percent to 29 percent. Another 12 percent of the TLs reported gains of between 30 percent and 39 percent. Gains exceeding 40 percent were reported by the top group of TL carriers.[134] Even the LTL sector did well, with almost 70 percent reporting traffic increases. Almost one-quarter of the LTLs reported gains of over 40 percent.[135] The survey did not distinguish between long-haul and regional LTLs, but much of the increase was likely due to transborder partnerships between Canadian and American regional LTLs. The long-haul LTL sector was in serious difficulty by then, but regional LTLs were expanding transborder operations with American partners, as will be seen later. Overall, the benefits have been balanced. In the National Transportation Agency survey, both TL and LTL carriers reported even gains between themselves and American carriers.[136]

Trucking and Trade: Regional Diversification

Ontario has always been the centre of transborder trucking, with almost half of Canada's Class 1 carriers located there.[137] Figure 6.1 shows a heavily regional concentration in 1989, with Quebec the only other province having a share of more than 20 percent of the transborder revenues. The tonnage patterns were almost the same. (In some of the graphs that follow, rounding of data produces totals of less than 100 percent.)

A similar regional concentration was true on the American side, as Figure 6.2 (top) shows, with the northern midwest (north-central) and northeastern states accounting for almost three-quarters of the southbound revenues. The same two regions accounted for 78 percent of the tonnage. The same pattern prevailed northbound, with these two regions originating 70 percent of the revenues. They were the source of 78 percent of the northbound tonnage (Figure 6.2 [bottom]). One reason for the concentration was Ontario's automobile industry. Motor vehicles and components moving to

Figure 6.1

Share of revenues in Canada, 1989

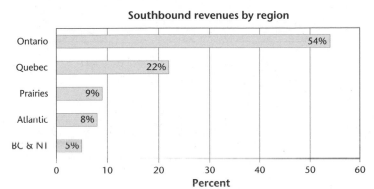

Southbound revenues by region

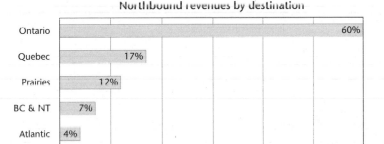

and from Ontario headed the 1989 list of transborder commodities by region. Iron, steel, and alloys, again from Ontario, were second.[138] On the American side, 23 percent of the transborder traffic had origins and destinations in Ohio and Michigan alone.[139] Ontario's industrial integration with the US northeast and upper midwest also showed in a relatively balanced commodity mix between import and export truck traffic.[140]

This was not long-haul trucking. Major LTL and TL carriers have average lengths of haul of 2,000 kilometres. Ontario carriers' trips to the northeastern and north-central states averaged 520 kilometres.[141] The short inter-regional distances give access to the enormous traffic pool of the US heartland but do not produce the revenues possible with longer trips. A Statistics Canada survey of 1992 trucking data showed per-ton carrier revenues increasing rapidly with distance.[142] Average trip kilometres from Ontario to the American south are 1,516; to the west they are 3,886. Those journeys are, indeed, more profitable than are the shorter ones. Revenues

Figure 6.2

Share of revenues in the United States, 1989

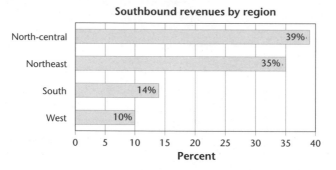

Southbound revenues by region

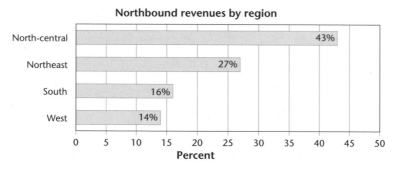

Northbound revenues by region

on Canadian traffic to the American north-central states exceeds tonnage by 1 percent, but on traffic to the south it exceeds tonnage by 10 percent. Serving those farther regions is desirable expansion. During the 1990s expansion away from the Great Lakes core occurred on both sides of the border.

On the Canadian side the largest traffic gains went to Quebec, the Prairie provinces, and British Columbia, as Figure 6.3 (top) shows. The southbound tonnage figures have the same distribution. The same pattern prevailed northbound, as is seen in Figure 6.3 (middle). Because the other provinces' traffic had expanded from much smaller bases, Ontario's portion of the total increase was still large, as Figure 6.3 (bottom) shows. A similar pattern held for tonnage.

Even so, Ontario's share of the overall increase represented a relative decline – from 57 percent of north- and southbound transborder revenues to 50 percent, and from 58 percent of the total transborder tonnage to 52 percent. Some of the other provinces' gains are impressive in their own right. Revenues on traffic between the Prairie provinces and the southern states, for example, increased from $26 million to $152 million.

Figure 6.3

Revenue increases in Canada, 1989-97

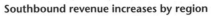

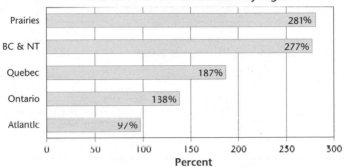

Southbound revenue increases by region

Region	Percent
Prairies	281%
BC & NT	277%
Quebec	187%
Ontario	138%
Atlantic	97%

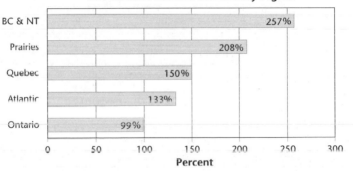

Northbound revenue increases by region

Region	Percent
BC & NT	257%
Prairies	208%
Quebec	150%
Atlantic	133%
Ontario	99%

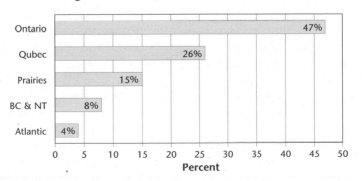

Regional shares of total southbound revenue increases

Region	Percent
Ontario	47%
Qubec	26%
Prairies	15%
BC & NT	8%
Atlantic	4%

Regional expansion was bilateral. In the United States, as Figure 6.4 (top) shows, the southern and western states showed the largest increases. The pattern was the same northbound, as Figure 6.4 (bottom) shows.

Figure 6.4

Revenue increases in the United States, 1989-97

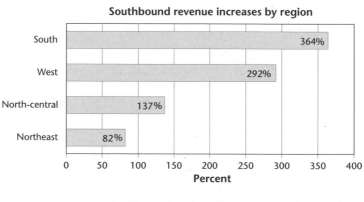

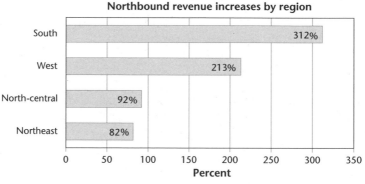

Remembering that trucking is a derived-demand industry and that carriers follow freight, and remembering that trucks transport two-thirds of Canada-US commerce, we can treat these figures as a rough logistical map of free trade. The gains were largest, as Figure 6.5 shows, in the formerly peripheral regions: British Columbia, the Prairies, and Quebec in Canada, and the south and west in the United States. Although the largest gains stemmed from small bases, the figures show the broadening involvement of the two countries' regional economies.

We can see the traffic shifts in another way with average trip kilometres. Increases show not only greater distance from the border, but also a wider

Figure 6.5

Top ten interregional trans-border increases in southbound revenue, 1989-97

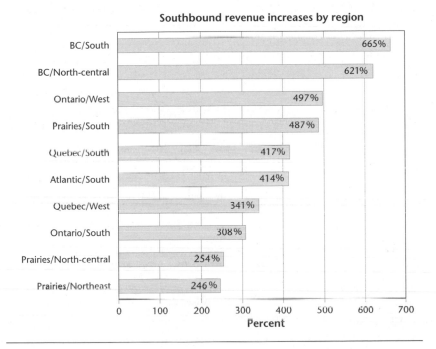

Southbound revenue increases by region

Region	Percent
BC/South	665%
BC/North-central	621%
Ontario/West	497%
Prairies/South	487%
Quebec/South	417%
Atlantic/South	414%
Quebec/West	341%
Ontario/South	308%
Prairies/North-central	254%
Prairies/Northeast	246%

coverage of points. In 1995 Quebec carriers doubled their distance in the north-central states. In the south, Ontario carriers travelled 20 percent more kilometres, and carriers from Manitoba, Saskatchewan, and Alberta travelled 10 percent more. Given the expanse of the American market and the distance between points, these increases reflect a greater presence of Canadian carriers and a wider array of shippers being served. Again, the biggest gains occurred beyond the Ontario-Great Lakes region, although even there kilometres were up by 4 percent – a not insignificant increase, given the region's proximity and density of traffic centres.[143]

Trucking and Trade: Commodity Diversification

Figure 6.6 shows the top-ten north- and southbound commodities in 1989 and 1997. They provide a useful gauge of activity, accounting for 54 percent of total transborder revenues and 53 percent of total tonnage in 1989, and for 59 percent of total revenues and 61 percent of total tonnage in 1997. According to the traditional image of the Canada-United States trade relationship, Canada imports manufactures and exports semi-processed goods. Supporting that image is general freight, 1997's top northbound

commodity. General freight includes all items falling outside basic industrial classifications and is a handy index of diverse goods. According to the
traditional image, however, general freight would have always ranked at
the top. In 1989, as Figure 6.6 shows, general freight ranked fifth – behind
motor vehicles, chemicals, machinery, and iron, steel, and alloys. These,
too, are manufactures, but their rankings sketch a more diverse image.
Motor vehicles reflect an integrated automotive sector. Chemicals are ingredients of industrial end products, as are iron, steel, and alloys, and non-
metallic basic products (second, fourth, and eighth on the list). Three of the
remaining commodities are food products. Machinery is the one other
commodity on 1989's northbound list that conforms to the traditional
image. Items in that category are often capital goods.

Now consider 1997's top-ten lists. General freight's move to first place
northbound is matched by its move into second place southbound. That
change itself can be interpreted as an index of more diverse trade. Motor

Figure 6.6

Top-ten north- and southbound commodities, 1989 and 1997

1989

Northbound	Southbound
Motor vehicles	Motor vehicles
Chemicals	Paper/paperboard
Machinery	Wood-fabricated products
Iron, steel, and alloys	Iron, steel, and alloys
General freight	Remaining end products
Vegetables	Non-metallic mineral basic products
Fruits	Chemicals
Non-metallic mineral basic products	Metal-fabricated basic products
Remaining end products	Non-ferrous metals
Other foods	Metal ores and related products

1997

General freight	Motor vehicles
Motor vehicles	General freight
Iron, steel, and alloys	Paper/paperboard
Vegetables	Wood-fabricated products
Chemicals	Iron, steel, and alloys
Metal-fabricated products	Furniture and fixtures
Machinery	Chemicals
Fruits	Non-metallic mineral basic products
Paper/paperboard	Remaining end products
Containers	Non-ferrous metals

Source: Statistics Canada, *Trucking in Canada 1989,* 117; Statistics Canada, *Trucking in Canada 1997,* 75.

vehicles, which dropped to second position on the northbound list, continues to occupy first position southbound, reflecting the automotive industry's importance. The same two-way traffic characterizes the key industrial commodities of iron, steel, and alloys. As the third largest northbound category and the fifth-largest southbound category, they show heavy commerce in both directions. The same is true of chemicals (fifth-ranked northbound and seventh-ranked southbound) and of paper/paperboard (third-ranked southbound and ninth-ranked northbound). As in 1989, commodities filling out the northbound list are not manufactures but foods – vegetables and fruit. Altogether, these rankings reflect a more diverse trade relationship than the traditional image would suggest. The importance of manufactures shows in their relative weighting. The first two southbound commodities in 1997, motor vehicles and general freight, account for almost 40 percent of top-ten revenues and almost one-quarter of all southbound revenues.

General freight appeared for the first time in the top-ten southbound ranking in 1993. Its 863 percent increase between 1990 and 1997 presents a striking profile of diversifying exports. Figure 6.7 charts revenue, and the same pattern characterizes tonnage.

Figure 6.7

Growth of southbound general commodities by revenue, 1990-97

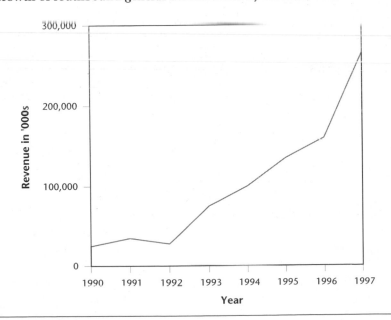

There is also a notable diversification regionally. Figure 6.8 shows 1997's top-ten ranking by province of origin and commodity, their rank in 1989, and the increases in revenue and tonnage. In reading the chart, for example, one can see motor vehicles from Ontario ranking first in both years. Showing the increase in motor vehicle shipments between 1989 and 1997, carrier revenues rose by 43 percent and tonnage by 33 percent.

Figure 6.8

Top-ten southbound commodities by region and revenue, 1997

	Rank in 1989	Revenue increase (%)	Tonnage increase (%)
1 Ontario/Motor vehicles	1	43	33
2 Ontario/General or unclassified freight	3	238	n/a
3 Quebec/Paper and paperboard	4	142	153
4 Qubec/General or unclassified freight	5	138	157
5 Ontario/Iron, steel, and alloys	2	65	41
6 BC/Wood fabricated materials	7	224	302
7 Quebec/Motor vehicles	6	95	155
8 Prairies/Meat and meat preparations	10	566	760
9 Atlantic/Paper and paperboard	8	96	91
10 BC/Paper and paperboard	9	318	321

Regions and manufactured commodities that moved up the ranking are: Ontario/General or unclassified freight, Quebec/General or unclassified freight, and British Columbia/Wood-fabricated materials. Ontario and Quebec wood-fabricated materials were among the top ten for 1997. Particularly noteworthy is the rapid growth of general freight from Ontario and Quebec. General freight entered Ontario's top-five list in 1993 and Quebec's in 1995. Ontario's 238 percent increase occurred in four years, and Quebec's 138 percent increase occurred in three years.

Transborder Operations

Among the long-haul LTLs, the major development was the purchase of Winnipeg-based Reimer Express by Roadway Express in 1997, through which it acquired a twenty-four-terminal network stretching from Montreal to Vancouver. Because Roadway closed twenty-two of its own Canadian terminals, the acquisition represented integration more than expansion. Roadway's strategy was to accommodate north-south traffic more efficiently. The reconfiguration added 6.6 percent to Roadway's total tonnage for the first quarter of 1997.[144] There has also been expansion from Canada. LTL operations into the United States are feasible in traffic lanes with sufficient volume to support terminals. Unlike traditional LTL, which sought to serve large areas, the emphasis is on a few terminals in key locations. Concord Transportation, which grew from a family business and operates 185 tractors and 275 trailers, has concentrated on overnight service in three carefully chosen corridors – Toronto-Montreal, Toronto-Chicago, and Vancouver-Seattle – and has additional terminals in San Francisco and Los Angeles.[145]

Regional LTLs have expanded by forming transborder partnerships. For the Canadian regional carriers, the partnerships are attractive because they provide access to the United States without the need to invest in terminals and hire American staff. By dealing with firms that are established in their territories, alliances also reduce risk.[146] In one combination, New Brunswick-based Day and Ross interchanges cargo with Massachusetts-based Plymouth Rock Transportation at Plymouth's terminal in New Jersey, giving the two carriers joint coverage of the New England and Mid-Atlantic states and the Atlantic provinces, Quebec, and Ontario. Another alliance involves New Jersey-based TNT Red Star Express and New Brunswick-based Midland Transport Ltd.[147] Cabano Transport of Quebec opened alliances with two American regional carriers (Old Dominion, giving access to the southern Atlantic states, and Churchill, giving access to the Midwest). In transborder refrigerated service, Erb Transport of Ontario formed an alliance with FEE Transportation.[148] Because of the traffic gains and low costs, alliances are attractive propositions. In the view of an Ernst and Young transport specialist, Canadian carriers who have not yet formed alliances with American carriers or invested in them should do so.[149]

Alliances blend integrated and independent operations. An example of integration can be seen in the partnership between Manitoulin Transport and Pennsylvania-based New Penn Motor Express. In the words of Manitoulin's marketing manager, "We're integrating our information systems and operations. It's almost like we're an extension of each other. That's ideally the relationship we want with each of the carriers we're dealing with in the States."[150] In addition to its partnership with New Penn, Manitoulin has alliances with six other American carriers, giving it service coverage of the entire country. Manitoulin also operates independently in the United States, with terminals in Chicago, Minneapolis, and Detroit.

With no need for terminal networks, the Canadian TL firms that expanded in the American market after deregulation in 1980 quickly began doing very well.[151] Others organized or expanded as free trade's prospects began to emerge. For carriers coping with deregulation and the 1990 recession, these moves were a gamble. In 1991, when other carriers were failing or cutting back, Ontario-based Challenger Motor Freight invested heavily in expansion.[152] Positioned as a transborder TL carrier specializing in auto parts, paper, furniture, and electronic equipment, Challenger benefited quickly from free trade, returning to profitability in 1993 and expanding its fleet to 700 tractors and 1,800 trailers. In 1994, soaring traffic allowed Challenger to expand its American operations by 30 percent.[153] Later that year, with the passage of NAFTA and the conclusion of a bilateral trucking agreement with Mexico, Challenger was the first Canadian carrier to offer through service.[154] Muskoka Transport, seen earlier as a target of aggressive competition by a large American TL, now does 55 percent of its business in the United States, compared to 15 percent in the late 1980s.[155]

The same conditions – abundant traffic and free truck movement – make transborder operations available to small firms. Garden Grove Produce Imports, a Winnipeg-based distributor, decided in 1992 to use its own trucks to bring produce from California and Texas. To provide backhauls, Garden Grove began soliciting agricultural and general freight in Canada, and by 1993 trucking accounted for half of Garden Grove's business. Free trade and deregulation, according to the firm's owner, "made it easier to move more product into Canada and easier to run trucks."[156]

Because TL carriers operate directly from shipper to receiver, their main operational requirement is having a load available at the point of delivery. Operating in purely domestic markets makes possible the continuous movement between shippers and receivers that vehicle utilization requires. With no restriction on movement, the next destination may be anywhere. That latitude increases the number of acceptable cargoes. Cabotage rules restrict that latitude for foreign carriers. Roughly symmetrical American and Canadian restrictions – principally customs duties on foreign equipment and immigration rules on foreign drivers – prevent foreign carriers from hauling cargoes between domestic points.[157] Cabotage is permitted in the two countries only under the limited circumstances of repositioning equipment and carrying cargoes that are "incidental" to an international trip.[158] Traffic that is off the line of travel to and from the border is generally unavailable, unless carriers use domestic equipment and drivers and have a domestic place of business. In practice, according to one carrier executive, "the customs definition [of cabotage] was so broad that it practically encompassed anything you did outside of deadheading straight back to where you came from."[159]

Because of the different dispersion of traffic centres in the two countries, cabotage restrictions affect American and Canadian carriers differently. For American carriers, the concentration of traffic potential in Canada's three major metropolitan areas, along with their proximity to the border, expands the prospects of having return loads nearby. For Canadian carriers, finding return loads far from the border depends on shippers near the point of delivery with cargoes for Canada. Two conditions improve Canadian carriers' prospects. The first is triangular routing, and the second, is direct expansion into the United States.

Triangular routes have two of their base points in Canada and their apex in the United States. By adding Canadian destinations, triangular routes increase the availability of return loads. An example of a triangular trip would be taking furniture from Ontario to the southern United States, travelling from there to a western province with general freight, and returning across Canada to Ontario with food products. Triangular routings enable Canadian carriers to maximize their opportunities to find cargoes in all parts of their operations and to compete more widely for transborder traffic.[160]

Efforts by shippers to achieve economies of scale by consolidating distribution into giant regional centres in order to serve both the United States and Canada favour triangular routes. "If you have a warehouse in Calgary, Chicago, and Seattle," one carrier executive observed, "you probably don't need them all."[161] Because of the number of points in a regional network, transborder distribution encourages triangular movements.[162] Taking advantage of integrated distribution was the objective of Ontario-based TNT Overland Express when it formed an alliance with three American carriers to create Express LINK. Its partners are Estes Express of Virginia, GI Trucking of California, and Lakeville Motor Express of Minnesota. For TNT, that set of partners expands the points TNT can offer its Canadian shippers. The carrier's vice-president attributed the strategy directly to trade.[163]

With traffic potential multiplying under NAFTA, cabotage restrictions became increasingly constraining. In 1994 the CTA (which became the Canadian Trucking Alliance in 1997) proposed to the ATA that they join forces to push for changes in the two countries' customs regulations governing foreign trucks. They succeeded in reaching agreement on allowing foreign carriers one free domestic trip for each international one.[164] Progress stalled in 1997 when the Canadian government sought to apply the GST to the value of the transport performed in Canada and, much more expensively, to the value of the US vehicles being used.[165] Agreed to instead was a reinterpretation of existing rules so that the domestic or international status of a shipment is determined by its origin and destination and not by the line of travel of its transport vehicle. That definition allows more flexibility in travelling domestically to pick up and deliver international cargoes. Immigration restrictions in both countries, however, continue to prohibit domestic movements from being handled by foreign drivers.

Cabotage restrictions can be eliminated by opening subsidiaries in the United States or by acquiring American firms. One attraction of direct expansion is retaining a single corporate management, thus facilitating integration on an extensive scale. Another is the ability to offer more elaborate combinations of domestic and international service. For carriers expanding from a large base in Canada, the prospects can be spacious. Trimac Ltd. acquired a Wyoming-based regional fuel carrier in 1989, adding to its other American carrier holdings in Kentucky, Texas, Washington, and California and broadening its service offerings.[166] In 1992 Trimac purchased a Seattle-based bulk carrier and consolidated its holdings in the Northwest into a single operation. Intrastate deregulation in 1995 opened those markets, allowing Trimac to bid on local fuel contracts.[167] Anticipating increased trade with Mexico, Trimac entered an interline agreement with a Mexican carrier, Transportes Norti-Mex, for bulk commodities service between the three countries.[168] In a similar move, Vitran Corp. of Toronto purchased Overland Group, an Ohio-based carrier, as the first step in assembling a North American distribution service. To provide flexible regional coverage, Vitran plans to use both contract and regional LTL carriage. Vitran's intermodal base in Canada enables it to expand into the Toronto-Chicago and Chicago-Los Angeles corridors.[169] In 1995, American operations accounted for 55 percent of Vitran's revenues.[170]

Cyber-Integration

At a Vancouver coffee shop in 1996, entrepreneur Michael Paterson met a stranded owner-operator from Tennessee who had delivered a load several days earlier but could not find a return load to get back home. This prompted Paterson to think of ways of making load information readily available and to allow small operators to bypass freight brokers – whose normal commission is 10 percent. In 1997 Paterson set up a trucker-run site on the Internet to enable carriers and shippers to contact each other directly and arrange transportation. There are now 21 load-matching sites on the Internet. Examples are getloaded.com, freight-terminal.com, and freightmarket.com. Sabre, the airline reservations system, operates TL and LTL support services at sabre.com.

When American and Canadian regulators withdrew from trucking, they left carriers and shippers to deal with one another directly. Cargo transactions on the Internet allow whatever combinations of shippers, cargoes, carriers, and destinations the participants agree to. This cheap and simple innovation democratizes the motor carrier industry, enabling the smallest firms and independent operators to find business and making price information generally available.[171] In the same extemporaneous and decentralized way, it creates a single continental marketplace.

Sociologists who study markets regard pricing as an interactive process in which suppliers use their formal and informal abilities to assess competitors' outputs and prices – the most visible indicators of the relationships among producers and buyers.[172] Although the Internet makes prices readily available, two aspects of deregulated trucking complicate the process. The first is the blend of public and confidential price information. The major carriers do post rates, but deregulation in both countries allows carriers and shippers to establish confidential rates and to negotiate discounts. The public rates are widely known and serve as marker prices, but it is the thousands of daily transactions between carriers and shippers that establish what is actually charged. That makes the Internet a spot market that augments a much larger field of price activity. Trucking also delivers a multitude of individual products, making them difficult to compare and producing a range of prices.[173] Together, these conditions greatly expand the task of conducting systematic assessments of competitors.[174] Ultimately, price floors are determined by a producer's costs, and ceilings are determined by a buyer's valuation of the product and awareness of alternatives. Within these boundaries there is much room for comparison, uncertainty, and negotiation.

Although deregulation has provided widespread access, and free trade has generated growing levels of traffic, carrier involvement varies. LTL carriers, as we have seen, are tied to fixed terminal networks, and most of the survivors are regional. The opportunities of private carriers to carry other shippers' cargoes are limited by the logistics patterns of their parent firms, while TL carriers have high mobility. Together, we can see carriers operating in niches created by their operational latitudes and their shippers' requirements. Some of these niches are local, others regional, and still others continental.[175] Together they constitute a rich network.

Conclusion

Free trade and deregulation proved to be complementary reforms. Deregulation prompted the industry to restructure according to actual demand, and free trade provided eventually substantial levels of traffic. The sectoral nature of the industry and the spatial location of traffic centres in the two countries supply an array of advantages and niches. TL carriers, with their unlimited mobility, are the ones best suited to profit. For American carriers, the fact that Canada's major traffic centres are located close to the border makes it easy and inexpensive to add international service. For Canadian carriers, the ability of TL carriers to range broadly puts the entire American market within reach. As carrier services have diversified, shippers have adopted specialized logistics and brought carriers into close relationships. As continent-wide traffic patterns develop, organizationally unified operations in the two countries become possible, either as close alliances of American and Canadian carriers or as single-firm enterprises. In these ways free trade and deregulated transport mutually reinforce one another. Their effects show in expansion and diversification, as thousands of vehicles trace various logistical patterns.

7
Conclusion

We have seen the potent force of economic efficiency – both prospective and achieved. Academic demonstrations of regulatory waste became a prospective remedy when stagflation prompted the American government to perceive a crisis in regulation. Facing the same circumstance the Canadian government ordered a major regulatory review. Because the two countries' motor carrier industries had always been regulated, removing controls led to courting the unknown. The actual sequence of deregulation resulted in the American experience being a demonstration case. Canadian advocates of reform could point to the gains related to lower shipping costs, while Canadian opponents of reform could point to turbulence and distress. As the process continued, efficiency expanded from being a primarily domestic concern to being an international concern. In the United States, falling logistics costs were part of a more general recovery of industrial advantages. In Canada, those costs could be used to address international competitiveness – a concern made salient by a major recession.

Prospective efficiency weakened the arguments of protected trucking industries. Successful in persuading Congress to stop short of full deregulation, those arguments did not stop a redirected ICC. In Canada, the industry's ability to forestall change owed much to its being within a federal jurisdiction. The motor carriers accurately foretold that there would be dislocation, and the real distress that occurred should not be minimized. Restructuring in both countries, particularly as it led to the failure and loss of long-established common carriers, seriously affected personal livelihoods. Survival involved more than adapting to price and service competition; it meant finding new and attractive ways of using carrier resources amidst severe cost pressures, service innovations, and increasingly demanding expectations from shippers. With controls removed on both sides of the border, that adaptation has been international.

An open and efficient trucking industry proved to be highly compatible with free trade. From a transborder base in Ontario and the American northeast and upper midwest, trucking has followed trade in an extending pattern of commercial movement. As in domestic transport, trucking's international advantages are speed and flexibility. Seeking lower costs and higher efficiency, industry has adopted more closely scheduled logistics (which, themselves, trace the evolution of free trade). Freed from regulatory restrictions, motor carriers are well positioned to adapt to them. These developments prompt more general reflections about the territorial organization of industry and commerce.

Jurisdiction and Movement

State boundaries, rather than reflecting the natural structure of economic activity, may merely enclose it within authority and rules. There may be no particular reason why some, if not most, economic activity should be confined within continuous frontiers.[1] Left on their own, industries with flexible technologies and international markets might operate fluidly and successfully across territorial jurisdictions.

This prospect itself is not new. Almost a half century ago international relations theorist Quincy Wright depicted "producing and trading systems ... and systems of communication and transportation" as converging naturally in particular areas, with jurisdictional boundaries resulting from the imposition of "legal and administrative systems." He was interested in the extent to which such boundaries reflect natural commerce and transportation and the "degree of discontinuity at frontiers of communication and transportation systems and the relative extensiveness of actual communication and trade across frontiers."[2] Viewing states as enclosures on a broader field of transactions, with boundaries not necessarily reflecting the actual perimeters of activity, Wright was interested in "the relative abruptness of changes at frontiers" and the "permeability" of the frontiers themselves. He saw states as "hampering the trend in a shrinking world toward a reduction of national differences" and looked towards a "more homogenous field in which national boundaries present less formidable barriers to communication ... and trade."[3]

A more recent study emphasizes natural routes and confluences – "canals, rivers, ports, highways, airline hubs and electronic networks." These, writes David Elkins, "may have been crucial in economic, social and political life. Especially crucial for economic development and urban growth have been instances where more than one means of communication or transportation intersected: for example, where a caravan route links up with a catchment area, or a canal ties a river system to a seaport, or a seaport like London or New York spawns a railroad network."[4]

These networks, and the economic activity they support, have become more autonomous. As that has happened, "territorial organization – especially contiguity – has declined in significance."[5] Economic activity establishes its own natural boundaries, and those may or may not coincide with state jurisdictions.

Industries can indeed have their own boundaries.[6] Recent research in economic sociology, drawing on network analysis, maps industries by transactions between buyers and sellers. The defining indicators are the overlapping of products and the level and intensity of the buyers' and sellers' relationships.[7] When the state is present as a regulator, and when controls govern market entry as they did in trucking, industrial boundaries are jurisdictional. When the state is absent after deregulation, industrial boundaries are transactional.

Whether an industry actually flows across international boundaries depends on the demand for its products and the mobility of its organization. Deregulation transformed trucking by replacing rules with prices.[8] When the American and Canadian governments adopted the same reform, the transformation became international. Decisions about investment, location, and operations became the carriers' sole discretion, and the border was open. Regulation's strikingly similar origins and standards in Canada and the United States produced two highly complementary neighbouring industries. Unbound from regulatory controls and able to move into new markets quickly, motor carriers were in ready supply. Deregulation was intended to increase efficiency in domestic trucking markets, but by allowing free travel among the commercial routes of Canada and the United States, deregulation achieved its final results internationally.

Free trade increased traffic and extended it from its previous concentration in automotive commodities between Ontario and the north-central states into more comprehensive patterns. Sectoral developments in trucking were highly compatible. Under deregulation, mobile and adaptive TL carriers were able to begin offering fast point-to-point service across the continent, expanding shippers' choices of service and multiplying the points of origin and delivery. TL is the ideal medium in just-in-time and integrated logistics schemes. Production, supply, and distribution have been rationalizing under free trade, generating complex patterns of transportation and demands for highly dependable service. The location of traffic centres favours large American LTL carriers, who can serve Canada from established networks in the United States. The same location favours Canadian TL carriers, whose mobility gives them free range of a vast American market.

Carrier-shipper relations, closely organized under regulation, have become directly interactive. The boundaries of movement are shaped by the shippers' logistical needs, which carriers compete to supply. Traffic is now contestable on a continent-wide basis for carriers of all sizes and specialties. The ultimate expression of deregulation and trade as complementary forces is found in the truckers' cargo websites. Access to supply and price information is cheap and universal, eliminating the size threshold to continent-wide operations and enabling any carrier to exploit its mobility.

Open Roads: A Globalizing Metaphor

Efficiency gains and expanded markets provide the incentives for integrated commercial activity. Low barriers to trade and investment provide access and capital. Telecommunications and transport furnish fast and inexpensive linkages. As one of a set of facilitating factors, cheap and efficient transportation encourages commercial movement. The advent of just-in-time and flow through logistics came when shippers realized the potential of the transport resources that were becoming available under deregulation. Integrated production and expanded markets become feasible when transporters can serve them. Converging streams of goods-laden vehicles at traffic centres and border crossings manifest a general convergence of liberal rules and free movement. As the means expand, so do the commercial horizons.

Notes

Chapter 1: Introduction

1 Statistics Canada, *Trucking in Canada 1995* (Ottawa: Statistics Canada, 1997), 71.
2 Thomas J. Courchene, with Colin R. Telmer, *From Heartland to North American Region State: The Social, Fiscal and Federal Evolution of Ontario* (Toronto: University of Toronto Centre for Public Management, 1998), 297.
3 Statistics Canada, *Trucking in Canada 1989*, 115-6; *Trucking in Canada 1997* (Ottawa: Statistics Canada, 1999), 10, 72.
4 The results have continued long beyond 1980. See, for example, "Motor Carrier Failures Reach Record Highs," *Transport Topics*, 8 April 1991, 17.
5 Daniel Bearth, "Two Majors Discuss Taking Control after Decontrol," *Transport Topics*, 4 February 1991, 9.
6 Harrison White, "Markets, Networks and Control," in *Interdisciplinary Perspectives on Organization Studies*, ed. Siegwart Lindenberg and Hein Schreuder (Oxford: Pergamon, 1993), 227.
7 On the replacement of the norms of regulation with the norm of open competition in domestic and international aviation and in maritime shipping, see Mark Zacher with Brent Sutton, *Governing Global Networks: International Regimes for Transportation and Communications* (Cambridge: Cambridge University Press, 1996), 76-8, 126. On intramural comparisons, price, and output decisions, see Harrison White, "Production Markets as Induced Role Structures," in *Sociological Methodology 1981*, ed. Samuel Leinhardt (San Francisco: Jossey Bass, 1981), 44-5; Harrison White, "Where Do Markets Come From?" *American Journal of Sociology* 87 (November 1981): 518; and Joel Podolny, "A Status-Based Model of Market Competition," *American Journal of Sociology* 98 (January 1993): 829-72.
8 Eric Leifer, "Markets as Mechanisms: Using a Role Structure," *Social Forces* 64 (December 1985): 446.
9 Jeffrey Frieden and Ronald Rogowski, "The Impact of the International Economy on National Policies: An Analytical Overview," in *Internationalization and Domestic Politics*, ed. Helen Milner and Robert Keohane (Cambridge: Cambridge University Press, 1996), 31.
10 Some reformers have been amazed by the forces they unleashed. For a statement by a drafter of the Motor Carrier Act, 1980, see Will Ris in the Management Outlook Forum, *Transport Topics*, 25 January 1993, 11, 15.
11 Statistics Canada, *Trucking in Canada 1997*, 72.
12 Ibid., 71.

Chapter 2: The State in Action

1 Huseyin Leblebici and Gerald Salancik, "Stability in Interorganizational Exchanges: Rulemaking Processes of the Chicago Board of Trade," *Administrative Science Quarterly 27* (June 1982): 228, 239.
2 John Meyer and Brian Rowan, "Institutionalized Organizations: Formal Structure as Myth and Ceremony," in *The New Institutionalism in Organizational Analysis*, ed. Walter Powell

and Paul DiMaggio (Chicago: University of Chicago Press, 1991), 52.

3 Ibid., 194.

4 Ibid.

5 Mitchell Koza, "Regulation and Organization: Environmental Niche Structure and Administrative Organization," in *Research in the Sociology of Organizations*, vol. 6, *1988*, ed. Nancy DiTomaso and Samuel Bacharach (Greenwich, CN: JAI Press, 1988), 189.

6 On the nature of multiproduct industries, see Ann F. Friedlaender and Elizabeth Bailey, "Market Structure and Multiproduct Industries," *Journal of Economic Literature* 20 (September 1982): 1024-48. The article treats trucking as an example of a multiproduct industry.

7 Koza, "Regulation and Organization," 170.

8 Udo Staber and Howard Aldrich, "Trade Association Stability and Public Policy," in *Organizational Theory and Public Policy*, ed. Richard Hall and Robert Quinn (Beverly Hills: Sage, 1983), 174.

9 Keith Provan, "The Federation as an Interorganizational Linkage Network," *Academy of Management Review* 8 (1983). 79.

10 Meyer and Rowan, "Institutionalized Organizations," 52

11 Ibid.

12 Frank Dobbin, *Forging Industrial Policy: The United States, Britain, and France in the Railway Age* (Cambridge: Cambridge University Press, 1994), 20-1.

13 Walter Powell, "Expanding the Scope of Institutional Analysis," in Powell and DiMaggio, *New Institutionalism*, 191.

14 For a colourful description of commercial travel on early roads, see Archibald Currie, *Canadian Transportation Economics* (Toronto: University of Toronto Press, 1967), 438-42.

15 Regulation, particularly size and weight restrictions, had a direct effect on vehicle design. In the western American states, bridge weight formulas produced truck tractors with very long wheelbases, resulting in many extra feet of unused space between cab and trailer.

16 Alexander L. Morton, "Is There an Alternative to Regulation for the Railroads?" in *Perspectives on Federal Transportation Policy*, ed. James Miller (Washington, DC: American Enterprise Institute, 1975), 28; Howard J. Darling, "Transport Policy in Canada: The Struggle of Ideologies versus Realities," in *Issues in Canadian Transport Policy*, ed. K.W. Studnicki-Gizbert (Toronto: Macmillan, 1974), 14-5.

17 The Supreme Court of the United States, 267 U.S. 307 (1925); 267 U.S. 317 (1925).

18 William Childs, *Trucking and the Public Interest: The Emergence of Federal Regulation 1914-1940* (Knoxville, TN: University of Tennessee Press, 1985), 70-81.

19 Thomas Gale Moore, *Freight Transportation Regulation* (Washington, DC: American Enterprise Institute, 1972), 25, 26.

20 Dudley Pegrum, "The Economic Basis of Public Policy for Motor Transport," *Land Economics* 28 (1952): 250; Childs, *Trucking and the Public Interest*, 84-9; Roger G. Noll, *Reforming Regulation: An Evaluation of the Ash Council Proposals* (Washington, DC: Brookings Institution, 1971), 38.

21 Childs, *Trucking and the Public Interest*, 94.

22 Eugene D. Anderson, "The Motor Carrier Authorities Game," *ICC Practitioners Journal* 47 (November/December 1979): 27.

23 A summary of the reports of the federal coordinator of transportation from 1933 to 1940 appears in Harvey Levine, *National Transportation Policy: A Study of Studies* (Lexington MA: Lexington, 1978), 131-5.

24 Dudley F. Pegrum, *Transportation Economics and Public Policy*, 3rd ed. (Homewood IL: Irwin, 1973), 333.

25 James March and Johan Olsen, *Rediscovering Institutions* (New York: Free Press, 1989), 38.

26 Childs, *Trucking and the Public Interest*, 120-2.

27 Ibid., 128.

28 Ibid.

29 Anderson, "The Motor Carrier Authorities Game," 32-6.

30 James C. Nelson, "Politics and Economics in Transport Regulation and Deregulation: A Century Perspective on the ICC's Role," *Logistics and Transportation Journal* 23 (March 1987): 14-5.

31 March and Olsen, *Rediscovering Institutions*, 54.

32 Frank Dobbin, *Forging Industrial Policy: The United States, Britain, and France in the Railway Age* (Cambridge: Cambridge University Press, 1994), 20.
33 Ibid., 21.
34 March and Olsen, *Rediscovering Institutions,* 39, 54.
35 James C. Nelson, "The Changing Economic Base for Surface Transport Regulation," in *Perspectives on Federal Transportation Policy*, ed. James Miller (Washington, DC: American Enterprise Institute, 1975), 14.
36 Harold Kaplan, *Policy and Rationality: The Regulation of Canadian Trucking* (Toronto: University of Toronto Press, 1989), 34.
37 Childs, *Trucking and the Public Interest,* 116-7.
38 Kaplan, *Policy and Rationality,* 34.
39 Royal Commission into Railways and Transportation, Report, 20 November 1931, 55, quoted in M.L. Rapoport, QC, "History of the Public Commercial Vehicles Act and Related Laws and Regulations," prepared for the Ontario PCV Review Committee, October 1981, 2.
40 Ibid., 4.
41 F.P. Nix and A.M. Clayton, *Motor Carrier Regulation: Institutions and Practices* (Ottawa: Economic Council of Canada, 1980), 12, 13.
42 Kaplan, *Policy and Rationality,* 42.
43 Ibid.
44 Nix and Clayton, *Motor Carrier Regulation,* 96.
45 Ibid.
46 Ibid., 98.
47 M.W. Westmacott and D.J. Phillips, "Transportation Policy and National Unity," in *Canada Challenged: The Viability of Confederation*, ed. R.B. Byers and Robert W. Reford (Toronto: Canadian Institute of International Affairs, 1979), 237.
48 Richard J. Shultz, *Federalism, Bureaucracy, and Public Policy: The Politics of Highway Transport Regulation* (Montreal: McGill-Queen's University Press, 1980), 14.
49 Rapoport, "History of the Public Commercial Vehicles Act," 14.
50 Schultz, *Federalism, Bureaucracy, and Public Policy,* 15.
51 Ibid.
52 Rapoport, "History of the Public Commercial Vehicles Act," 15.
53 Ibid., 16.
54 Kaplan, *Policy and Rationality,* 41.
55 Nix and Clayton, *Motor Carrier Regulation,* 43.
56 Ibid., 115-9.
57 Rapoport, "History of the Public Commercial Vehicles Act," 16.
58 Interstate Commerce Commission, 1 M.C.C. 190, 202 (1936).
59 Ibid.
60 Interstate Commerce Commission, 1 M.C.C., 712, 715-16 (1937).
61 Robert Fellmeth, *The Interstate Commerce Omission: The Public Interest and the ICC* (New York: Grossman, 1970), 120.
62 Anderson, "The Motor Carrier Authorities Game," 41.
63 For more information on the workings of route and commodity restrictions, see Fellmeth, *Interstate Commerce Omission,* 121-3.
64 Ron Hirschhorn, *Trucking Regulation in Canada: A Review of the Issues,* Working Paper no. 26 (Ottawa, Economic Council of Canada, December 1981), 16.
65 Interdepartmental Committee on Competition and Regulation in Transportation, *Competition and Regulation in Inter-City Trucking in Canada* (Ottawa: Transport Canada, 1982), 15.
66 Hirschhorn, *Trucking Regulation in Canada,* 24.
67 Norman Bonsor, "The Development of Regulation in the Highway Trucking Industry in Ontario," in *Government Regulation, Issues and Alternatives: 1978* (Toronto: Economic Council of Ontario, 1978), 116.
68 Richard Lande, "Changing Canadian Trucking Laws Affect U.S. Carriers," *Transport Topics,* 25 May 1987, 9-10.
69 Bonsor, "Development of Regulation," 119.
70 Nix and Clayton, *Motor Carrier Regulation,* 66.
71 Michel Boucher, "Regulation of the Quebec Trucking Industry: Institutions, Practices and

Analytical Considerations," in *Studies of Trucking Regulation,* vol. 2., ed. Norman C. Bonsor, Michel Boucher, J.J. McRae, D.M. Prescott, R.J. Lord and J. Shaw (Ottawa: Economic Council of Canada, 1990), 72-5, 91.

72 Bonsor, "Development of Regulation," 116.
73 "Line-Haul Costs," *Transport Topics,* 19 December 1988, 4.
74 Taff, *Commercial Motor Transportation,* 199.
75 Ibid., 108, 109.
76 Robyn, *Braking the Special Interests,* 18.
77 Fellmeth, *Interstate Commerce Omission,* 60.
78 "Gain with No Pain," *Canadian Transportation Logistics* 99 (December 1996): 15.
79 For regulations by province, see Interdepartmental Committee on Competition and Regulation in Transportation, *Competition and Regulation in Inter-City Trucking in Canada,* 3-18, under heading "Service Provisions."
80 Cairns and Kirk, *Canadian For-Hire Trucking,* 14; Rapoport, "History of the Public Commercial Vehicles Act," 8.
81 Garland Chow, *Rate and Cost Analysis of For-Hire Trucking: Provincial Comparisons* (Ottawa: Bureau of Competition Policy, Consumer and Corporate Affairs Canada, 1982); James J. McRae, *Definition and Characteristics of the Trucking Markets: A Statistical Analysis* (Ottawa: Strategic Policy Directorate, Transport Canada, 1980); M.B. Cairns and B.D. Kirk, *Canadian For-Hire Trucking and the Effects of Regulation: A Cost-Structure Analysis* (Ottawa: Research Branch, Canadian Transport Commission, 1980); Interdepartmental Committee on Competition and Regulation in Transportation, *Competition and Economic Regulation in Transportation: Summary Report* (Ottawa: Transport Canada, 1982).
82 Bonsor, "Development of Regulation," 116.
83 Adil Cubukgil and Richard M. Soberman, *Impact of Proposed Regulatory Reform* (Transmode Consultants, 1980), 25. For an argument favouring expanding contract carriage in Canada, see James J. McRae and David M. Prescott, "Second Thoughts on Tariff Bureaus," *Canadian Public Policy* 9 (June 1983): 200-9.
84 "Trucking's Future Belongs to the Swift and Sure Handed," *Transport Topics,* 17 July 1989, 8.
85 *Transport Topics, Management Outlook Forum,* 22 January 1990, 14.
86 *Annual Review of the National Transportation Agency of Canada, 1993* (Ottawa: National Transportation Agency of Canada, 1994), 211, fig. 9.13. That tabulation does not distinguish LTL results.
87 Nelson, "Politics and Economics in Transport Regulation," 24.
88 Andrew F. Daugherty, Forrest D. Nelson, and William R. Vigdor, "An Econometric Analysis of the Cost and Production Structure of the Trucking Industry," in *Analytical Studies in Transport Economics,* ed. Andrew F. Daugherty (Cambridge: Cambridge University Press, 1985), 66.
89 Dorothy Robyn, *Braking the Special Interests: Trucking Deregulation and the Politics of Policy Reform* (Chicago: University of Chicago Press, 1987), 18-9.
90 Ibid.
91 James J. McRae and David M. Prescott, "Second Thoughts on Tariff Bureaus," *Canadian Public Policy* 9 (June 1983): 202.
92 Interdepartmental Committee on Competition and Regulation in Transportation, *Competition and Regulation,* 17-8.
93 Currie, *Canadian Transportation Economics,* 459.
94 Nix and Clayton, *Motor Carrier Regulation,* 46.
95 Bonsor, "Development of Regulation," 118.
96 Boucher, "Regulation of the Quebec Trucking Industry," 101-2.
97 Currie, *Canadian Transportation Economics,* 459.
98 Ibid., 460.
99 Personal communications, 1986-92.
100 Kaplan, *Policy and Rationality,* 80-90.

Chapter 3: The State Withdraws

1 Michael Atkinson and William Coleman, "Strong States and Weak States: Sectoral Policy Networks in Advanced Capitalist Economies," *British Journal of Political Science* 19 (January

1989): 51.
2 Ibid., 52.
3 Paul Sabatier, "Policy Change over a Decade or More," in *Policy Change and Learning: An Advocacy Coalition Approach*, ed. Paul Sabatier and Hank Jenkins-Smith (Boulder: Westview, 1993), 13-39.
4 Anthony Brown and Joseph Stewart, Jr., "Competing Advocacy Coalitions, Policy Evolution and Airline Deregulation," in Sabatier and Smith, *Policy Change and Learning*, 84.
5 Hank Jenkins-Smith and Paul Sabatier, "The Dynamics of Policy-Oriented Learning," in Sabatier and Jenkins-Smith, *Policy Change and Learning*, 45-8.
6 Brown and Stewart, "Competing Advocacy Coalitions," 101.
7 Ibid., 85-6; Mark Zacher with Brent Sutton, *Governing Global Networks: International Regimes for Transportation and Communications* (Cambridge: Cambridge University Press, 1996), 115.
8 On assumed rationality as a source of institutional persistence, see Frank Dobbin, *Forging Industrial Policy: The United States, Britain, and France in the Railway Age* (Cambridge: Cambridge University Press, 1994), 21.
9 James C. Nelson, "Politics and Economics in Transport Regulation: A Century Perspective of the ICC's Role," *Logistics and Transportation Review* 23 (March 1987): 18.
10 James C. Nelson, "New Concepts in Transportation Regulation," *Transportation and National Policy* (Washington, DC: US Government Printing Office, 1942), 197-243.
11 Nelson's report was published as *Federal Regulatory Restrictions upon Motor and Water Carriers*, Senate Document 78, 79th Congress, 1st session. (Washington, DC: US Government Printing Office, 1945).
12 Dudley F. Pegrum, "The Economic Basis for Public Policy for Motor Transport," *Land Economics* 28 (1952): 244-63.
13 Robert A. Nelson, "The Economic Structure of the Highway Carrier Industry in New England" (Boston: New England Governor's Conference on Public Transportation, 1957), 313-4.
14 Dudley F. Pegrum, *Public Regulation of Business*, 2nd ed. (Homewood, IL: Irwin, 1965), 620.
15 John W. Snow, "The Problem of Motor Carrier Regulation and the Ford Administration's Proposal for Reform," in *Regulation of Entry and Pricing in Truck Transportation*, ed. Paul W. MacAvoy and John W. Snow (Washington, DC: American Enterprise Institute, 1977), 37.
16 John B. Lansing, *Transportation and Public Policy* (New York: Free Press, 1966), 262.
17 Presidential Advisory Committee on Transport Policy and Organization, *Revision of Federal Transportation Policy* (Washington, DC: US Government Printing Office, 1955).
18 James C. Miller, III, "Introduction," in *Perspectives on Federal Transportation Policy*, ed. James C. Miller III (Washington, DC: American Enterprise Institute, 1975), 5.
19 For a useful typology of aggressive entrants into markets, see William A. Brock and David S. Evans, "Creamskimming," in *Breaking Up Bell: Essays on Industrial Organization and Regulation*, ed. David S. Evans (New York: North-Holland, 1983), 69.
20 Transportation Act, 1972, Hearings before the Subcommittee on Transportation and Aeronautics of the Committee on Interstate and Foreign Commerce, House of Representatives, 92nd Congress, 2nd session (Washington, DC: US Government Printing Office, 1972).
21 Dudley F. Pegrum, *Transportation: Economics and Public Policy* (Homewood, IL: Irwin, 1968), 401.
22 Ibid., 402.
23 Martha Derthick and Paul J. Quirk, *The Politics of Deregulation* (Washington, DC: Brookings Institution, 1985), 36.
24 Paul Emery, "An Empirical Approach to the Motor Carrier Economics Controversy," *Land Economics* 41 (August 1965): 285-9; Michael L. Lawrence, "Economies of Scale in the General Freight Motor Common Carrier Industry: Additional Evidence," *Proceedings of the Seventeenth Annual Meeting of the Transportation Research Forum* (Oxford, IN: Cross, 1976), 169-96; Mark Ladenson and Allan Stoga, "Returns to Scale in the U.S. Trucking Industry," *Southern Economic Journal* 30 (January 1974): 390-6; Stanley Warner, "Cost Models, Measurement Error and Economies of Scale in Trucking," in *The Cost of Trucking: Econometric Analysis* (Dubuque, IA: Brown, 1965), 1-46.
25 Arthur DeVany and T.R. Saving, "Product Quality, Uncertainty, and Regulation: The Trucking Industry," *American Economic Review* 67 (December 1977): 583-94.

26 Mark Keaton, "The Structure of Costs in the U.S. Motor Carrier Industry," *Proceedings of the Nineteenth Annual Meeting of the Transportation Research Forum* (Oxford, IN: Cross, 1978), 356-64.

27 Victoria Ann Daily, "The Certificate Effect: The Impact of Federal Entry Controls on the Growth of the Motor Common Carrier Firm" (PhD diss., University of Virginia, 1973), 78-98.

28 Merrill Roberts, "Some Aspects of Motor Carrier Costs: Firm Size, Efficiency, and Financial Health," *Land Economics* 32 (August 1956): 228-38; Robert Nelson, "The Economics of Scale in the Motor Industry: A Reply," *Land Economics* 35 (May 1959): 180-5; John Meyer, et al., *The Economics of Competition in the Transportation Industry* (Cambridge: Harvard University Press, 1959).

29 Garland Chow, "The Status of Economies of Scale in Regulated Trucking: A Review of the Evidence and Future Directions," in *Proceedings of the Nineteenth Annual Meeting of the Transportation Research Forum* (Oxford, IN: Cross, 1978), 365-73.

30 Roger Koenker, "Optimal Scale and the Size Distribution of American Trucking Firms," *Journal of Transport Economics and Policy* 9 (January 1977): 54-67; Ann Friedlaender, "Hedonic Costs and Economies of Scale in the Regulated Trucking Industry," *CTS Report 77-5* (Center for Transportation Studies, Massachusetts Institute of Technology, 1977).

31 Stephen Breyer, *Regulation and Its Reform* (Cambridge: Harvard University Press, 1982), 224; George W. Hilton, "Ending the Ground-Transportation Cartel," in *Instead of Regulation: Alternatives to Federal Regulatory Agencies*, ed. Robert W. Poole, Jr. (Lexington, MA: Lexington, 1982), 51.

32 Richard Klem, "Market Structure and Conduct," in *Regulation of Entry and Pricing in Truck Transportation*, ed. Paul W. MacAvoy and John W. Snow (Washington, DC: American Enterprise Institute, 1977), 137-8.

33 Ann F. Friedlaender and Elizabeth Bailey, "Market Structure and Multiproduct Industries," *Journal of Economic Literature* 20 (September 1982): 1,034-5.

34 Judy S. Wang, and Ann F. Friedlaender, "Output Aggregation, Network Effects, and the Measurement of Trucking Technology," *Review of Economics and Statistics* 66 (May 1984): 267-76; Wang and Friedlaender, "Truck Technology and Efficient Market Structure, *Review of Economics and Statistics* 67 (May 1985): 250-8; Laurits Christenson and John Huston, "A Reexamination of the Cost Structure for Specialized Motor Carriers," *Logistics and Transportation Review* 23 (December 1987): 339-52.

35 Janet Thomas and Scott Callan, "Constant Returns to Scale in the Post-Deregulatory Period: The Case of Specialized Motor Carriers," *Logistics and Transportation Review* 25 (September 1989): 271-89.

36 Garland Chow and Michael Tretheway, "Productivity in the U.S. Trucking Industry: The Early Deregulation Experience" (Vancouver: Faculty of Commerce and Business Administration, University of British Columbia, 1988); Curtis Grimm, Thomas Corsi, and Judith Jarrell, "U.S. Motor Carrier Cost Structure under Deregulation," *Logistics and Transportation Review* 25 (September 1989): 231-50.

37 Theodore Keeler, "Deregulation and Scale Economies in the U.S. Trucking Industry: An Econometric Extension of the Survivor Principle," *Journal of Law and Economics* 32 (October 1989): 229-53; John Ying, "Regulatory Reform and Technical Change: New Evidence of Scale Economies in Trucking," *Southern Economic Journal* 56 (April 1990): 996-1,010.

38 Robert Kling, "Deregulation and Structural Change in the LTL Motor Freight Industry," *Transportation Journal* 30 (Spring 1990): 47-53.

39 Hickling Corporation, Division of Economics and Policy in association with Garland Chow, *Economics of the Trucking Industry in Transborder Markets: Final Report*, prepared for the Minister of Transport's Task Force on Trucking Issues, 1991, 2-8.

40 Breyer, *Regulation and Its Reform*, 32.

41 Ibid., 224.

42 Lansing, *Transportation and Public Policy*, 62.

43 Roger G. Noll and Bruce M. Owen, "The Predictability of Interest Group Arguments," in *The Political Economy of Deregulation: Interest Groups in the Regulatory Process*, ed. Roger G. Noll and Bruce M. Owen (Washington, DC: American Enterprise Institute, 1983), 54.

44 Breyer, *Regulation and Its Reform*, 224.

45 Ibid., 31-2.
46 Richard N. Farmer, "The Case for Unregulated Truck Transportation," *Journal of Farm Economics* 46 (May 1964): 403.
47 Ibid., 408.
48 Thomas Gale Moore, *Freight Transportation Regulation* (Washington, DC: American Enterprise Institute, 1972), 62.
49 D. Daryl Wyckoff and David H. Maister, *The Motor-Carrier Industry* (Lexington, MA: Lexington, 1977), xli.
50 J.L. Cavinato and A.G. Stenger, "Purchasing Transportation in the Changing Trucking Industry," *Journal of Purchasing and Materials Management* 19 (Spring 1983): 3.
51 Donald F. Wood and James C. Johnson, *Contemporary Transportation* (Tulsa: Penwell, 1983), 514.
52 Paul W. MacAvoy, ed., *Unsettled Questions on Regulatory Reform* (Washington, DC: American Enterprise Institute, 1978), 10.
53 Friedlaender and Bailey, "Market Structure and Multiproduct Industries," 1042.
54 Ibid.
55 Sabatier and Jenkins-Smith, "Policy Change over a Decade or More," 34.
56 Roger Noll, *Reforming Regulation: An Evaluation of the Ash Council Proposals* (Washington, DC: Brookings Institution, 1971), 110.
57 Ibid., 100.
58 On the impact of stagflation and the rise of regulatory reform, see Alan Altshuler and Roger Teal, "The Political Economy of Airline Deregulation," in *Current Issues in Transportation Policy*, ed. Altshuler and Teal (Lexington, MA: DC Heath, 1979), 43-4.
59 Gary L. Seevers, "Prospects for Regulatory Reform," in *Perspectives on Federal Transportation Policy*, ed. James Miller (Washington, DC: American Enterprise Institute, 1975), 203.
60 Ibid., 202.
61 Fred Thompson, "Regulatory Reform and Deregulation in the United States," in *Government Regulation: Scope, Growth, Process*, ed. W.T. Stanbury and Fred Thompson (Montreal: Institute for Research on Public Policy, 1980), 193.
62 Ibid.
63 D. Daryl Wyckoff and David H. Maister, *The Motor-Carrier Industry* (Lexington, MA: Lexington, 1977), 183-5.
64 Samuel Eastman, "We Can Do More than Just Talk about Motor Carrier Regulatory Reform, *ICC Practitioners' Journal* 46 (July-August 1979): 675.
65 National Transportation Policy Study Commission, *National Transportation Policies through the Year 2000* (Washington, DC: Government Printing Office, June 1979), 248-52.
66 Joseph Steinfeld, "Regulation versus Free Competition: The Current Battle over Deregulation of Entry into the Motor Carrier Industry," *ICC Practitioners' Journal* 45 (July-August 1978): 600.
67 110 M.C.C. 514 (1969).
68 419 U.S. 281 (1974).
69 James C. Johnson and James P. Rakowski, "The Reed-Bulwinkle Act (1948): A Thirty Year Prospective," in *Proceedings of the Nineteenth Annual Meeting of the Transportation Research Forum* (Oxford, IN: Cross, 1978), 24.
70 Marcus Alexis, "Regulation of Surface Transportation," in *The Political Economy of Deregulation: Interest Groups in the Regulatory Process*, ed. Roger G. Noll and Bruce M. Owen (Washington, DC: American Enterprise Institute, 1983), 126.
71 Ibid.
72 Paul J. Quirk, *Industry Influence in Federal Regulatory Agencies* (Princeton: Princeton University Press, 1981), 85, 94; Johnson and Rakowski, "The Reed-Bulwinkle Act (1948)," 24.
73 Steinfeld, "Regulation versus Free Competition," 606.
74 Alexis, "Regulation of Surface Transportation," 123.
75 Roger Noll and Bruce Owen, "Conclusion," in Noll and Owen, *The Political Economy of Deregulation,* 156-7.
76 Ibid.
77 Steinfeld, "Regulation versus Free Competition," 608.
78 Interstate Commerce Commission, Ex Parte No. MC-121.

79 Ibid., *131 MC 573, 575-76.*
80 Paul F. Dempsey, "Erosion of the Regulatory Process in Transportation: The Winds of Change," *ICC Practitioners' Journal* 47 (March-April 1980): 316.
81 Alexis, "Regulation of Surface Transportation," 123-4.
82 *ICC 80: Ninety-Fourth Annual Report of the Interstate Commerce Commission* (Washington, DC: Government Printing Office, 1981), 15.
83 Altshuler and Teal, "Political Economy of Airline Deregulation," 50.
84 Noll and Owen, *Political Economy of Deregulation,* 159.
85 *ICC 80: Ninety-Fourth Annual Report of the Interstate Commerce Commission,* 15, 20, 21.
86 Derthick and Quirk, *Politics of Deregulation,* 121-3.
87 Robyn, *Braking the Special Interests,* passim.
88 Donald V. Harper, "The Federal Motor Carrier Act of 1980: Review and Analysis," *Transportation Journal* 20 (Winter 1980): 9.
89 Thomas Gale Moore, *Freight Transportation Regulation* (Washington, DC: American Enterprise Institute, 1972), 45; Kevin Horn, "Shipper Support and Entry into Regulated Trucking," *Logistics and Transportation Review* 20 (June 1984): 111-26.
90 Michael de Courcy Hinds, "Regulatory Officials' Unusual Ideas Voiced in Free-Wheeling Closed Session," *New York Times,* 12 December 1982, 22. The applicant in question was serving time for drug trafficking and second-degree murder. "How do you find a man like that fit?" Taylor asked a year later. "I don't know. This case was absolutely outrageous." Commissioner Frederic Andre, according to Taylor, apologized to the inmate's family for not granting the application sooner. John Parker, "ICC Members Bare Squabbles During Hill Hearing on Regulation," *Transport Topics,* 21 November 1983, 24.
91 Robert E. Mabley and Walter D. Strack, "Deregulation: A Green Light for Trucking," *Regulation* 6 (July-August 1982): 42, 56.
92 In the ICC's words: "Carriers are to apply for broad, unencumbered authority. Restrictions on authorities generally are disallowed except in unusual instances." *ICC 81: Ninety-Fifth Annual Report of the Interstate Commerce Commission* (Washington, DC: Government Printing Office, 1982), 46.
93 "ATA General Counsel Blasts ICC's 'Mistaken' Ideas on Entry," *Transport Topics,* 1 December 1980, 6.
94 For a concise summary of these developments, see *Highway Common Carrier Newsletter,* 16 November 1983, 8-10.
95 Regular Common Carrier Conference, *Trucking De-regulation/Economic Recession: The Facts* (reprint of testimony before Senate oversight hearings) (Washington, DC: Regular Common Carrier Conference, American Trucking Associations, 1983), 2, 15.
96 "Rate Wars, Overcapacity Are Linked to ICC Action, ATA Tells Congress," *Transport Topics,* 28 June 1982, 1, 11, 41. This story covers testimony before the House oversight hearings.
97 General Accounting Office, *Effects of Regulatory Reform on Unemployment in the Trucking Industry,* GAO/CED-82-90, 11 June 1982.
98 John Meyer and Brian Rowan, "Institutionalized Organizations: Formal Structure as Myth and Ceremony," in *The New Institutionalism in Organizational Analysis,* ed. Walter Powell and Paul DiMaggio (Chicago: University of Chicago Press, 1991), 59.
99 Daniel Bearth, "Trucking Failures Hit Record in 1991," *Transport Topics,* 22 June 1992, 2.
100 Nicholas A. Glaskowsky, *Effects of Deregulation on Motor Carrier* (Westport, CN: Eno Foundation for Transportation, 1986), 21-2.
101 Glaskowsky, *Effects of Deregulation,* 36.
102 Ibid., 21.
103 Bearth, "Trucking Failures Hit Record in 1991," 17.
104 Regular Common Carrier Conference, *Trucking Deregulation/Economic Recession,* 11.
105 Glaskowsky, *Effects of Deregulation,* 19.
106 Ronald D. Roth, "Industry Casualties: 6 Fleets a Day in 1985," *Transport Topics,* 30 June 1986, 13.
107 "Motor Carrier Failures Reach Record Highs," *Transport Topics,* 8 April 1991, 17.
108 "Motor Carrier Profits in Free-Fall," *Transport Topics,* 5 February 1990, 2.
109 Daniel Bearth, "Static LTL Trucking is Losing Profitability, Say Economists," *Transport Topics,* 25 March 1991, 4.

110 "Fleets Still Failing at Record Clip," *Transport Topics,* 2 September 1991, 3.
111 Daniel Bearth, "Two Majors Discuss Taking Control after Decontrol," *Transport Topics,* 4 February 1991, 9.
112 "Trucking's Future Belongs to the Swift and Sure-Handed," *Transport Topics,* 17 July 1989, 8.
113 Glaskowsky, *Effects of Deregulation,* 26.
114 "No Conclusive Evidence of Predatory Pricing in Trucking, GAO Says," *Transport Topics,* 13 April 1987, 3.
115 David L. Sparkman, "Lifschutz Appeal Rejected," *Transport Topics,* 9 July 1993, 7.
116 "Deregulation: You're Stronger for It, If It Doesn't Kill You, Young Says," *Transport Topics,* 9 November 1987, 12.
117 Patricia Cavanaugh, "Analyst sees 'Incredible' Turnover Since Deregulation," *Transport Topics,* 18 July 1988, 8.
118 David L. Sparkman, "Roadway to Leave Rate Bureaus," *Transport Topics,* 29 January 1992, 1, 39.
119 Ibid.
120 Daniel Bearth, "Carolina's Mayhew Predicts Demise of Rate Regulation," *Transport Topics,* 16 July 1990, 9.
121 "Deregulation: You're Stronger for It," 12.
122 Harrison White, "Where Do Markets Come From," *American Journal of Sociology* 87 (November 1981): 519-20.
123 On a firm's reputation as a proxy for the quality of its goods, and on the interactive origins of reputations, see Joel Podolny, "A Status-Based Model of Market Competition," *American Journal of Sociology* 98 (January 1993): 830.
124 Glaskowsky, *Effects of Deregulation on Motor Carriers,* 15.
125 John Schulz, "TL Carriers Planning New Rate Strategy Keyed to Matching Cost of Servicing Shippers," *Traffic World,* 18 March 1991, 7, 8.
126 Glaskowsky, *Effects of Deregulation,* 44.
127 Udo Staber and Howard Aldrich, "Trade Association Stability and Public Policy," in *Organizational Theory and Public Policy,* ed. Richard Hall and Robert Quinn (Beverly Hills: Sage, 1983), 170.
128 David L. Sparkman, "Task Force Proposes Changes in ATA Policies on Regulation," *Transport Topics,* 19 January 1987, 1.
129 Thomas M. Strah, "Sen Packwood 'Ready Again' to Push Decontrol," *Transport Topics,* 8 February 1988, 7.
130 Kevin Hall, "Truckers Group Ducks the Issue on Intrastate Motor Deregulation," *Traffic World,* 2 March 1992, 20. See also John D. Schulz, "Bush Administration Weighs in on Latest Push for Deregulation," *Traffic World,* 6 April 1992, 21.
131 "Special Report: Truckload Freight," *Traffic World,* 30 January 1995, 34.
132 George Bohlander and Martin Farris, "Collective Bargaining in Trucking: The Effects of Deregulation," *Logistics and Transportation Review* 20 (September 1985): 224.
133 Ibid., 232.
134 "Carey a Hit on Capitol Hill," *Traffic World,* 6 April 1992, 23.
135 Donald Harmatuck, "The Effects of Economic Conditions and Regulatory Changes upon Motor Carrier Tonnages and Revenues," *Transportation Journal* 24 (Winter 1984): 38.
136 Daniel Bearth, "Tentative Agreement Ends 24-Day Strike," *Transport Topics,* 9 May 1994, 1.
137 *Globe and Mail,* 10 October 1984, B3.
138 Bohlander and Farris, "Collective Bargaining in Trucking," 229.
139 Daniel Bearth, "Tentative Agreement Ends 24-Day Strike," 30.
140 "After the Strike," *Transport Topics,* 9 May 1994, 30.
141 Daniel Bearth, "Teamsters Face Financial Crisis," *Transport Topics,* 7 June 1993, 1, 22.
142 John Schulz, "Teamsters Red Ink Flowing," *Traffic World,* 2 May 1994, 10.
143 "Sen Packwood 'Ready Again' to Push Decontrol," *Transport Topics,* 8 February 1988, 7.
144 Thomas Strah, "DOT's Trucking Dereg Bill Sent to Congress," *Transport Topics,* 25 May 1987, 1, 2.
145 Thomas M. Strah, "ATA Takes Decontrol Stance," *Transport Topics,* 4 July 1994, 19.
146 "Skinner Focuses on Deregulation," *Transport Topics,* 9 April 1990, 7, 31.
147 "Card Stumps for Deregulation," *Transport Topics,* 6 July 1992, 5.

148 Oliver B. Patton, "On Hill: Decontrol, Undercharges," *Transport Topics,* 9 March 1992, 1, 42.
149 "How We Got Where We Are: A Chronology," *Transport Topics,* 15 August 1994, 23.
150 Strah, "ATA Takes Decontrol Stance," 19.
151 John Schultz, "Life with Donohue," *Traffic World,* 16 June 1997, 35.
152 "Congress Passes Intrastate Deregulation," *Transport Topics,* 15 August 1994, 1, 23.
153 "DOT Opposes ICC Sunset Proposal," *Regular Common Carrier Newsletter,* 18 October 1993, 3.
154 William B. Cassidy, "Clinton Signs Regulatory Reform Act," *Transport Topics,* 5 September 1994, 7.
155 *New York Times,* 29 November 1995, B12; 1 January 1996, A1.

Chapter 4: Deregulation, Discrimination, and Diplomacy
1 Ronald J. Wonnacott, *Aggressive U.S. Reciprocity Evaluated with a New Approach to Trade Conflicts* (Montreal: Institute for Research on Public Policy, 1984), 6.
2 Ibid., 9.
3 Aggressive reciprocity is suggested by Eugene M. Ludwick, "Strategic Considerations for Transportation Planning in a Deregulated and Free Trade Environment," in *Proceedings of the Twenty-Second Annual Meeting of the Canadian Transportation Research Forum* (Saskatoon: University of Saskatchewan Printing Services, 1987), 610.
4 Discrimination is also a trade principle and is prohibited by GATT. With trucking regulation, the absence of an international agreement made this a problem of diffuse reciprocity and removed direct remedy under GATT.
5 Robert O. Keohane, "Reciprocity In International Relations," *International Organization* 40 (Winter 1986): 4.
6 Ibid., 4, 22-4.
7 Ibid., 4. This, according to Keohane, is the normal meaning of reciprocity in economics and game theory.
8 Wonnacott, *Aggressive U.S. Reciprocity,* 10.
9 Alvin Gouldner, "The Norm of Reciprocity: A Preliminary Statement," *American Sociological Review* 25 (April 1960): 164.
10 Ibid., 177.
11 Keohane, "Reciprocity in International Relations," 16-9.
12 Michael Atkinson and William Coleman, "Strong States and Weak States: Sectoral Policy Networks in Advanced Capitalist Economies," *British Journal of Political Science* 19 (January 1989): 51.
13 Robert Putnam, "Diplomacy and Domestic Politics: The Logic of Two Level Games," *International Organization* 42 (Summer 1988): 427-60.
14 Where cited, information for this and the following chapter was gathered in a series of interviews, conducted between 1981 and 1983, with officials in the American and Canadian federal governments, the ATA, the CTA, the Ontario Ministry of Transportation and Communications, officials in the highway transport boards of Manitoba and Alberta, and transport lawyers and consultants in both countries. Their generous help in explaining matters to me is gratefully acknowledged. Responsibility for interpretations and any errors is mine.
15 Interstate Commerce Commission, Ex Parte MC No. 157 (1982), Investigation into Canadian Law and Policy Regarding Applications of American Motor Carriers for Canadian Operating Authority, 3.
16 Canada, Department of External Affairs, "Information on the Policies and Practices of the Canadian Provincial and Federal Governments in Regard to the Trucking Industry," Attachment to Department of External Affairs Note GNT-314, 19 May 1982, 16.
17 Garland Chow and James J. MacRae, "Non-Tariff Barriers and the Structure of the U.S.-Canadian (Transborder) Trucking Industry," *Transportation Journal* 30 (Winter 1990): 7.
18 John Heads, Barry E. Prentice, and Mahlon Harvey, *The Transborder Competitiveness of Canadian Trucking* (Winnipeg: Transport Institute, University of Manitoba, 1991), 27.
19 Ibid., 11-4.
20 Ron Hirschhorn, *Trucking Regulation in Canada: A Review of the Issues,* Working Paper no. 26 (Ottawa: Economic Council of Canada, December 1981), 22.
21 Ibid.

22 Before the Interstate Commerce Commission, Ex Parte No. MC-157, "Investigation into Canadian Law and Policy Regarding Application of American Motor Carriers for Canadian Entry, Joint Brief of Canadian Respondents E.J. Bourque Transport, Ltd., Provost Cartage, Inc., and Transx Ltd.," 26 May 1982, 20.

23 For a brief summary of American cabotage policy prior to 1991, see Barry Holmes, "International Hardball," *Motor Truck*, 1 August 1992, 18.

24 Interview, Department of Transportation, July 1982.

25 "Canada, Mexico Are Winners in MC Act, ATA Tells Congress," *Transport Topics*, 23 February 1981, 14.

26 Ibid., 14.

27 Interviews, Canadian Embassy and American Trucking Association, Washington, DC, July 1982.

28 Mark Larratt-Smith, Ontario Ministry of Transportation and Communications, presentation to conference of Canadian-American Motor Carrier Association, Toronto, 30 September 1982.

29 Chow and MacRae, "Non-Tariff Barriers," 8.

30 Ibid.

31 Interview, American Trucking Association, December 1983.

32 Patricia Lisciandro, *1982 Financial Analysis of the Motor Carrier Industry*, Washington, DC: American Trucking Associations, 1983, 20.

33 Ibid.

34 "Canada, Mexico are Winners in MC Act, ATA Tells Congress," *Transport Topics*, 23 February 1981, 14.

35 *Globe and Mail*, 12 February 1982.

36 Interview, Department of Transportation, April 1982.

37 "U.S. Entry Controls Must be Tighter, Kane Tells Canadians," *Transport Topics*, 13 July 1981, 8.

38 Interview, Canadian Embassy, Washington, DC, April 1982.

39 Interview, Washington, DC, December 1983.

40 House of Representatives, Committee on Public Works and Transportation, Report to accompany H.R. 3663, 97th Congress, 1st session, 17 November 1981, 36.

41 "Canadian Carrier's Plea for Restriction Removal Contested," *Transport Topics*, 4 January 1982, 1, 23.

42 Ex Parte MC No. 157, Tr. 1472.

43 Interviews, Washington, DC, July 1982, December 1983.

44 Department of Transportation, "Before the Interstate Commerce Commission: Response of the United States Department of Transportation to Comments of Transportes del Valle S.S. de C.V. and Auto Express Mexicano Regarding Reciprocity," 13 November 1981, 2.

45 Interview, Canadian Embassy, Washington, DC, July 1982; Interview, Office of the US Trade Representative, December 1983.

46 "U.S. Carriers Fail to Block Canadian Carrier from Entry," *Transport Topics*, 26 October 1981, 21.

47 "Canada Policy Not Grounds for U.S. Protest," *Transport Topics*, 14 December 1981, 1, 43.

48 Interview, Department of State, April 1982.

49 "Rep. Nowak Asks Hold on Canada, Mexico Grants, *Transport Topics*, 11 January 1982, 1, 25.

50 "ICC Weighing Reciprocity Issue, Rep. Nowak Told," *Transport Topics*, 8 February 1982, 1, 26.

51 Interview, Senate Committee on Commerce, Science, and Transportation, April 1982.

52 "Senate Asks Halt on Grants to Foreigners," *Transport Topics*, 15 February 1982, 1, 8.

53 Interview, Interstate Commerce Commission, April 1982.

54 Interview, Washington, DC, December 1983.

55 Interstate Commerce Commission, Ex Parte No. MC-157, 2.

56 Ibid., 4.

57 Ibid., 7.

58 Ibid., 8.

59 Interview, Washington, DC, December 1983.

60 For a thorough exploration of that sentiment, see Stephen Clarkson, *Canada and the Reagan Challenge* (Toronto: Lorimer, 1981).

61 Interview, Canadian Embassy, Washington, DC, April 1982.
62 Interview, Canadian Embassy, July 1982; Interview, Department of External Affairs, November 1983.
63 Interview, Department of State, April 1982.
64 Interview, American Trucking Association, 5 April 1982.
65 Before the Interstate Commerce Commission, Ex Parte No. MC-157, Comments of American Trucking Associations, Inc., Common Carrier Conference: Irregular Route, National Tank Truck Carriers, Inc., Regular Common Carrier Conference, and Specialized Carriers and Rigging Association, 23 March 1982, 3-4.
66 Ibid., 6, 7.
67 Interview, US House of Representatives, April 1982.
68 "Discrimination Not the Issue, Whitlock Informs Canadians," *Transport Topics*, 8 March 1982, 1, 68.
69 *U.S. National Study on Trade in Services*, Washington, DC: Office of the United States Trade Representative, December 1983.
70 Tim Dickson, "Road Haulage Single Market Is Still a Long Way from Reality," *Financial Times*, 23 October 1989, 11.
71 Interview, Department of State, April 1982.
72 Canada-U.S. Meeting on International Trucking, Ottawa, ON, 4 March 1982 (interdepartmental minutes, Departments of State, Transportation, and Commerce), 3, 4.
73 Ibid., 7, 8.
74 Ernest Holsendolph, "U.S. Trucking Decontrol Held Boon to Canadians," *New York Times*, 18 March 1982, D18.
75 Harold Hongju Koh, "A Legal Perspective," *Perspectives on a U.S.-Canadian Free Trade Agreement*, ed. Robert Stern, Philip Trezise, John Whalley (Washington, DC/Ottawa: Brookings Institution/Institute for Research on Public Policy, 1987), 103.
76 Canada-U.S. Meeting on International Trucking, Ontario, 4 March 1982 (interdepartmental minutes), 10.
77 Interview, Department of Transportation, April 1982.
78 "ICC-Canada," *Transport Topics*, 29 March 1982, 1, 4.
79 Before the Interstate Commerce Commission, Ex Parte No. MC-157, Joint Brief of Canadian Respondents E.J. Bourque Transport Ltd., Provost Cartage Inc., and Transx Ltd., 26 May 1982, passim.
80 Ex Parte No. MC-157, Verified Statement of Stephen Paul Flott, 23 March 1982, 18.
81 Interview, Washington, DC, November 1983.
82 Canadian Embassy, Washington, DC, Diplomatic Note No. 179, 13 April 1982.
83 Exchange of correspondence between Morris/Bright/Rose and IU International Management and the US Embassy, Ottawa, concerning the disallowance of the IU International/Canadian Motorways Ltd. takeover, 12 May 1982.
84 Canadian Embassy, Washington, DC, Diplomatic Note No. 314, 19 May 1982.
85 The amendment is contained in the *Congressional Record: Senate*, 30 June 1982, 7,701.
86 "Senate Handed Bill that Ties Foreign Rights to Reciprocity," *Transport Topics*, 17 May 1982, 1, 28.
87 Drew Lewis, Secretary of Transportation, to Senator John Danforth, 21 May 1982.
88 Interview, Department of Transportation, July 1982.
89 Interview, Office of the US Trade Representative, December 1983.
90 Interview, Transport Canada, December 1982.
91 Charles Doran, *Forgotten Partnership: Canadian-American Relations Today* (Baltimore: Johns Hopkins University Press, 1984), 59-61.
92 Interview, Office of the US Trade Representative, December 1983.
93 *Congressional Record: Senate*, 30 June 1982, 7,707.
94 Interview, Department of State, November 1983.
95 Interview, Department of Transportation, July 1982.
96 Notes for an Address by the Honourable William G. Davis, Premier of Ontario, to Great Lakes Water Resources Conference, Mackinac Island, Michigan, 11 June 1982.
97 Canadian Embassy, Washington, DC, Diplomatic Note No. 338, 16 July 1982.
98 "Canada Asks U.S. to Veto Measure Setting Moratorium on Truck Rights," *Traffic World*, 26

July 1982, 13, 14.

99   Robert M. Butler, "Canadians Are Considering 'Options' in Retaliation on Trucking Situation," *Traffic World,* 16 August 1982, 25.

100 Michael T. Kaufman, "Canada Protests Trucking Bill," *New York Times,* 23 August 1982, D1.

101 Samuel Uskiw, Manitoba Minister of Highways and Transportation, to Mark McGuigan, Secretary of State for External Affairs, 24 August 1982.

102 *Financial Post,* 18 September 1982.

103 Carey French, "U.S. Trucking Firm Crying Foul over Decision to Bar Expansion," *Globe and Mail,* 27 September 1982, B9.

104 "ICC Instructed on Canada Rights, Issues Filing Order," *Transport Topics,* 4 October 1982, 1, 21.

105 Canadian-American Motor Carriers Association, memorandum, 21 September 1982.

106 "More Canadian Carriers' Certificates Delayed Pending Probe Findings," *Traffic World,* 26 July 1982, 35.

107 "Canadian Applications for U.S. Truck Rights Delayed Again by ICC," *Traffic World,* 30 August 1982, 30.

108 David L. Sparkman, "Reagan Signs Bus Bill, Lifts Licensing Ban on Canadian Carriers," *Transport Topics,* 28 September 1982, 1, 28.

109 Department of External Affairs, Press Release, 24 September 1982.

110 Jennifer Hunter, "Canadians Not Keen to Retaliate against U.S. Truck Restrictions," *Globe and Mail,* 4 October 1982, B4.

111 John King, "U.S. and Canadian Officials Confused about Trucking Rules," *Globe and Mail,* 22 September 1982, B15.

112 "Trucking War Looms Ahead," *Canadian Transportation and Distribution Management,* August 1982, 15.

113 Interstate Commerce Commission, Ex Parte No. MC-157, "Investigation into Canadian Law and Policy Regarding Applications of American Motor Carriers for Canadian Operating Authority," 8 October 1982, 11-13.

114 Garland Chow, "Canadian-U.S. Transborder Trucking: The Impact of U.S. Trucking Deregulation," paper presented at the annual meeting of the American Economics Association, New York, 29 December 1982, 17.

115 William Brock, United States Trade Representative, to Allan Gotlieb, Ambassador of Canada, 17 November 1982; Allan Gotlieb, Ambassador of Canada, to William Brock, United States Trade Representative, 24 November 1982. (Both letters contain identical wording regarding the five principles.)

116 John King, "Reagan Ends Cross-Border Trucking Feud," *Globe and Mail,* 1 December 1982, 1, 2.

117 Canadian Trucking Association, memo to International Committee and Provincial Managers, 12 January 1983.

118 Rolf Lockwood, "Roadway vs. the OTA," *Bus and Truck Transport,* January 1983, 24, 25.

119 Barbara Cook, "Ontario Truckers Out to Put Brake on U.S. Entry," *Financial Post,* 30 April 1983, 43.

120 Lockwood, "Roadway vs. the OTA," 24, 25.

121 Canadian Trucking Association, memo to International Committee and Provincial Managers, 12 January 1983.

122 "U.S. Carriers Still Eye Ontario Despite Past License Refusals," *Financial Post,* 7 April 1984, S7.

123 "License Refusal May Spark Strong US Protest," *Motor Truck,* March 1984, 1, 16.

124 Interview, Department of Transportation, December 1983.

125 John N. Turner, "There Is More to Trade than Trade: An Analysis of the U.S./Canada Trade Agreement 1988," *California Management Review* 33 (Winter 1991): 109-10.

126 Sources within a large literature include Roger Frank Swanson, "The United States as a National Security Threat," *Behind The Headlines* 26 (1970); Ian Lumsden, ed., *Close the 49th Parallel Etc.: The Americanization of Canada* (Toronto: University of Toronto Press, 1970); John Hutcheson, *Dominance and Dependency: Liberalism and National Policies in the North Atlantic Triangle* (Toronto: McClelland and Stewart, 1978); Daniel Drache, "Canada in the American Empire," *Canadian Journal of Political and Social Theory* 12 (1988): 212-28; Glen Williams, "Canadian Sovereignty and the Free Trade Debate," in *Knocking on the Back Door:*

Canadian Perspectives on the Political Economy of Freer Trade with the United States, ed. Allan M. Maslove and Stanley L. Winer (Halifax: Institute for Research on Public Policy, 1987). For a more recent statement, see Daniel Drache, "Assessing the Benefits of Free Trade," in *The Political Economy of North American Free Trade,* ed. Ricardo Grinspun and Maxwell A. Cameron (Montréal and Kingston: McGill-Queen's University Press, 1993).

127 For a concise summary of dependency assumptions in analyses of Canadian foreign policy, see David Dewitt and John H. Kirton, *Canada as a Principal Power: A Study in Foreign Policy and International Relations* (Toronto: Wiley, 1983), 28-36. For a review and critique of these assumptions in Canadian political economy, see Glen Williams, "On Determining Canada's Location Within the International Political Economy," *Studies in Political Economy* 25 (Spring 1988): 107-40.

128 Williams, "Canadian Sovereignty," 102.

129 Ibid.

130 Robert Laxer, "The Political Economy of Canada," in *(Canada) Ltd.: The Political Economy of Dependency,* ed. James Laxer (Toronto: McClelland and Stewart, 1973), 28.

131 Williams, "Determining Canada's Location," 133.

132 Garth Stevenson, "Continental Integration and Canadian Unity," in *Continental Community? Independence and Integration in North America,* ed. W. Andrew Axline et al. (Toronto: McClelland and Stewart, 1974), 210-4.

133 Williams, "Canadian Sovereignty," 104.

134 Stephen Clarkson, *Canada and the Reagan Challenge,* 2nd ed. (Toronto: Lorimer, 1985), 297.

135 Donald Smiley, "A Note on Canadian-American Free Trade and Canadian Policy Autonomy," in *Trade-Offs on Free Trade,* ed. Marc Gold and David Leyton-Brown (Toronto: Carswell, 1988), 444.

136 Stephen Krasner, "Trade Conflicts and the Common Defense: The United States and Japan," *Political Science Quarterly* 101 (Winter 1986): 801.

137 A recent conceptual analysis of interdependence defines its basic element as "events that take place within one state [having] an impact on events taking place in another state." See John A. Kroll, "The Complexity of Interdependence," *International Studies Quarterly* 37 (September 1993): 323

138 Robert O. Keohane and Joseph S. Nye, *Power and Interdependence,* 2nd ed. (Glenview, IL: Foresman, 1989), 203-5. Doran, *Forgotten Partnership,* 60-1. Clarkson, too, credits the Canadian government with the ability to focus closely on the United States and to formulate coherent policies. See Clarkson, *Canada and the Reagan Challenge,* 294-6. Applying a "complex neo-realist perspective," Dewitt and Kirton often reach similar conclusions. See Dewitt and Kirton, *Canada as a Principal Power,* 36-46, 403-5.

139 Gotlieb was appointed Ambassador to the United States in December 1981.

140 Mitchell Sharp, "Canada-U.S. Relations: Options for the Future," *International Perspectives* (Fall 1972, Special issue): 1, 17. The other two options were continuing current policies and pursuing closer integration.

141 For a brief summary of the Nixon shocks and the origins of the Third Option, see Peter Dobell, *Canada in World Affairs,* Vol. 17, *1971-1973* (Toronto: Canadian Institute of International Affairs, 1985), 13-29, 48-53.

142 Harald von Riekhoff, "The Third Option in Canadian Foreign Policy," in *Canada's Foreign Policy: Analysis and Trends,* ed. Brian Tomlin (Toronto: Methuen, 1978), 98.

143 For an account and critique, see Jack Granatstein and Robert Bothwell, *Pirouette: Pierre Trudeau and Canadian Foreign Policy* (Toronto: University of Toronto Press, 1990), 58-177.

144 Allan Gotlieb and Jeremy Kinsman, "Reviving the Third Option," *International Perspectives* (January/February 1981): 3.

145 Ibid.

146 For a discussion of these ideas and developments, see Ernie Keenes, "Rearranging the Deck Chairs: A Political Economy Approach to Foreign Policy Management in Canada," *Canadian Public Administration* 35 (Fall 1992): 381-401.

147 Gordon Osbaldeston, "Reorganizing Canada's Department of External Affairs," *International Journal* 37 (Summer 1982): 460.

148 Doran, *Forgotten Partnership,* 61.

149 Keohane and Nye, *Power and Interdependence,* 206-7.

150 Ibid., 203-5.
151 Doran, *Forgotten Partnership*, 59.
152 William Coleman and Grace Skogstad, "Policy Communities and Policy Networks: A Structural Approach," in *Policy Communities and Policy Networks in Canada: A Structural Approach*, ed. William Coleman and Grace Skogstad (Mississauga: Copp Clark Pitman, 1990), 15.

Chapter 5: The State Withdraws
1 Arthur Kroeger, "A Perspective on Transportation in Canada," *Optimum* 14 (November 1983): 7-8.
2 Jeffrey Frieden and Ronald Rogowski, "The Impact of the International Economy on National Policies: An Analytical Overview," in *Internationalization and Domestic Politics*, ed. Helen Milner and Robert Keohane (Cambridge: Cambridge University Press, 1996), 43.
3 Eric Helleiner, *States and the Reemergence of Global Finance: From Bretton Woods to the 1990s* (Ithaca: Cornell University Press, 1994), 18-9.
4 Susan Strange, *The Retreat of the State: The Diffusion of Power in the World Economy* (Cambridge: Cambridge University Press, 1996), 79.
5 Richard Rose, *Lesson-Drawing in Public Policy: A Guide to Learning Across Time and Space* (Chatham, NJ: Chatham, 1993), 125.
6 James March and Johan Olsen, *Rediscovering Institutions: The Organizational Basis of Politics* (New York: Free Press, 1989), 94.
7 Michael Atkinson and William Coleman, "Strong States and Weak States: Sectoral Policy Networks in Advanced Capitalist Economies," *British Journal of Political Science* 19 (January 1989): 51.
8 Murray G. Smith, "A Canadian Perspective," in *Perspectives on a U.S.-Canadian Free Trade Agreement*, ed. Robert M. Stern, Phillip H. Trezise, John Whalley (Washington, DC/Ottawa: Brookings Institution/Institute for Research on Public Policy, 1987), 52.
9 Ron Hirschhorn, *Trucking Regulation in Canada: A Review of the Issues,* Working Paper no. 26 (Ottawa: Economic Council of Canada, December 1981), 10.
10 Statistics Canada, *Trucking in Canada 1989* (Ottawa: Statistics Canada, 1991), 115-6, 123.
11 Lynne Calderwood, "Trucking and Trade: New Directions," *Bus and Truck Transport*, June 1984, 23, 24.
12 Julius M.L. Gorys, "The Role of U.S. Gateways in Transporting Ontario's Exports," *Transportation Quarterly* 44 (January 1990): 122.
13 "Tank Carriers Focus on Image, Education, Safety, Data," *Transport Topics*, 1 October 1984, 49.
14 Lou Volpintesta, "Would an Open Border Improve Trucking Service?" *Canadian Transportation and Distribution Management*, February 1984, 32; Andrew Tausz, "Ontario Trucking Reform Creates Shipper Rift," *Canadian Transportation and Distribution Management*, January 1984, 32.
15 John McManus, "On the 'New' Transportation Policy after Ten Years," in *Studies of Regulation in Canada*, ed. W.T. Stanbury (Montreal: Institute for Research on Public Policy, 1978), 217-8.
16 F.W. Anderson, "The Philosophy of the MacPherson Royal Commission and the National Transportation Act: A Retrospective Essay," in *Issues in Canadian Transport Policy*, ed. K.W. Studnicki-Gizbert (Toronto: Macmillan, 1974), 53.
17 Howard Darling, "Transport Policy in Canada: The Struggle of Ideologies versus Realities," in ibid., 14-34.
18 Harold Kaplan, *Policy and Rationality: The Regulation of Canadian Trucking* (Toronto: University of Toronto Press, 1989), 82-7.
19 Ibid., 51.
20 W.T. Stanbury and Fred Thompson, *Regulatory Reform in Canada* (Montreal: Institute for Research on Public Policy, 1982), 22, 23.
21 Ibid., 7.
22 Economic Council of Canada, *Responsible Regulation: An Interim Report by the Economic Council of Canada, November 1979* (Ottawa: Ministry of Supply and Services, 1979), Appendix A.
23 Andrew Klymchuk, *Trucking Industry: Analysis of Performance, Research Monograph 14* (Research Branch, Bureau of Competition Policy, Consumer and Corporate Affairs Canada,

1983), Foreword.

24 For a list of those studies, see *Competition and Economic Regulation in Transportation, Summary Report* (Ottawa: Interdepartmental Committee on Competition and Regulation in Transportation, 1982), Appendix I.

25 The studies are: M. Cairns and B. Kirk, *Canadian For-Hire Trucking and the Effects of Regulation,* Report 10-80-03, Interdepartmental Committee on Competition (Ottawa: Canadian Transport Commission, 1980); Garland Chow, *An Analysis of Selected Aspects of Performance of For-Hire Motor Carriers in Canada* (Ottawa: Department of Consumer and Corporate Affairs, 1982); James MacRae and David Prescott, *Regulation and Performance in the Canadian Trucking Industry* (Ottawa: Economic Council of Canada, 1981).

26 Klymchuk, *Trucking Industry,* 22.

27 Andrew Klymchuk, *Private Trucking: Analysis and Implications,* Research Monograph 15 (Research Branch, Bureau of Competition Policy, Consumer and Corporate Affairs Canada, 1983), 70.

28 Pam Cooper, *Literature Review of Foreign Experience of Regulated and Deregulated Trucking* (Ottawa: Department of Consumer and Corporate Affairs, 1980).

29 Klymchuk, *Trucking Industry,* summary.

30 Ibid., 67, 68.

31 G.B. Renchenthaler, "Direct Regulation in Canada," in *Studies on Regulation in Canada.* ed. W.T. Stanbury (Toronto: Butterworth, 1978), 77.

32 Economic Council of Canada, *Responsible Regulation: An Interim Report by the Economic Council of Canada, November 1979* (Ottawa: Ministry of Supply and Services, 1979), 1.

33 Economic Council of Canada, *Reforming Regulation* (Ottawa: Ministry of Supply and Services, 1981), 21, 143.

34 Anthony Ellison, "Regulatory Reform in Transport: A Canadian Perspective," *Transportation Journal* 23 (Summer 1984): 4.

35 Stephen Clarkson, *Canada and the Reagan Challenge: Crisis and Adjustment, 1981-1985* (Toronto: Lorimer, 1985), 20-1.

36 Stanbury and Thompson, *Regulatory Reform in Canada,* 119-22.

37 Norman Bonsor, *Transportation Economics: Theory and Canadian Policy* (Toronto: Butterworths, 1984), 149.

38 R. Kent Weaver, *The Politics of Industrial Change: Railway Policy in North America* (Washington, DC: Brookings Institution, 1985), 82-5.

39 Ontario Public Commercial Vehicles Act Review Committee, *Responsible Trucking: New Directions* (Toronto: Ontario Ministry of Transportation and Communications, June 1983), 59.

40 Ibid., 4.

41 Remarks by the Honourable James Snow, Minister of Transportation and Communications, on the inauguration of the PCV Review Committee, 9 June 1981, 3.

42 Rolf Lockwood, "Unfinished Business," *Bus and Truck Transport,* August 1983, 22.

43 Report of the Ontario Highway Transport Board to the Honourable James W. Snow, Minister of Transportation and Communications, on the Balance of Trade in Trucking Services between the United States and Canada, Toronto, Ontario Highway Transport Board, July 30, 1983.

44 Rolf Lockwood, "U.S. Carriers Claim Entry Rules Unfair," *Financial Post,* 3 April 1982, S1.

45 "How to Have Deregulation without Really Meaning To," *Financial Post,* 23 April 1983, 17.

46 Peter Carlyle-Goudge, "Task Force to Review Truck Regulations," *Financial Post,* 1 January 1983, 5.

47 This interpretation appeared in testimony before the Commons Standing Committee on Transport and was given by Nick Mulder, Administrator of the Canadian Surface Transportation Administration of Transport Canada. *Minutes of the Proceedings and Evidence of the Standing Committee on Transport,* 32nd Parliament, 2nd session, 5 April 1984, 11:44.

48 "The U.S. Experience: Can Canada Cash In?" *Canadian Transportation and Distribution Management,* August 1984, 19.

49 Lockwood, "US Carriers Claim Entry Rules Unfair."

50 These costs relate to LTL carriage and terminals. As was seen in Chapter 2, truckload (TL) carriers can serve vast areas without terminals and require much lower capital outlays. That is the principal reason for TL's rapid expansion in the two countries after deregula-

tion as well as for Canadian TL carriers' subsequent prosperity in the American market.

51 "Rates Will Drop: Open-Border Supporters," *Canadian Transportation and Distribution Management,* February 1984, 37.

52 Ibid.

53 Interview, Canadian Manufacturers Association, November 1983.

54 "Rates Will Drop," 37.

55 Report of the Ontario Highway Transport Board to the Honourable James W. Snow, Minister of Transportation and Communications, on the Balance of Trade in International Trucking Services between the United States of America and Canada, Toronto, Ontario Highway Transport Board, 30 July 1983, 42, 43.

56 Interview with transport consultant, Toronto, November 1983.

57 "International Guidelines Set," *Bus and Truck Transport,* September 1984, 8.

58 "Ontario Writes New Trucking Regulations," *Canadian Transportation and Distribution Management,* October 1984, 12.

59 "Axworthy Wants to Deregulate Airlines and Trucking," *Motor Truck,* April 1984, 57.

60 "ATPC Demands Regulatory Reform," *Canadian Transportation and Distribution Management,* August 1982, 13.

61 Rob Robertson, "Manitoba's Trucking Industry Will Remain 'Regulated': Plohman," *Motor Truck,* May 1984, 19.

62 Rob Robertson, "Illegal Truckers Who Dodge Taxes and Overload Vehicles Cost Taxpayers $200 Million and Must Be Stopped: QTA," *Motor Truck,* May 1985, 13, 14.

63 Michel Boucher, "L'Inspiration Américaine de la Déréglementation en Transport Routier," *Canadian Public Policy* 12 (March 1986): 193-4.

64 Eugene Ludwick, "Strategic Considerations for Transportation Planning in a Deregulated and Free Trade Environment," *Proceedings of the Twenty-Second Annual Meeting of the Canadian Transportation Research Forum* (Saskatoon: University of Saskatchewan Printing Services, 1987), 609.

65 "Axworthy Wants to Deregulate Airlines and Trucking," *Motor Truck,* April 1984, 22 ; Christopher Waddell, "Deregulation Question Keeps Industry Sectors Dangling on a String," *Financial Post,* 12 May 1984, 27.

66 David Stewart-Patterson, "Axworthy Dissatisfied with New CTC Report," *Globe and Mail,* 31 August 1984, B8.

67 James Rusk, "The Axworthy Empire," *Globe and Mail,* 4 December 1984, 1, 12.

68 David Stewart-Patterson, "Axworthy Pushes CTC to Cut Rules More," *Globe and Mail,* 25 May 1984, B1.

69 James Rusk, "Political Friends Ran Axworthy Empire," *Globe and Mail,* 5 December 1984, 1, 5.

70 Christopher Waddell, "Deregulation Question Keeps Industry Sectors Dangling on String," *Financial Post,* 12 May 1984, 27.

71 Edward Greenspon, "Deregulation Route Backed at Transport Conference," *Financial Post,* 11 September 1982, 4.

72 Christopher Waddell, "CTC Takes New Line on Regulations," *Financial Post* 12 May 1984, 28.

73 Anon., "Interim Report on Air Fares in the Wind," *Financial Post,* 12 May 1984, 27.

74 Testimony of Nick Mulder, Administrator, Surface Transportation Administration, Transport Canada, *Minutes of Proceedings and Evidence of the Standing Committee on Transport,* 32nd Parliament, 2nd session, 5 April 1984, 11:43.

75 "Axworthy Set to Take Charge," *Bus and Truck Transport,* June 1984, 3.

76 Christopher Waddell, "Truckers Steering Clear of Axworthy," *Financial Post,* 9 June 1984, 7.

77 Interview, Canadian Conference of Motor Transport Administrators, November 1983.

78 "Axworthy Set to Take Charge," 3.

79 Robert English, "Trucking: Hurting All Over But Still Hanging In," *Financial Post,* 3 April 1982, S1.

80 G. Bruce Doern and Brian W. Tomlin, *Faith and Fear: The Free Trade Story* (Toronto: Stoddart, 1991), 17-19.

81 Ibid., 21.

82 Brian Tomlin, "The Stages of Prenegotiation: The Decision to Negotiate North American Free Trade," *International Journal* 44 (Spring 1989): 263-6, 276.

83 Department of External Affairs, *A Review of Canadian Trade Policy: A Background Document to Canadian Trade Policy for the 1980s* (Ottawa: Ministry of Supply and Services, 1983), 58-59.

84 Department of External Affairs, *Canadian Trade Policy for the 1980s: A Discussion Paper* (Ottawa: Ministry of Supply and Services, 1983), 18. A brief description of the recession's impact on the economy appears on 3-5.

85 Richard Simeon, "Inside the Macdonald Commission," *Studies in Political Economy* 22 (Spring 1987): 173.

86 Edward A. Carmichael, Wendy Dobson, Richard G. Lipsey, "The Macdonald Report: Signpost or Shopping Basket?" *Canadian Public Policy* 12 (Supplement, February 1986): 23.

87 Royal Commission on the Economic Union and Development Prospects for Canada, *Report*, vol. 1 (Ottawa: Minister of Supply and Services, 1985), 270.

88 Simeon, "Inside the Macdonald Commission," 174.

89 Ibid., 173.

90 Royal Commission, *Report*, vol. 1, 50.

91 Nora Silzer and Mark Krasnick, "The Free Flow of Goods in the Canadian Economic Union," in *Perspectives on the Canadian Economic Union*, ed. Mark Krasnick (Toronto: University of Toronto Press, 1986), 164-5.

92 Richard Schultz and Alan Alexandroff, *Economic Regulation and the Federal System* (Toronto: University of Toronto Press, 1985).

93 Royal Commission on the Economic Union and Development Prospects for Canada, *Report*, vol. 2 (Ottawa: Ministry of Supply and Services, 1985), 256. The Crow's Nest Pass Freight Rate is noted briefly in connection with agricultural exports on 432-3, and the high cost of moving coal from mine to port is noted on 473. A general reference to American deregulation in banking, airlines, and telecommunication appears on 209-11.

94 John Langford, "'Transport Canada and the Transport Ministry: The Attempt to Retreat to Basics," in *How Ottawa Spends Your Tax Dollars: National Policy and Economic Development, 1982*, ed. G. Bruce Doern (Toronto: Lorimer, 1982), 147-53, 162-6.

95 Arthur Kroeger, "Hard Going: Transportation Development in Lean Times," *Policy Options* 2 (July/August 1981): 13-6.

96 *Minutes of Proceedings and Evidence of the Standing Committee on Transport*, 33rd Parliament, 2nd session, 5 April 1984, 11:43.

97 The Memorandum of Understanding's provisions appear in *Freedom to Move: A Framework for Transportation Reform* (Ottawa: Transport Canada, 1985), 32.

98 Barry Holmes, "Ministers Set Dates for Reregulating Trucking," *Motor Truck*, November 1984, 13.

99 Ibid.

100 Andrew Tausz, "Proposals Get Mixed Reviews," *Canadian Transportation and Distribution Management*, October 1985, 30.

101 Keith Nickson, "Deregulation: The Push is On," *Canadian Transportation and Distribution Management*, October 1985, 24.

102 Barry Holmes, "Enough! Truckers Alarmed as Reg Reform Program Sinks Deeper and Deeper into the Quagmire of Indecision," *Motor Truck*, November 1985, 39.

103 Cecil Foster, "Trucking Companies Gearing up for Deregulation," *Globe and Mail*, 26 August 1985, B4.

104 Edward Greenspon, "Deregulation Route Backed at Transportation Conference," *Financial Post*, 11 September 1982, 4.

105 "MP Predicts Dereg of Trucking," *Motor Truck*, June 1984, 22.

106 "New Transport Minister Mazankowski Says Some Form of Truck Deregulation Inevitable," *Motor Truck*, October 1984, 23, 24.

107 Tausz, "High Cost of Failing to Deregulate," 102.

108 *Freedom to Move: A Framework for Transportation Reform* (Ottawa: Transport Canada, 1985), 31-3.

109 Andrew Tausz, "Proposals Get Mixed Reviews," *Canadian Transportation and Distribution Management*, October 1985, 30.

110 *Minutes of Proceedings and Evidence of the Standing Committee on Transport*, 33rd Parliament, 2nd session, 5 April 1984, 11:42.

111 Ibid., 11:45.

112 Ibid., 11:44.
113 *Minutes of Proceedings and Evidence of The Standing Committee on Transport,* House of Commons, 33rd Parliament, 2nd session, 17 February 1987, 11:6.
114 Doug Hunter, "Proposed Changes Give Shippers a Better Deal," *Financial Post,* 11 May 1987, 34.
115 *Minutes and Proceedings,* 10 March 1987, 16:18-27.
116 Ibid., 9 March 1987, 15:18.
117 Ibid., 5 March 1987, 14:70-1.
118 *House of Commons Debates,* 33rd Parliament, 2nd session, 10 February 1987, 3280.
119 Greenspon, "Deregulation Route Backed," 4.
120 Andrew Tausz, "The High Cost of Failing to Deregulate," *Report on Business Magazine,* October 1985, 108.
121 Garland Chow and James J. MacRae, "Non-Tariff Barriers and the Structure of the U.S.-Canadian (Transborder) Trucking Industry," *Transportation Journal* 30 (Winter 1990): 5.
122 Robert V. Delaney, "The North American Scene: A Macro-Economic View," *Transportation Quarterly* 46 (January 1992): 21-2, 25.
123 For a study from that period, see Bruce Wilkinson, *Canada in the Changing World Economy* (Montreal: C.D. Howe Research Institute, 1980).
124 Tausz, "High Cost of Failing to Deregulate," 108.
125 *Minutes of Proceedings and Evidence of the Standing Committee on Transport,* 33rd Parliament, 1st session, 31 October 1985, 30:5-7.
126 Cecil Foster, "Transportation Firms Adapt to Changes," *Globe and Mail,* 23 June 1986, B1; Ludwick, "Strategic Considerations for Transportation Planning," 609.
127 Doug Hunter, "Transport Bill Collison Looms," *Financial Post,* 32 March 1987, 5.
128 James Pollock, "Deregulation Spells Turmoil in Transport: But Manufacturers Should Stand to Gain," *Financial Post,* 9 November 1985, 37.
129 "Mazankowski Infers New NTA Will Do Everything Except Fly Planes and Steer Trucks," *Motor Truck,* April 1986, 20.
130 *Minutes of Proceedings and Evidence from the Standing Committee on Transport,* 9 March 1987, 15:27-8.
131 Ibid., 10 March 1987, 16:36-7.
132 William Crampton, "Truckers Driven to Conclude Deregulation Inevitable," *Globe and Mail,* 3 December 1984, B20.
133 Cecil Foster, "Deregulation Bill Lacks Support from Truckers," *Globe and Mail,* 26 November 1984, IB6.
134 "Some Transport Ministers Now Advocating 'Fitness Only' Test," *Motor Truck,* April 1986, 40.
135 *Minutes of Proceedings and Evidence of the Standing Committee on Transport,* 33rd Parliament, 1st session, 21 November 1985, 39:25.
136 Barry Holmes, "Plohman Says Mazankowski Double-Crossed Provincial Ministers on Reg Agreement, *Motor Truck,* September 1986, 26.
137 "Shocked CTA Accuses Maz of Promising One Thing, Doing Another," *Motor Truck,* September 1986, 27, 45.
138 The question of taxes and operating costs was taken up in a series of federal studies begun in 1981. The results are reviewed in the Chapter 6.
139 "Crosbie Concedes to Provinces on Dereg Bill," *Motor Truck,* May 1987, 1.
140 Cecil Foster, "Survey Finds Shippers Now Favor Deregulation," *Globe and Mail,* 4 March 1984, B15.
141 For a lengthy statement of the CTA' s position, see *Minutes of Proceedings and Evidence of the Standing Committee on Transport,* 33rd Parliament, 1st session, 25 October 1985, 29:5-29:35.
142 "Some Transport Ministers Now Advocating 'Fitness Only' Test," *Motor Truck,* April 1986, 40.
143 "Relaxed Entry Controls May Give Provincial Boards Some Flexibility in Denying or Granting Route Authorities," *Motor Truck,* October 1987, 22.
144 Mary Hepburn, "Dropped," *Truck Fleet,* November 1987, 5.
145 Jo-Anne Sommers, "Free Trade with the U.S.: What Do Shippers Stand to Gain?" *Canadian Transportation and Distribution Management,* September 1985, 43.
146 "StatsCan Delivers Both Private and For-Hire Stats," *Motor Truck,* October 1986, 67-70.

147 Fred Nix, "Whose Truck Costs are Less, Canada or US?" *Motor Truck*, March 1988, 17.
148 Harold Hongju Koh, "A Legal Perspective," in Stern, Trezise, and Whalley, *Perspectives*, 103-5.
149 Richard Simeon, "Federalism and Free trade," in *The Future on the Table: Canada and the Free Trade Issue*, ed. Michael D. Henderson (North York, ON: Masterpress, York University, 1987), 80-1.
150 Kenneth Norrie, Richard Simeon, and Mark Krasnick, *Federalism and Economic Union in Canada* (Toronto: University of Toronto Press, 1986), 334.
151 Murray G. Smith, "Services," in *Free Trade: The Real Story*, ed. John Crispo (Agincourt, ON: Gage, 1988), 40.
152 Telephone interview, ATA, July 1988.
153 Cecil Foster, "Ontario Truckers Group Hits Snag in Its Licensing Fight Win," *Globe and Mail*, 31 October 1988, B7.
154 Barry Holmes, "No Dereg until Ontario Reciprocates, QTA Urges," *Motor Truck*, July 1988, 1.
155 "Trucking Action Vote," *Traffic World*, March 14, 1988, 36.
156 "Some Ministers Now Advocating 'Fitness Only' Test," *Motor Truck*, April 1986, 39.
157 "Manitoba Will Maintain Strict Entry Controls: Norquay," *Motor Truck*, June 1988, 44.
158 Motor Carrier Policy and Programs, Policy Coordination Group, Transport Canada, *Review of Subsections 8(3) to 8(5) of the Motor Vehicle Transport Act 1987*, Report to Parliament, May 1992, pp. ii, iii.
159 Colin Bennett, "What Is Policy Convergence and What Causes It?" *British Journal of Political Science* 21 (April 1991): 229-32; on the influential role of the Bank of International Settlements in the harmonization of monetary and investment policies, see Helleiner, *States and the Reemergence of Global Finance*, 199.
160 Ibid., 229.
161 Grace Skogstad, "Agricultural Policy," in *Border Crossings: The Internationalization of Canadian Public Policy*, ed. G. Bruce Doern, Leslie Pal, and Brian Tomlin (Toronto: Oxford University Press, 1996), 145.
162 Richard Schultz and Mark Brawley, "Telecommunications Policy," in ibid., 106.

Chapter 6: After Deregulation

1 Statistics Canada, *Trucking in Canada 1995* (Ottawa: Statistics Canada, 1996), 76, 79; Statistics Canada, *Trucking in Canada, 1997* (Ottawa: Statistics Canada, 1998), 71, 74.
2 Statistics Canada, *Trucking in Canada 1997*, 69, 77-80.
3 Ibid., *Trucking in Canada 1990*, 115; Ibid., *Trucking in Canada 1997*, 72.
4 Barry Holmes, "Truckers' Protests Alarm a Nation," *Motor Truck*, July 1990, 11.
5 National Transportation Agency of Canada, *Annual Review of the National Transportation Agency of Canada 1991, 1994* (Ottawa: Ministry of Supply and Services, 1992, 1995), 109, 118.
6 Daniel Bearth, "Competition Heats Up U.S.-Canada Relations," *Transport Topics*, 9 July 1990, 27.
7 National Transportation Agency of Canada, *Annual Review 1989* (Ottawa: Ministry of Supply and Services, 1990), 77, 78.
8 "Now All of a Sudden, We're in Serious Trouble," *Motor Truck*, December 1989, 14.
9 These terms are Statistics Canada's and the National Transportation Agency's. Statistics Canada quotes an operating ratio of ninety-seven as "viable" (*Trucking in Canada 1995*, 8), and the National Transportation Agency (*Annual Review 1994*, 133) quotes ninety-five as "healthy."
10 National Transportation Agency of Canada, *Annual Review 1994*, 133.
11 Ibid., *Annual Review 1993*, 210.
12 Ibid., *Annual Review 1991*, 144.
13 *The Competitiveness of the Ontario Transborder Trucking Industry* (Toronto: Deloitte Touche Management Consultants, 1991), 10.
14 National Transportation Agency of Canada, *Annual Review 1991*, 112-3.
15 Ibid., *Annual Review 1993*, 59.
16 The studies are: *Transborder Trucking Survey 1991* (Ottawa: Statistics Canada Transportation Division, April 1991); F.E. Collins, J.F. Woods, and D.B. Toms, *Review of Transborder Trucking*

Markets (Montreal: KPMG Peat Marwick Stevenson and Kellogg, Management Consultants, 1991); *Economics of the Trucking Industry in Transborder Markets* ([n.p.]: Hickling Corporation Division of Economics and Policy in association with Garland Chow, 1991); *The Financial Performance of Canadian Trucking Firms* (Vancouver: Price Waterhouse, 1991); *Comparison of Canadian and U.S. Trucking Costs in Transborder Markets* (Calgary: Trimac Consulting Services, 1991) ; *The Effect of Taxation on Canada-U.S. Trucking Competitiveness* (Toronto: Peat Marwick Thorne, 1991); *Implications of Alternative Cabotage Rules* (Toronto: Transmode Consultants, 1991); John Heads, Barry E. Prentice, Mahlon Harvey, *The Transborder Competitiveness of Canadian Trucking* (Winnipeg: Transport Institute, University of Manitoba, 1991). A study appearing subsequently was entitled *Owner Operator Costs and Earnings Comparison in Canada-U.S. Transborder Trucking* (Calgary: Trimac Consulting Services, 1991).

17   *The Competitiveness of the Ontario Transborder Trucking Industry*.
18   Ibid., 31. Heads, Prentice, and Harvey, *Transborder Competitiveness*, 95, 96.
19   Heads, Prentice, and Harvey, *Transborder Competitiveness*, 96.
20   *Effect of Taxation on Canada-U.S. Trucking Competitiveness* (Toronto: Peat Marwick Thorne, 1991).
21   *The Competitiveness of the Ontario Transborder Trucking Industry*, 10, 11.
22   *Comparison of Canadian and U.S. Trucking Costs*, 14, 15.
23   Ibid., 20.
24   Ibid., 20-3.
25   *Ontario Transborder Trucking Industry*, 24; National Transportation Agency of Canada, *Annual Review 1991*, 120.
26   Heads, Prentice, Harvey, *Transborder Competitiveness*, xii.
27   Ibid., 101-2.
28   Ibid., 102.
29   Colins, Woods, Toms, *A Review of Transborder Trucking Markets*, 48.
30   Bearth, "Competition Heats Up U.S.-Canada Relations," 27.
31   Heads, Prentice, Harvey, *Transborder Competitiveness*, 109.
32   Geoffrey Rowan, "Ottawa's Relief to Truckers Falls Short of Demands," *Globe and Mail*, 7 December 1991, B3.
33   *The Competitiveness of the Ontario Transborder Trucking Industry*, 26, 27.
34   Ibid.
35   *Implications of Alternative Cabotage Rules* (Transmode Consultants in association with Fred Nix and Gough and Gray Group, 1991), 52.
36   Ibid., *Ontario Transborder Trucking Industry*, 23.
37   Clarence Woudsma and Pavlos Kanaroglou, "The Impacts of Trucking Deregulation in Ontario: A Market-Specific Approach," *Canadian Public Policy* 22 (Winter 1996): 374-5.
38   Charles A. Taff, *Commercial Motor Transportation* (Homewood, IL: Irwin, 1955), 506-8.
39   Chow, *Rate and Cost Analysis of For-Hire Trucking*, 17-9.
40   In 1979, the year before deregulation, there were seventy-seven ICC-certificated freight forwarders; four years after deregulation there were 3,000. Adil Cubukgil and Richard Soberman, *The Impact of Proposed Regulatory Reform on Extraprovincial Trucking* (Toronto: Transmode Consultants, 1986), 34. On American freight brokers' growth under deregulation, see Michael Crum, "The Expanded Role of Motor Freight Brokers in the Wake of Regulatory Reform," *Transportation Journal* 24 (September 1985): 5-15.
41   Cubukgil and Soberman, *Proposed Regulatory Reform*, 29.
42   Mark Keaton, "Economies of Density and the Structure of the LTL Motor Carrier Industry Since Deregulation," Transportation Executive Update 8 (November/December 1994): 18.
43   Nicholas A. Glaskowsky, *Effects of Deregulation on Motor Carriers* (Westport, CN: Eno Foundation for Transportation, 1986), 26.
44   Ibid., 35; "Line-Haul Costs," *Transport Topics*, 19 December 1988, 4.
45   *Transport Topics*, Management Outlook Forum, 22 January 1990, 14.
46   "Trucking's Future Belongs to the Swift and Sure-Handed," *Transport Topics*, 17 July 1989, 17. For an exploration of whether hub-and-spoke systems would improve the operations of high-volume TL carriers, see Tarek T. Taha and G. Don Taylor, "An Integrated Modeling Framework for Evaluating Hub-and-Spoke Networks in Truckload Tracking," *Logistics and*

Transportation Review, 30 June 1994, 141-66.
47 Curtis M. Grimm, Thomas M. Corsi, Judith L. Jarrell, "U.S. Motor Carrier Cost Structure under Deregulation," *Logistics and Transportation Review* 25 (September 1989): 244.
48 *Value Line Investment Survey,* June 24, 1994, 273, 275.
49 "Change of Thinking," *Canadian Transportation Logistics* 99 (September, 1996): 44.
50 Jeffrey S. Medford, "1994 – Beyond: The Long-Haul Teamster Carriers Are Facing a Catch-22 Dilemma," *Transportation Executive Update* 8 (September/October 1994). 8-9.
51 William Cassidy, "The 99.7% Factor," *Transport Topics,* 14 February 1994, 7.
52 Bill Vance, "The Mackie Group," *Globe and Mail,* 11 May 1995, Insert 6, 7.
53 On the use of satellite communications and tracking in motor carriage, see Brenda Yarrow, "Techno Trucking," *Canadian Transportation Logistics* 97 (January 1994): 16.
54 Shawn Coates, "Flexible Advantage," *Western Commerce and Industry* 47 (August 1995): 24-5.
55 Cubukgil and Soberman, *Proposed Regulatory Reform,* 29.
56 These, it should be noted, are not line-haul costs, which were shown earlier to favour small TL operations.
57 David L. Sparkman, "Return of the Big Three," *Transport Topics,* 11 August 1997, 20.
58 Mark Hallman, "Dark Omen Seen in Motorways' End," *Financial Post,* 23 November 1993, 7.
59 National Transportation Agency of Canada, *Annual Review 1993,* 59.
60 The two LTLs have retained their names.
61 For a comparison of airline and LTL hub-and-spoke systems, see Tarek T. Taha and G. Don Taylor, "An Integrated Modeling Framework for Evaluating Hub-and-Spoke Networks in Truckload Trucking," *Logistics and Transportation Review* 30 (June 1994): 142-7.
62 Taha and Taylor, "An Integrated Modeling Framework," 146-7.
63 "LTL Carriers Struggle Back to Profitability," *Modern Purchasing* 38 (October 1996): 28.
64 "Shakeout," *Materials Management and Distribution* 42 (March 1997): 24.
65 Hallman, "Dark Omen," 7.
66 Daniel Bearth, "Canada's Motorways Ltd. Closes," *Transport Topics* 27 December 1993, 2.
67 Statistics Canada, *Trucking in Canada 1995,* 110.
68 Statsitics Canada, *Trucking in Canada 1990* (Ottawa: Statistics Canada, 1993), 67; Statistics Canada, *Trucking in Canada 1995,* 57.
69 Noreen Rasbach, "A Fresh Start for CP Express," *Globe and Mail,* 10 March 10 1995, B13.
70 "1994 – Beyond," 8-9.
71 Keaton, "Economies of Density," 22.
72 Ibid., 8.
73 Statistics Canada, *Trucking in Canada 1992* (Ottawa: Minister of Industry, Science and Technology, 1995), 61.
74 John Schultz, "Trucking's 'Rolls Royce,'" *Traffic World,* 2 June 1997, 11.
75 Statistics Canada, *Trucking in Canada, 1995,* 48.
76 Mark Hallman, "Vitran Called a Vehicle for the Long Haul," *Financial Post,* 28 June 1995, 23.
77 Ibid., 62.
78 Bernard LaLonde and Martha Cooper, *Partnerships in Providing Customer Service: A Third-Party Perspective* (Oak Brook, IL: Council on Logistics Management, 1989), 13, 18. An expanded study appears in LaLonde and Cooper, "The Competitive Edge," *Transportation Executive Update* 3 (September/October 1989), 6, 7.
79 "ICC Proposed End to Contract Rules," *Transport Topics,* July 15, 1991, 1, 31.
80 "Transborder Savings Bonanza," *Modern Purchasing* 38 (March 1996): 22.
81 Roy Dale Voorhees, Benjamin Allen, Dale Pinnekamp, "An Examination and Analysis of the 'Invisible' Full Service Truck Leasing Industry," *Transportation Journal* 22 (Spring 1983): 65.
82 National Transportation Agency of Canada, *Annual Review, 1993,* 62.
83 Gene Bergoffen and Donald E. Tepper, "After a Tough Decade, Picture Improves for Private Carriage," *Transport Topics,* 30 September 1991, 18.
84 Thomas Strah, "Private Truck Fleets Reflect More Efficient Management," *Transport Topics,* 17 May 1993, 6.
85 David L. Sparkman, "Private Fleets: Value vs. Costs," *Transport Topics,* 30 April 1990, 15.

86 Ibid.
87 John Perser, "Corporate Logistics Managers often Lead Drive to Outsource, but Final Decision Is Moving Up," *Traffic World,* 14 November 1994, 26.
88 LaLonde and Cooper, "Competitive Edge," 8.
89 Daniel Bearth, "Serving the Auto Industry," *Transport Topics,* 14 February 1994, 6.
90 Ibid.
91 Daniel Bearth, "Truckload Fleets on a Roll," *Transport Topics,* 17 October 1994, 90.
92 Ibid.
93 Bob Rast, "Chrysler Presses Cutting Edge of Technology to Streamline Supply Chain, Fine Tune J-I-T," *Traffic World,* 17 October 1994, 33.
94 Bearth, "Serving the Auto Industry," 6.
95 Donald V. Harper and Karen S. Goodner, "Just-In-Time and Inbound Transportation," *Transportation Journal* 30 (Winter 1990): 29.
96 Adam Corelli, "JIT Strategy Works Even with Ford's Global Supply Line," *Globe and Mail,* 1 March 1994, B24.
97 Harper and Goodner, "Just-In-Time," 30.
98 Bearth, "Truckload Fleets on a Roll," 90.
99 "Economist Predicts Good Year Ahead for Trucking Industry," *Truck News,* October 1993, 16.
100 Andrew Tausz, "The Logistics Revolution," *Globe and Mail,* 9 March 1993, C3.
101 "Non-Stop Logistics Takes Quick Response to Another Level," *Transport Topics,* 14 November 1994, 9.
102 Bonnie Toews, "See No Boundaries," *Canadian Transportation Logistics* 97 (March 1994): 28, 30.
103 "Oshawa Foods Embracing Latest Computer Technologies," *Truck News,* October 1994, 24.
104 Ibid.
105 David L. Sparkman, "Where We Are Going," *Transport Topics,* 6 June 1994, 12.
106 James Farrell and Tony Reed, "The Lessons Learned by the Winners," *Transport Topics,* 8 October 1990, 16.
107 Ibid.
108 Management Outlook, *Transport Topics,* 22 January 1990, 13.
109 Mark, "Holding the Line," 38.
110 Bearth, "Serving the Auto Industry," 5, 6.
111 LaLonde and Cooper, *Partnerships,* 21, 22.
112 "Core Carrier Concept," *Transport Topics,* 16 April 1990, 11.
113 "Helping Hand: Companies Use Third-Party Logistics," *Materials Management and Distribution* 41 (September 1996): 40, 42.
114 Grant M. Davis and William Cunningham, "Identifying Markets for Contract Logistics Services," *Transportation Quarterly* 48 (Autumn 1994): 434.
115 Ibid.
116 Davis and Cunningham, "Identifying Markets," 434.
117 "The Power of Partnerships," *Canadian Transportation Logistics* 99 (September 1996): 14-5.
118 Daniel Bearth, "The Saturn-Ryder Partnership," *Transport Topics,* 4 October 1993, 8.
119 "Leasing vs. Owning," *Truck News,* March 1994, 46.
120 National Transportation Agency of Canada, *Annual Review, 1993,* 113.
121 Mark, "Holding the Line," 37.
122 Collins, Woods, Toms, *Review of Transborder Trucking Markets,* 1; Heads, Prentice, Harvey, *Transborder Competitiveness,* 6, 7.
123 Heads, Prentice, Harvey, *Transborder Competitiveness,* 10; Daniel Bearth, "Competition Heats Up U.S.-Canada Relations," *Transport Topics,* 9 July 1990, 27.
124 Statistics Canada, *Trucking in Canada 1989,* 88; Statistics Canada, *Trucking in Canada 1993,* 54-7; Statistics Canada, *Trucking in Canada 1995,* 50-3; Statistics Canada, *Trucking in Canada 1997,* 48-51.
125 Ibid., 111.
126 Ibid., 118.
127 National Transportation Agency of Canada, *Annual Review 1994,* 117.
128 Ibid., 118.

129 William Cassidy, "Canadian Fleets Find Strength in U.S. Partnerships," *Transport Topics*, 24 July 1995, 8.
130 National Transportation Agency of Canada, *Annual Review 1993*, 112.
131 Price Waterhouse, *Financial Performance of Canadian Trucking Firms*, 11.
132 Ibid.
133 Statistics Canada, *Trucking in Canada 1997*, 69.
134 Price Waterhouse, *Financial Performance of Canadian Trucking Firms*, 11.
135 Ibid.
136 National Transportation Agency of Canada, *Annual Review 1994*, 131, 132.
137 The figures in the following section were tabulated from data in Statistics Canada, *Trucking in Canada 1989*, 115-6 and 123; and from Statistics Canada, *Trucking in Canada 1997*, 71, 74.
138 Statistics Canada, *Trucking in Canada 1989*, 118-20.
139 Collins, Woods, Toms, *Review of Transborder Trucking Markets*, Exhibit II-3.
140 Ibid., 10. For a more detailed breakdown of Ontario's industrial commodities trade with the United States, see *The Competitiveness of the Ontario Transborder Trucking Industry*, appendices to Stages I and II, Appendix A. 12.
141 Ibid., 53.
142 Statistics Canada, *Trucking in Canada 1992* (Ottawa: Minister of Industry, Science and Technology, 1995), 61.
143 Ibid.
144 "LTL Fleets Continue to Prosper," *Transport Topics*, 28 July 1997, 1.
145 "Building for the Future," *Canadian Transportation Logistics* 99 (September 1996): 18.
146 William Cassidy, "Canadian Fleets Find Strength in U.S. Partnerships," *Transport Topics*, 24 July 1995, 8.
147 William B. Cassidy, "Day & Ross Latest Canadian to Strike a Deal Down South," *Truck News*, November 1993, 25.
148 Ibid.
149 Catherine Harris, "Keep on Trucking," *Financial Post*, 1 June 1996, 35.
150 Cassidy, "Canadian Fleets Find Strength in U.S. Partnerships," 8.
151 Cubukgil and Soberman, *Proposed Regulatory Reform*, 41.
152 "Trucker to Hire 140 Drivers," *Globe and Mail*, 19 March 1994, B6.
153 Wilfrid List, "18 Wheels and a Satellite Dish," *Globe and Mail*, 6 April 1993, B24; "Trucker to Hire 140 Drivers," *Globe and Mail*, March 19, 1994, B6.
154 Dena Brooker, "Binvenidos a Challenger," *Materials Management and Distribution* 39 (November 1994): 70.
155 Harris, "Keep on Trucking," 35.
156 Kip Park, "Border Breakers," *Manitoba Business* 16 (December 1994): 8.
157 For a review and comparison of relevant legislation and statutes, see *Implications of Alternative Cabotage Rules* (Transmode Consultants), 13-39.
158 Ibid., 16-9.
159 Roger King, "U.S.-Canada Cabotage Overhauled," *Transport Topics* June 30, 1997, 6.
160 *Implications of Alternative Cabotage Rules*, 44.
161 "North-South Link to a Promising Future," *Western Commerce and Industry* 48 (September/October 1996): 68-9.
162 "Less-Than-Lucrative," *Materials Management and Distribution* 41 (March 1996): 20, 22.
163 "Helping Hand: Companies Use Third Party Logistics," *Materials Management and Distribution* 41 (September 1996): 40, 42.
164 Dan Lang, "U.S. Grants Cabotage Rights to Canadian Trucks," *Transport Topics*, February 22, 1999, 3.
165 Darren Prokop, "In 1998 We Freed Trade. Now Let's Free Transport," *Policy Options* 20 (June 1999) 39.
166 "Trimac Targets Growth in Share of Changing North American Bulk Market," *Modern Bulk Transporter*, November 1987, 18-30; Daniel Bearth, "Trimac System of Canada Buys Wyoming Bulk Hauler," *Transport Topics*, 20 February 1989, 4.
167 "Transborder Savings Bonanza," *Modern Purchasing* 38 (March 1996): 21, 23.
168 National Transportation Agency of Canada, *Annual Review 1993*, 59, 61.

169 Mark Hallman, "Vitran Makes Inroads into US with Buy," *Financial Post*, November 16, 1994, 11.
170 Hallman, "Vitran," 23.
171 On universal price information and competition, see Ronald Burt and Ilan Talmud, "Market Niche," *Social Networks* 15 (1993): 136.
172 Harrison White, "Markets, Networks and Control," in *Interdisciplinary Perspectives on Organization Studies*, ed. Siegwart Lindenberg and Hein Schreuder (Oxford: Pergamon, 1993), 227.
173 Eric Leifer, "Markets as Mechanisms: Using a Role Structure," *Social Forces* 64 (December 1985): 446.
174 Harrison White, "Where Do Markets Come From?" *American Journal of Sociology* 87 (November 1981): 518.
175 For a formal discussion of niches, networks, and markets, see Burt and Talmud, "Market Niche," 133-49.

Chapter 7: Conclusion

1 David Elkins, *Beyond Sovereignty: Territory and Political Economy in the Twenty-First Century* (Toronto: University of Toronto Press, 1995), 126.
2 Quincy Wright, *The Study of International Relations* (New York: Appleton-Century-Crofts, 1955), 539-69.
3 For a more recent treatment, emphasizing the often adventitious nature of national boundaries, see Friedrich Kratochwil, "Of Systems, Boundaries and Territory," *World Politics* 38 (October 1986): 1-26.
4 Elkins, *Beyond Sovereignty*, 126.
5 Ibid.
6 For a typology of analytic approaches, see Paul Hirsch, "The Study of Industries," in *Research in the Sociology of Organizations*, vol. 4, *1985*, ed. Samuel Bacharach and Stephen Mitchell (Greenwich, CN: JAI, 1985), 217-310.
7 For a market topology of the American economy, see Ronald Burt, *Structural Holes: The Social Structure of Competition* (Cambridge: Harvard University Press, 1992), 82-114. For an identification of "market-areas" based on Statistics Canada Standard Industrial Classification data, see S.D. Berkowitz, "Markets and Market-Areas: Some Preliminary Formulations," in *Social Structures: A Network Approach*, ed. Barry Wellman and S.D. Berkowitz (Cambridge: Cambridge University Press, 1988), 275-80.
8 William Ouchi, "Markets, Bureaucracies, and Clans," *Administrative Science Quarterly* 25 (March 1980): 136-7.

Bibliography

Regulation and Market Structures

Atkinson, Michael, and William Coleman. "Strong States and Weak States: Sectoral Policy Networks in Advanced Capitalist Economies." *British Journal of Political Science* 19 (January 1989): 47-69.

Berkowitz, S.D. "Markets and Market-Areas: Some Preliminary Formulations." In *Social Structures: A Network Approach,* ed. Barry Wellman and S.D. Berkowitz. Cambridge: Cambridge University Press, 1988.

Burt, Ronald. *Structural Holes: The Social Structure of Competition.* Cambridge: Harvard University Press, 1992.

Burt, Ronald, and Debbie Carlton. "Another Look at the Network Boundaries of American Markets." *American Journal of Sociology* 95 (November 1989): 723-53.

Burt, Ronald S., and Ilan Talmud. "Market Niche." *Social Networks* 15 (1993): 136-40.

DiMaggio, Paul. "State Expansion and Organizational Fields." In *Organizational Theory and Public Policy,* ed. Richard Hall and Robert Quinn, Beverley Hills: Sage, 1983.

Dobbin, Frank. *Forging Industrial Policy: The United States, Britain, and France in the Railway Age.* Cambridge: Cambridge University Press, 1994.

Hirsch, Paul. "The Study of Industries." In *Research in the Sociology of Organizations.* Vol. 4, 1985, ed. Samuel Bacharach and Stephen Mitchell. Greenwich, CN: JAI, 1985.

Jenkins-Smith, Hank, and Paul Sabatier. "The Dynamics of Policy-Oriented Learning." In *Policy Change and Learning. An Advocacy Coalition Approach,* ed. Paul Sabatier and Hank Jenkins-Smith. Boulder. Westview, 1993.

Koza, Mitchell. "Regulation and Organization: Environmental Niche Structure and Administrative Organization." In *Research in the Sociology of Organizations.* Vol. 6, 1988, ed. Nancy DiTomaso and Samuel Bacharach. Greenwich, CN: JAI, 1988.

Leblebici, Huseyin, and Gerald Salancik. "Stability in Interorganizational Exchanges: Rule-making Processes of the Chicago Board of Trade." *Administrative Science Quarterly* 27 (June 1982): 227-42.

Leifer, Eric. "Markets as Mechanisms: Using a Role Structure." *Social Forces* 64 (December 1985): 442-72.

March, James G., and Johan P. Olsen. *Rediscovering Institutions: The Organizational Basis of Politics.* New York: Free Press, 1989.

Meyer, John, and Brian Rowan. "Institutional Organizations: Formal Structure as Myth and Ceremony." In *The New Institutionalism and Organizational Analysis,* ed. Walter Powell and Paul DiMaggio. Chicago: University of Chicago Press, 1991.

Oliver, Christine. "Determinants of Interorganizational Relationships: Integration and Future Directions." *Academy of Management Review* 15 (April 1990): 241-65.

Ouchi, William. "Markets, Bureaucracies, and Clans." *Administrative Science Quarterly* 25 (March 1980): 129-41.

Podolny, Joel. "A Status-Based Model of Market Competition." *American Journal of Sociology*

98 (January 1993): 829-72.

Powell, Walter. "Expanding the Scope of Institutional Analysis." In *The New Institutionalism and Organizational Analysis,* ed. Walter Powell and Paul DiMaggio. Chicago: University of Chicago Press, 1991.

Provan, Keith. "The Federation as and Interorganizational Linkage Network." *Academy of Management Review* 8 (1983): 79-89.

Sabatier, Paul. "Policy Changes over a Decade or More." In *Policy Change and Learning: An Advocacy Coalition Approach,* ed. Paul Sabatier and Hank Jenkins-Smith. Boulder, CO: Westview, 1993.

Scott, W. Richard. "The Organization of Environments: Network, Cultural, and Historical Elements." In *Organizational Environments: Ritual and Rationality,* ed. John Meyer and W. Richard Scott. Newbury Park: Sage, 1992.

Scott, W. Richard, and John Meyer. "The Organization of Societal Sectors: Propositions and Early Evidence." In *The New Institutionalism and Organizational Analysis,* ed. Walter Powell and Paul DiMaggio. Chicago: University of Chicago Press, 1991.

Staber, Udo, and Howard Aldrich. "Trade Association Stability and Public Policy." In *Organizational Theory and Public Policy,* ed. Richard Hall and Robert Quinn. Beverly Hills: Sage, 1983.

Stanbury, W.T., and Fred Thompson. "The Scope and Coverage of Regulation in Canada and the United States: Implications for the Demand for Reform." In *Government Regulation: Scope, Growth, Process,* ed. W.T. Stanbury. Montreal: Institute for Research on Public Policy, 1980.

Weaver, R. Kent. *The Politics of Industrial Change: Railway Policy in North America.* Washington, DC: Brookings, 1985.

White, Harrison. "Markets, Networks, and Control." In *Interdisciplinary Perspectives on Organization Studies,* ed. Siegwart Lindenberg and Hein Schreuder. Oxford: Pergamon, 1993.

—. "Production Markets as Induced Role Structures." In *Sociological Methodology 1981,* ed. Samuel Leinhardt. San Francisco: Jossey Bass, 1981.

—. "Where Do Markets Come From?" *American Journal of Sociology* 87 (November 1981): 517-47.

Zucker, Lynne. "Institutional Theories of Organization." In *Annual Review of Sociology.* Vol. 13, *1987,* ed. W. Richard Scott and James Short. Palo Alto: Annual Reviews, 1987.

Economics and Transport

Baker, Gwendolyn H. "The Carrier Elimination Decision: Implications for Motor Carrier Marketing." *Transportation Journal* 24 (Fall 1984): 20-9.

Baumol, William, and Robert Willig. "Fixed Cost, Sunk Cost, Entry Barriers and Sustainability of Monopoly." *Quarterly Journal of Economics* 95 (August 1981): 405-31.

Baumol, William C., John C. Panzar, and Robert Willig. "On the Theory of Perfectly Contestable Markets." In *New Developments in the Analysis of Market Structure,* ed. Joseph E. Stiglitz and G. Frank Mathewson. Cambridge: MIT Press, 1986.

Baumol, William J., and Dietrich Fischer. "Cost Minimizing Number of Firms and Determination of Industry Structure." *Quarterly Journal of Economics* 92 (August 1978): 439-67.

Bohlander, George, and Martin Farris. "Collective Bargaining in Trucking: The Effects of Deregulation." *Logistics and Transportation Review* 20 (September 1985): 223-39.

Bonsor, Norman. *Transport Economics: Theory and Canadian Policy.* Toronto: Butterworths, 1984.

Brock, William A., and David S. Evans. "Creamskimming." In *Breaking Up Bell: Essays on Industrial Organization and Regulation,* ed. David S. Evans. New York: North-Holland, 1983.

Bruning, Edward, and Edward Morash. "Deregulation and the Cost of Equity Capital: The Case of Publicly Held Motor Carriers." *Transportation Journal* 20 (Winter 1983): 72-81.

Cairns, M.B., and B.D. Kirk. *Canadian For-Hire Trucking and the Effects of Regulation: A Cost-Structure Analysis.* Ottawa: Research Branch, Canadian Transport Commission, 1980.

Caves, Richard E., and Michael E. Porter. "Barriers to Exit." In *Essays on Industrial Organization in Honor of Joe S. Bain,* ed. Robert T. Masson and P. David Qualls. Cambridge: Ballinger, 1976.

Chow, Garland. "Canadian-U.S. Transborder Trucking: The Impact of U.S. Trucking Deregulation." Paper presented at the annual meeting of the American Economics Association, New York, 29 December 1982.

—. *Rate and Cost Analysis for For-Hire Trucking: Provincial Comparisons*. Ottawa: Bureau of Competition Policy, Consumer and Corporate Affairs Canada, 1982.

—. "The Status of Economies of Scale in Regulated Trucking: A Review of the Evidence and Future Directions." In *Proceedings of the Nineteenth Annual Meeting of the Transportation Research Forum*. Oxford, IN: Richard B. Cross, 1978.

Chow, Garland, and James J, McRae. "Non-Tariff Barriers and the Structure of the US-Canadian (Transborder) Trucking Industry." *Transportation Journal* 30 (Winter 1990): 4-22.

Chow, Garland, and Michael Tretheway. "Productivity in the U.S. Trucking Industry: The Early Deregulation Experience." Vancouver: Faculty of Commerce and Business Administration, University of British Columbia, 1988.

Christenson, Laurits, and John Huston. "A Reexamination of the Cost Structure for Specialized Motor Carriers." *Logistics and Transportation Review* 23 (December 1987): 339-52.

Collins, F.E., J.F. Woods, and D.B. Toms. *Review of Transborder Trucking Markets*. Montreal: Peat Marwick Stevenson and Kellogg, Management Consultants, 1991.

Crum, Michael. "The Expanded Role of Motor Freight Brokers in the Wake of Regulatory Reform." *Transportation Journal* 24 (September 1985): 5-15.

Cubukgil, Adil, and Richard Soberman. *The Impact of Proposed Regulatory Reform on Extraprovincial Trucking*. Toronto: Transmode Consultants, 1986.

Currie, Archibald. *Canadian Transportation Economics*. Toronto: University of Toronto Press, 1967.

Dailey, Victoria Ann. "The Certificate Effect: The Impact of Federal Entry Controls on the Growth of the Motor Common Carrier Firm." PhD diss., University of Virginia, 1973.

Daugherty, Andrew F., Forrest D. Nelson, and William R. Vigdor. "An Econometric Analysis of the Cost and Production Structure of the Trucking Industry." In *Analytical Studies in Transport Economics*, ed. Andrew F. Daugherty. Cambridge: Cambridge University Press, 1985.

Deloitte and Touche Management Consultants. *The Competitiveness of the Ontario Transborder Trucking Industry*. Toronto: Deloitte and Touche Management Consultants, September 1991.

DeVany, Arthur, and T.R. Saving. "Product Quality, Uncertainty, and Regulation: The Trucking Industry." *American Economic Review* 67 (December 1977): 583-94.

Emery, Paul. "An Empirical Approach to the Motor Carrier Economics Controversy." *Land Economics* 42 (August 1965): 285-9.

Farahbod, Kamvar, and Laddie Logan. "A Conjoint Analysis Approach to Service in the Motor Carrier Industry." *Logistics and Transportation Review* 27 (June 1991): 185-97.

Friedlaender, Ann F. "Hedonic Costs and Economies of Scale in the Regulated Trucking Industry." CTS Report 77-5, Center for Transportation Studies, Massachusetts Institute of Technology, 1977.

Friedlaender, Ann F., and Elizabeth Bailey. "Market Structure and Multiproduct Industries." *Journal of Economic Literature* 20 (September 1982): 1024-48.

Glaskowsky, Nicholas A. *Effects of Deregulation on Motor Carriers*, Westport. CN: Eno Foundation for Transportation, 1986.

Gorys, Julius M.C. "Ontario-United States Border Truck Movements." *Transportation Quarterly* 41 (July 1987): 347-64.

Grimm, Curtis, Thomas Corsi, and Judith Jarrell. "U.S. Motor Carrier Cost Structure under Deregulation." *Logistics and Transportation Review* 25 (September 1989): 231-50.

Harmatuck, Donald. "The Effects of Economic Conditions and Regulatory Changes upon Motor Carrier Tonnages and Revenues." *Transportation Journal* 24 (Winter 1984): 31-40.

Harrison, Glenn W. "Experimental Evaluation of the Contestable Market Hypothesis." In *Public Regulation: New Perspectives on Institutions and Policies*, ed. Elizabeth E. Bailey. Cambridge: MIT Press, 1987.

Heads, John, Barry E. Prentice, and Mahlon Harvey. *The Transborder Competitiveness of Canadian Trucking*. Winnipeg: Transport Institute, University of Manitoba, 1991.

Hilton, George. "Ending the Ground Transportation Cartel." In *Instead of Regulaiton: Alternatives to Federal Regulatory Agencies,* ed. Rowbert W. Poole, Jr. Lexington, MA: Lexington, 1982.

Hinkling Corporation in cooperation with Garland Chow. *Economics of the Trucking Industry in Transborder Markets, Final Report.* N.p.: Hinkling Corporation, Division of Economics and Policy, 1991.

Horn, Kevin. "Shipper Support and Entry into Regulated Trucking." *Logistics and Transportation Review* 20 (June 1984): 111-26.

Keaton, Mark. "Economies of Density and the Structure of the LTL Motor Carrier Industry Since Deregulation." *Transportation Executive Update* 8 (November/December 1994): 12, 16-24.

—. "The Structure of Costs in the U.S. Motor Carrier Industry." *Proceedings of the Nineteenth Annual Meeting of the Transportation Research Forum.* Oxford, IN: Cross, 1978.

Klem, Richard. "Market Structure and Conduct." In *Regulation of Entry and Pricing in Truck Transportation,* ed. Paul W. MacAvoy and John W. Snow. Washington, DC: American Enterprise Institute, 1977.

Kling, Robert. "Deregulation and Structural Change in the LTL Motor Freight Industry." *Transportation Journal* 30 (Spring 1990): 47-53.

Klymchuk, Andrew. *Private Trucking: Analysis and Implications, Research Monograph 15.* Research Branch, Bureau of Competition Policy, Consumer and Corporate Affairs Canada, 1983.

Koenker, Roger. "Optimal Scale and the Size distribution of American Trucking Firms." *Journal of Transport Economics and Policy* 9 (January 1977): 54-67.

Ladenson, Mark, and Allan Stoga. "Returns to Scale in the U.S. Trucking Industry." *Southern Economic Journal* 30 (January 1974): 390-6.

LaLonde, Bernard, and Martha Cooper. *Partnerships in Providing Customer Service: A Third-Party Perspective.* Oak Brook, IL: Council on Logistics Management, 1989.

Lawrence, Michael L. "Economies of Scale in the General Freight Motor Common Carrier Industry: Additional Evidence." *Proceedings, Seventeenth Annual Meeting, Transportation Research Forum.* Oxford, IN: Cross, 1976.

MacRae, James J. *Definition and Characteristics of the Trucking Markets: A Statistical Analysis.* Ottawa: Strategic Policy Directorate, Transport Canada, 1980.

MacRae, James J., and David Prescott. *Regulation and Performance in the Canadian Trucking Industry.* Ottawa: Economic Council of Canada, 1981.

Meyer, John R., et al. *The Economics of Competition in the Transportation Industries.* Cambridge: Harvard University Press, 1964.

Nelson, Robert A. "The Economic Structure of the Highway Carrier Industry in New England." Boston: New England Governor's Conference on Public Transportation, 1957.

—. "The Economies of Scale in the Motor Industry: A Reply." *Land Economics* 35 (May 1959): 180-5.

Panzar, John, and Robert Willig. "Economies of Scale in Multi-Output Production." *Quarterly Journal of Economics* 91 (August 1977): 481-94.

Peat Marwick Thorne. *The Effect of Taxation on Canada-U.S. Trucking Competitiveness.* Toronto: Peat Marwick Thorne, 1991.

Price Waterhouse. *The Financial Performance of Canadian Trucking Firms.* Vancouver: Price Waterhouse, 1991.

Spence, Michael. "Contestable Markets and the Theory of Industrial Structure: A Review Article." *Journal of Economic Literature* 21 (September 1983): 981-90.

Statistics Canada. 1991. *Transborder Trucking Survey, 1991.* Ottawa: Statistics Canada, Transportation Division.

—. Published annually. *Trucking in Canada.* Ottawa: Statistics Canada.

Thomas, Janet, and Scott Callan. "Constant Returns to Scale in the Post-Deregulatory Period: The Case of Specialized Motor Carriers." *Logistics and Transportation Review* 25 (September 1989): 271-89.

Transmode Consultants. *Implications of Alternative Cabotage Rules.* Toronto: Transmode Consultants, 1991.

Transport Canada. *Competition and Economic Regulation in Transportation: Summary Report.*

Ottawa: Transport Canada, 1982.

Trimac Consulting Services. *Comparison of Canadian and U.S. Trucking Costs in Transborder Markets*. Calgary: Trimac Consulting Services, 1991.

—. *Owner Operator Costs and Earnings Comparison in Canada-U.S. Transborder Trucking*. Calgary: Trimac Consulting Services, 1991.

Wang, Judy S., and Ann Friedlaender. "Output Aggregation, Network Effects, and the Measurement of Trucking Technology." *Review of Economics and Statistics* 66 (May 1984): 267-76.

Wang, Judy S., and Ann Friedlaender. "Truck Technology and Efficient Market Structure." *Review of Economics and Statistics* 57 (May 1985): 250-8.

Woudsma, Clarence, and Pavlos Kanaroglou. "The Impacts of Trucking Deregulation in Ontario: A Market-Specific Approach." *Canadian Public Policy* 22 (Winter 1996): 374-5.

Wyckoff, D. Daryl, and David H. Maister. *The Motor-Carrier Industry*. Lexington, MA: Lexington, 1977.

Regulation: Canada

Advisory Committee on Truck Transportation. *Report of the Advisory Committee on Truck Transportation*. Downsview, ON: Ontario Ministry of Transportation 1991.

Anderson, F.W. "The Philosophy of the MacPherson Royal Commission and the National Transportation Act: A Retrospective Essay." In *Issues in Canadian Transport Policy*, ed. K.W. Studnicki-Gizbert. Toronto: Macmillan, 1974.

Baldwin, John. "Transportation Policy and Jurisdictional Issues." *Canadian Public Administration* 18 (Winter 1975): 630-41.

Bennett, Colin. "What Is Policy Convergence and What Causes It?" *British Journal of Political Science* 21 (April 1991): 215-34.

Bonsor, Norman. "The Development of Regulation in the Highway Trucking Industry in Ontario." In *Government Regulation: Issues and Alternatives, 1978*. Toronto: Ontario Economic Council, 1978.

Boucher, Michel. "L'Inspiration Americaine de la Dereglementation en Transport Routier." *Canadian Public Policy* 12 (March 1986): 189-201.

—. "Regulation of the Quebec Trucking Industry. Institutions, Practices and Analytical Considerations." In *Studies of Trucking Regulation*. Vol. 2, ed. Norman Bonsor, et al. Ottawa: Economic Council of Canada, 1990.

Cairns, Robert. *Rationales for Regulation*, Technical Report 2. Ottawa: Economic Council of Canada, 1980 .

Coleman, William D., and Tony Porter. "Banking and Securities Policy." In *Border Crossings: The Internationalization of Canadian Public Policy*, ed. G. Bruce Doern, Leslie Pal, and Brian Tomlin. Toronto: Oxford University Press, 1996.

Coleman, William D., and Grace Skogstad. "Policy Communities and Policy Networks: A Structural Approach." In *Policy Communities and Public Policy in Canada: A Structural Approach*, ed. William Coleman and Grace Skogstad. Toronto: Copp Clark, 1990.

Cooper, Pam. *Literature Review of Foreign Experience of Regulated and Deregulated Trucking*. Ottawa: Department of Consumer and Corporate Affairs, 1980.

Darling, Howard, J. "Transport Policy in Canada: The Struggle of Ideologies versus Realities." In *Issues in Canadian Transport Policy*, ed. K.W.Studnicki-Gizbert. Toronto: Macmillan, 1974.

Doern, G. Bruce, et al. "The Structure and Behaviour of Canadian Regulatory Boards and Commissions: Multidisciplinary Perspectives." *Canadian Public Administration* 18 (Fall 1975): 189-215.

Economic Council of Canada. *Responsible Regulation: An Interim Report by the Economic Council of Canada, November 1979*. Ottawa: Ministry of Supply and Services, 1979.

—. *Reforming Regulation* Ottawa: Ministry of Supply and Services, 1981.

Ellison, Anthony. "Regulatory Reform in Canada: A Different Ball Game." In *Regulatory Regimes in Conflict: Problems of Regulation in a Continental Perspective*, ed. Fred Thompson. Lanham, MD: University Press of America, 1984.

—. "Regulatory Reform in Transport: A Canadian Perspective." *Transportation Journal* 23 (Summer 1984): 4-19.

Hirschhorn, Ron. *Trucking Regulation in Canada: A Review of the Issues, Working Paper 26.* Ottawa: Economic Council of Canada, December 1981.

Interdepartmental Committee on Competition and Regulation in Canada. *Competition and Economic Regulation in Transportation, Summary Report.* Ottawa: Interdepartmental Committee on Competition and Regulation in Canada, 1982.

Interdepartmental Committee on Competition and Regulation in Transportation. *Competition and Regulation in Inter-City Trucking in Canada.* Ottawa: Transport Canada, 1982.

Kaplan, Harold. *Policy and Rationality: The Regulation of Canadian Trucking.* Toronto: University of Toronto Press, 1989.

Klymchuk, Andrew. *Trucking Industry: Analysis of Performance, Research Monograph 14.* Research Branch, Bureau of Competition Policy, Consumer and Corporate Affairs Canada, 1983.

Langford, John. "Transport Canada and the Transport Ministry: The Attempt to Retreat to Basics." In *How Ottawa Spends Your Tax Dollars: National Policy and Economic Development 1982,* ed. G. Bruce Doern. Toronto: Lorimer, 1982.

McManus, John. "On the 'New' Transportation Policy after Ten Years." In *Studies of Regulation in Canada,* ed. W.T. Stanbury. Montreal: Institute for Research on Public Policy, 1978.

MacRae, James J., and David M. Prescott. "Second Thoughts on Tariff Bureaus." *Canadian Public Policy* 9 (June 1983): 200-9.

National Transportation Agency of Canada. *Annual Report of the National Transportation Agency of Canada* (1990-1994). Ottawa: National Transportation Agency of Canada.

Nix, F.P., and A.M. Clayton. *Motor Carrier Regulation: Institutions and Practices.* Ottawa: Economic Council of Canada, 1980.

Ontario Highway Transport Board. *Report of the Ontario Highway Transport Board to the Honourable James W. Snow, Minister of Transportation and Communications, on the Balance of Trade in Trucking Services between the United States and Canada.* Toronto: Ontario Highway Transport Board, July 30, 1983.

Ontario Public Commercial Vehicles Act Review Committee. *Responsible Trucking: New Directions.* Toronto: Ontario Ministry of Transportation and Communications, June 1983.

Rapoport, M.L. "History of the Public Commercial Vehicles Act and Related Laws and Regulations." Paper prepared for the Ontario PCV Review Committee, October 1981. (Mimeo.)

Renchenthaler, G.B. "Direct Regulation in Canada: Some Policies and Problems." In *Studies on Regulation in Canada,* ed. W.T. Stanbury. Toronto: Butterworths, 1978.

Rose, Richard. *Lesson-Drawing in Public Policy: A Guide to Learning across Time and Space.* Chatham, NJ: Chatham, 1993.

Royal Commission on the Economic Union and Development Prospects for Canada. *Report.* Vol. 2. Ottawa, Ministry of Supply and Services, 1985.

Schultz, Richard, and Alan Alexandroff. *Economic Regulation and the Federal System.* Toronto: University of Toronto Press, 1985.

Schultz, Richard J. *Federalism, Bureaucracy, and Public Policy: The Politics of Highway Transport Regulation.* Montreal: McGill-Queen's University Press, 1980.

Schultz, Richard, and Mark Brawley. "Telecommunications Policy." In *Border Crossing: The Internationalization of Canadian Public Policy,* ed. G. Bruce Doern, Leslie A. Pal, and Brian W. Tomlin. Toronto: Oxford University Press, 1996.

Skogstad, Grace. "Agricultural Policy." In *Border Crossings: The Internationalization of Canadian Public Policy,* ed. G. Bruce Doern, Leslie A. Pal, and Brian W. Tomlin. Toronto: Oxford University Press, 1996.

Studnicki-Gizbert, K.W. "The Administration of Transport Policy: The Regulatory Problems." *Canadian Public Administration* 18 (Winter 1975): 642-58.

Transport Canada. *Freedom to Move: A Framework for Transportation Reform.* Ottawa: Transport Canada, 1985.

Regulation: United States

Adams, Walter, and James B. Hendy. *Trucking Mergers, Concentration and Small Business: An Analysis of Interstate Commerce Policy 1950-1956.* Select Committee on Small Business,

U.S. Senate, 85th Congress, 1st Session, 1957.

Alexis, Marcus. "Regulation of Surface Transportation." In *The Political Economy of Deregulation: Interest Groups in the Regulatory Process*, ed., Roger G. Noll and Bruce M. Owen. Washington, DC: American Enterprise Institute, 1983.

Altshuler, Alan, and Roger Teal. "The Political Economy of Airline Deregulation." In *Current Issues in Transportation Policy*, ed., Alan Altshuler and Roger Teal. Lexington: DC Heath, 1979.

Anderson, Eugene D. "The Motor Carrier Authorities Game." *ICC Practitioners' Journal* 47 (November/December 1979): 22-43.

Breyer, Stephen. *Regulation and Its Reform*. Cambridge: Harvard University Press, 1982.

Brown, Anthony, and Joseph Stewart, Jr. "Competing Advocacy Coalitions, Policy Evolution and Airline Deregulation." In *Policy Change and Learning: An Advocacy Coalition Approach*, ed. Paul Sabatier and Hank Jenkins-Smith. Boulder, CO: Westview, 1993.

Childs, William. *Trucking and the Public Interest: The Emergence of Federal Regulation 1914-1940*. Knoxville, TN: University of Tennessee Press, 1985.

Dempsey, Paul F., "Erosion of the Regulatory Process in Transportation: The Winds of Change," *ICC Practitioners' Journal* 47 (March-April 1980) 303-20.

Derthick, Martha, and Paul J. Quirk. *The Politics of Deregulation*. Washington, DC: Brookings Institution, 1985.

Fellmeth, Robert. *The Interstate Commerce Commission: The Public Interest and the ICC*. New York: Grossman, 1970.

Friedlaender, Ann, and Richard Spady. *Freight Transport Regulation: Equity, Efficiency and Competition in the Rail and Trucking Industries*. Cambridge: MIT Press, 1981.

General Accounting Office. *Effects of Regulatory Reform on Unemployment in the Trucking Industry*. GAO/CED-82-90, June 11, 1982.

Harper, Donald V. "The Federal Motor Carrier Act of 1980. Review and Analysis." *Transportation Journal* 20 (Winter 1980): 5-33.

House of Representatives, Committee on Public Works and Transportation, Report to Accompany H.R. 3663, 97th Congress, 1st Session, 17 November 1981

Interstate Commerce Commission. *ICC 80: Ninety-Fourth Annual Report of the Interstate Commerce Commission*. Washington, DC: Government Printing Office, 1981.

—. *ICC 81: Ninety-Fifth Annual Report of the Interstate Commerce Commission*. Washington, DC: Government Printing Office, 1982.

Johnson, James C., and James P. Rakowski. "The Reed-Bulwinkle Act (1948): A Thirty Year Prospective." In *Proceedings, Nineteenth Annual Meeting of the Transportation Research Forum*. Oxford, IN: Cross, 1978.

Levine, Harvey. *National Transportation Policy: A Study of Studies*. Lexington: Lexington, 1978.

MacAvoy, Paul W., ed. *Unsettled Questions on Regulatory Reform*. Washington, DC, American Enterprise Institute, 1978.

Moore, Thomas Gale. *Freight Transportation Regulation*. Washington, DC: American Enterprise Institute, 1972.

National Transportation Policy Study Commission. *National Transportation Policies through the Year 2000*. Washington, DC: Government Printing Office, June 1979.

Nelson, James C. "Politics and Economics in Transport Regulation and Deregulation: A Century Perspective on the ICC's Role." *Logistics and Transportation Journal* 23 (March 1987): 5-32.

Noll, Roger G. *Reforming Regulation: An Evaluation of the Ash Council Proposals*. Washington, DC: Brookings, 1971.

Noll, Roger G., and Bruce M. Owen. "The Predictability of Interest Group Alignments." In *The Political Economy of Deregulation: Interest Groups in the Regulatory Process*, ed. Roger G. Noll and Bruce M. Owen. Washington, DC: American Enterprise Institute, 1983.

Pegrum, Dudley, "The Economic Basis of Public Policy for Motor Transport," Land Economics 28 (1952) 244-63.

—. *Public Regulation of Business*, 2nd ed. Homewood, IL: Irwin, 1965.

—. *Transportation Economics and Public Policy*, 3rd ed. Homewood, IL: Irwin, 1973.

Robyn, Dorothy. *Braking the Special Interests: Trucking Deregulation and the Politics of Policy Reform*. Chicago: University of Chicago Press, 1987.

Snow, John W. "The Problem of Motor Carrier Regulation and the Ford Administration's Proposal for Reform." In *Regulation of Entry and Pricing in Truck Transportation*, ed. Paul W. MacAvoy and John W. Snow. Washington, DC: American Enterprise Institute, 1977.

Steinfeld, Joseph. "Regulation versus Free Competition: The Current Battle over Deregulation of Entry into the Motor Carrier Industry." *ICC Practitioners' Journal* 45 (July-August 1978): 590-609.

Thompson, Fred. "Regulatory Reform and Deregulation in the United States." In *Government Regulation: Scope, Growth, Process*, ed. W.T. Stanbury and Fred Thompson. Montreal: Institute for Research on Public Policy, 1980.

Transportation Act, 1972. Hearings before the Subcommittee on Transportation and Aeronautics of the Committee on Interstate and Foreign Commerce, House of Representatives, 92nd Congress, 2nd Session. Washington, DC: US Government Printing Office, 1972.

Trade and Transport

Appleton, Barry. *Navigating NAFTA*. Toronto: Carswell, 1994.

Brock, William. United States Trade Representative, letter to Allan Gotlieb, Ambassador of Canada, 17 November 1982; Alan Gotlieb, Ambassador of Canada, letter to William Brock, United States Trade Representative, 24 November 1982.

Canada. Department of External Affairs, Information on the Policies and Practices of the Canadian Provincial and Federal Governments in Regard to the Trucking Industry, Notes GNT-179, 314, 338 (1982).

Carmichael, Edward A., Wendy Dobson, and Richard G. Lipsey, "The Macdonald Report: Signpost or Shopping Basket?" *Canadian Public Policy* 12 (Supplement, February 1986): 23-39.

Congressional Record. Senate, 30 June 1982.

Delagran, Leslie. "Conflict in Trade Policy: The Role of Congress and the Provinces in Negotiating and Implementing the Canada-U.S. Free Trade Agreement." *Publius* 22 (Fall 1992): 15-30.

Department of External Affairs. *A Review of Canadian Trade Policy: A Background Document to Canadian Trade Policy for the 1980s*. Ottawa: Ministry of Supply and Services, 1983.

—. *Canadian Trade Policy for the 1980s: A Discussion Paper*. Ottawa: Ministry of Supply and Services, 1983.

Dicken, Peter. *Global Shift: The Internationalization of Economic Activity*, 2nd ed. London: Chapman, 1992.

Doern, G. Bruce, and Brian W. Tomlin. *Faith and Fear: The Free Trade Story*. Toronto: Stoddart, 1991.

Elkins, David. *Beyond Sovereignty: Territory and Political Economy in the Twenty-First Century*. Toronto: University of Toronto Press, 1995.

Finnemore, Martha. "Norms, Culture, and World Politics: Insights from Sociology's Institutionalism." *International Organization* 50 (Spring 1996): 325-48.

Frieden, Jeffrey, and Ronald Rogowski. "The Impact of the International Economy on National Policies: An Analytical Overview." In *Internationalization and Domestic Politics*, ed., Helen Milner and Robert Keohane. Cambridge: Cambridge University Press, 1996.

Gibbins, Roger. "Canadian Federalism: The Entanglement of Meech Lake and the Free Trade Agreement." *Publius* 19 (Summer 1989): 185-98.

Godwin, Stephen. "The North American Free Trade Agreement: Implications for Transportation." *Government Finance Review* 9 (June 1993): 11-4.

Helleiner, Eric. *States and the Reemergence of Global Finance: From Bretton Woods to the 1990s*. Ithaca: Cornell University Press, 1994.

Interstate Commerce Commission. Ex Parte Mc No. 157 (1982), Investigation into Canadian Law and Policy Regarding Applications of American Motor Carriers for Canadian Operating Authority. Washington, DC: Interstate Commerce Commission, 1982.

Keenes, Ernie. "Rearranging the Deck Chairs: A Political Economy Approach to Foreign

Policy Management in Canada." *Canadian Public Administration* 35 (Fall 1992): 381-401.

Keohane, Robert O. "Reciprocity in International Relations." *International Organization* 40 (Winter 1986): 1-28.

Keohane, Robert O., and Joseph S. Nye. *Power and Interdependence*, 2nd ed. Glenview, IL: Foresman, 1989.

Koh, Harold Hongju. "A Legal Perspective." In *Perspectives on a U.S.-Canada Free Trade Agreement*, ed. Robert Stern, Philip Trezise, John Whalley. Washington, DC/Ottawa: Brookings Institution/Institute for Research on Public Policy, 1987.

Krasner, Stephen. "Trade Conflicts and the Common Defense: The United States and Japan." *Political Science Quarterly* 101 (Winter 1986): 787-806.

Kroll, John A. "The Complexity of Interdependence." *International Studies Quarterly* 37 (September 1993): 321-48.

Ludwick, Eugene M. "Strategic Considerations for Transportation Planning in a Deregulated and Free Trade Environment." *Proceedings of the Twenty Second Annual Meeting of the Canadian Transportation Research Forum*. Saskatoon: University of Saskatchewan Printing Services, 1987.

Putnam, Robert. "Diplomacy and Domestic Politics: The Logic of Two-Level Games." *International Organization* 42 (Summer 1988): 427-60.

Royal Commission on the Economic Union and Development Prospects for Canada. *Report*. Vol. 1. Ottawa: Ministry of Supply and Services, 1985.

Silzer, Nora, and Mark Krasnick. "The Free Flow of Goods in the Canadian Economic Union." In *Perspectives on the Canadian Economic Union*, ed., Mark Krasnick. Toronto: University of Toronto Press, 1986.

Simeon, Richard. "Federalism and Free Trade." In *The Future on the Table: Canada and the Free Trade Issues*, ed. Michael D. Henderson. North York, ON: Masterpress, York University, 1987.

—. "Inside the Macdonald Commission." *Studies in Political Economy* 22 (Spring 1987): 167-79.

Smiley, Donald. "A Note on Canadian-American Free Trade and Canadian Policy Autonomy." In *Trade-Offs on Free Trade*, ed. Marc Gold and David Leyton-Brown. Toronto: Carswell, 1988.

Spruyt, Hendrik. "Institutional Selection in International Relations: State Anarchy as Order." *International Organization* 48 (Autumn 1994): 527-59.

Stevenson, Garth. "The Agreement and the Dynamics of Canadian Federalism." In *Trade-Offs on Free Trade*, ed. Marc Gold and David Leyton-Brown. Toronto: Carswell, 1989.

—. "Continental Integration and Canadian Unity." In *Continental Community? Independence and Integration in North America*, ed. W. Andrew Axline et al. Toronto: McClelland and Stewart, 1974.

Strange, Susan. *The Retreat of the State: The Diffusion of Power in the World Economy*. Cambridge: Cambridge University Press, 1996.

Tomlin, Brian. "The Stages of Prenegotiation: The Decision to Negotiate North American Free Trade." *International Journal* 44 (Spring 1989): 254-79.

US National Study on Trade in Services. Washington, DC: Office of the United States Trade Representative, December 1983.

Williams, Glen. "Canadian Sovereignty and the Free Trade Debate." In *Knocking on the Back Door: Canadian Perspectives on the Political Economy of Freer Trade with the United States*, ed. Allan M. Maslove and Stanley L. Winer. Halifax: Institute for Research on Public Policy, 1987.

—. "On Determining Canada's Location within the International Political Economy." *Studies in Political Economy* 25 (Spring 1988): 107-40.

Wonnacott, Ronald J. *Aggressive U.S. Reciprocity Evaluated with a New Approach to Trade Conflicts*. Montreal: Institute for Research on Public Policy, 1984.

Wright, Quincy. *The Study of International Relations*. New York: Appleton-Century-Crofts, 1955.

Zacher, Mark, with Brent Sutton. *Governing Global Networks: International Regimes in Transportation and Communication*. Cambridge: Cambridge University Press, 1996.

News and Reportage
Bus and Truck Transport
Canadian Pacific Limited, Annual Report (1988-1993)
Canadian Transportation and Distribution Management
Canadian Transportation Logistics
Financial Post
Financial Times
Globe and Mail
Highway Common Carrier Newsletter
Manitoba Business
Materials Management and Distribution
Modern Purchasing
Motor Truck
New York Times
Trade and Commerce
Traffic World
Transport Topics
Truck Fleet
Truck News
Western Commerce and Industry

Index

Set in Stone by Darlene Remus
Printed and bound in Canada by Friesens
Copy editor: Joanne Richardson
Proofreader: Ron Phillips

Canada and International Relations
Kim Nossal and Brian Job, General Editors